NO OTHER LIGHT

... with no other light
Except for that which in my heart was burning.
—John of the Cross

Mary Wolff-Salin

NO OTHER
LIGHT

POINTS OF CONVERGENCE
IN PSYCHOLOGY
AND SPIRITUALITY

CROSSROAD · NEW YORK

1986
The Crossroad Publishing Company
370 Lexington Avenue, New York, N.Y. 10017

Printed in the United States of America

Library of Congress Cataloging in Publication Data

Wolff-Salin, Mary.
No other light.

Bibliography: p.
1. Spirituality—Psychology. I. Title.
BL624.W65   1986   248'.01'9   85-29972
ISBN 0-8245-0748-7

Acknowledgments

Grateful acknowledgment is made to the following publishers for permission to use extended quotations from copyrighted works:

Cistercian Publications for material from *The Sayings of the Desert Fathers: The Alphabetical Collection*, translated by Benedicta Ward.

Franciscan Herald Press for material from *Teach Us to Pray: Learning a Little about God* by André Louf. Reprinted by Permission.

ICS Publications for material from *The Collected Works of St. John of the Cross*, translated by Kieran Kavanaugh and Otilio Rodriquez, copyright © 1979 Washington Province of Discalced Carmelites, ICS Publications, 2131 Lincoln Rd., N.E., Washington, D.C. 20002.

Princeton University Press for material from *The Collected Works of C.G. Jung*, trans. R.F.C. Hull, Bollingen Series XX. Vol. 7: *Two Essays on Analytical Psychology*, copyright 1953, © 1966 by Princeton University Press. *The Collected Works of C.G. Jung*, trans. R.F.C. Hull, Bollingen Series XX. Vol. 11: *Psychology and Religion: West and East*, copyright © 1958, 1969 by Princeton University Press. *The Collected Works of C.G. Jung*, trans. R.F.C. Hull, Bollingen Series XX. Vol. 14: *Mysterium Coniunctionis*, copyright © 1965, 1970 by Princeton University Press. Reprinted by permission of Princeton University Press.

To those who have been help on the journey.

CONTENTS

FOREWORD

The various wisdom traditions are unanimous and emphatic on one point: that the development that opens up before the human being is unimaginably vast; that the difference between a fully realized self and a "normal" self makes the very idea of a single species called man problematic. Now on this point, the psychoanalytic tradition stemming from Freud and Jung is at one with the traditional wisdom. More specifically, they, like it, see human fulfilment as involving the painful death of our ordinary ego-consciousness into a consciousness whose subject is incomparably wider and deeper than the ego.

Anyone who has some experience of this hazardous adventure, and who is familiar with the psychoanalytic tradition, will see that the latter's *witness* to the cost and grandeur of the spiritual journey is far more important than the differences that exist between the ancient and the modern versions of it. We desperately need all the help we can get for the journey beyond ego-centered consciousness, especially at this crucial moment in our history. Least of all may we dispense with those insights into it that are born of our modern culture. To miss this point, and to see the psychoanalytic and the ascetical-mystical tradition as dealing respectively with different areas of concern, is to fail to hear the witness of our contemporary culture to the abiding reality of a mysterious ground of consciousness. And if I do not hear the call of God in the accents of my own culture, it is to be doubted whether I hear it at all.

This splendid book is built upon a clear understanding that the common ground and complementarity of the two traditions are what are of primary importance. Mary Wolff-Salin gives to the great

spiritual ideas of antiquity vital breathing in the air of our contemporary self-understanding. And they are transformed in the
process. St. Benedict's degrees of humility shed layers of later
monastic moralistic commentary, and stand out as brilliantly observed stages in the progression from an ego-centered to a self-
directed life. What is especially interesting here is that the extreme
images of Scripture about our wretchedness — "I am a worm and no
man," etc. — are *restored* in their pristine vigour by modern psychology, alive to "the narcissistic personality with its grandiosity,
need for attention, inability to take criticism, unconcern for others,
seen as the opposite pole to the humble personality," whereas a
commentary innocent of psychology will incline to soften the harshness of the old images. A similar process may be observed in our
understanding of the central concern with salvation. For the psychoanalytic tradition takes us deeper than a concept of sin as wilful-
ness — remediable, if one is logical, by a change of will — to a concept
of sin as compulsiveness, in which we are trapped until we are
drawn into a process whose springs lie quite beyond our control,
the process whereby the total self, image of the Godhead, becomes
the directing principle in a person's life.

The dialectic of ego and self has a central role in this book. Here
again, the author sticks to the fruitful common ground between the
two traditions, refusing to get bogged down in questions raised by
the admittedly ambiguous way in which Jung writes of the self — is
it transcendent, or is it too transcended? An important question, in
the proper place. But within the admirably consistent methodology
of Wolff-Salin's book, it suffices that the concept of the self as
opposed to the ego is a vital agent in spiritual transformation. Is
not this concept the experiential form of what theology calls the
Imago Dei? And is not the lack of a strong experiential referent for
this traditional description of the human being responsible for the
weakness in our Christology? "Have you ever *felt* yourself as the
image of God?" "Well yes, when my lifelong companion Ego
collapsed on me and something else that I didn't understand, only
it sort of *was* me, seemed to be trying to take over."

Very exciting, too, is what happens to the traditional primacy
accorded to contemplation when the two traditions are allowed to
converge. It remains — but loses a certain elitist, intellectualist connotation. It asserts that we have to die to our ego-based consciousness and learn to live, emotionally and intellectually, in the real
order.

These are only a few of the points touched by this thorough—and thoroughly readable—book. The reader will come away from it with a fresh and more practical understanding of all the key concepts in the mystical tradition: work (a wonderful section), solitude, discretion, virtue, silence of the heart, will (*thelēma* rather than *voluntas*), memory, contemplation; and of the modern terms: transference, projection, animus-anima (a very nuanced treatment), persona, ego, self, and so forth. It's a book I've been waiting for for a very long time, and I'm certainly not alone.

I should like to conclude these remarks with two quotes from Peter Shaffer's play *Shrivings*.

> Remember, as animals we are failures, and as aggressive beings also. We have to come at last to see Ego in a new way. As a pod, evolved for our protection during our years through pre-history, but which has now become our prison. If we are not to suffocate in it, we have to burst it open.

> Oh yes! Stand up! Square up! Come outside! Come on the battlefield! History of the world! Put your fists where your faith is! Marvellous! . . . (*Harshly*) And that's what you want too, with all your long hair, sweet looks! . . . All of you, just the same . . . (*Pause. He stands for a moment, with eyes closed.*) (*Quietly: very calm*) To let go. Just to let go that *indulgence*. Fill up instead with true passiveness. A feeling so total, it's *like* violence. An immense Nothing inside you. A sledgehammer Nothing which alone can break that crust of Ego . . . Fasts—Vigils—all those tricks: what are they about, except this?—to fill up in a new way!

Sebastian Moore

PREFACE

In what seems another age — that is, before Vatican II — when I was a junior in the community to which I belong, I used to spend some hours daily reading Thomas Aquinas. I used to wonder that things that to us were so neatly compartmentalized — philosophy and theology, art and science — to him seemed to form a single organic whole. I could almost have believed, then, in "the thirteenth, greatest of centuries."

The remark is sometimes made of late — I have heard it attributed to Karl Rahner — that if Aquinas lived today, it would have been the findings of depth psychology, rather than of Aristotle, that he would have used as a basis for his work.

The pages that follow can have no such exhaustive aim, for the thoroughness and comprehensiveness required even to begin such a project are excluded. But the desire to write this book was indeed born of a perception of unity or, in this case, of the convergence of the disciplines of depth psychology and spirituality, in at least some of their themes.

It is obvious that, as someone remarked to me, Jung and especially Freud would turn over in their graves at what I have done. (Actually, Jung might well not, but honesty requires stating that it is only some of his thought that has been used in this book. He is a deeply spiritual writer but also very deliberately free and "heterodox." The fact that I have not used some of his quotations which diverge from, rather than converge with, classical Christian tradition in no way denies that these quotations exist. Appendix 2 discusses some of them in detail.)

These are vast fields, so I have limited my reflections quite severely. I speak much more, though not exclusively, of the West than of the East; more of Christianity than of other faiths; more of Jung than of Freud, simply because these are the areas where I am a little more informed. I also speak more of the early foundations of Western spirituality rather than of its later literature—let alone its postconciliar forms. These are present choices. In the past I have done otherwise.

I also use throughout some terminology that can be misleading. Words like *spiritual, spirituality, soul* suggest to many a set of dichotomies: spiritual/material, soul/body, spiritual life/daily ordinary life. It is important to state very strongly that these terms are used below in almost the opposite meaning. The whole human body-person is involved in the discussion of "soul." The "spiritual life" involves eating, drinking, working, living. These questions will emerge in more detail below, but the limitations of language require making this point from the beginning.

My hope in writing is simply to open further a path where others have already done some walking and where I hope that still others will continue to work, as I hope to do myself. It seems to me that there is nothing but gain that will result as we come to see where people examining human life from different perspectives come to somewhat parallel judgments of truth.

A venture like this has serious questions connected with it, especially with regard to the meaning of a concept like "convergence." What, for example, is the relationship between the individuation process as Jung sees it—notably when it has reached its highest point—and the transformation in Christ of Christian spiritual theology? Is John of the Cross speaking of something different from Jung? And, if so, how different? Any opinion is possible on a continuum between two extremes, one of which sees the two states as entirely different and the other of which identifies them. A point along that continuum seems to me a most likely choice, doubtless tending toward the pole of similarity. In various stages of the book I say that pointing out similarities and convergences does not imply an identification of the two states under discussion. This is my basic position. I am speaking of points of convergence throughout, but convergence of theme is not identity. On the other hand, however, who is to say where a clear line can be drawn? Theologically speaking, for example, would it be possible, without grace, to reach a state of full individuation? And where there is grace, is there not the seed of transformation? Who is to say to what degree this seed has come to flower? Karl Rahner spoke of the anonymous Christian; what of the anonymous saint? If any further judgment than this is to be made, surely it must be a question of individual cases and not of generalities. There is still another level where it is important to specify what this book does and does not try to do. No attempt has been made at a scholarly presentation of the thought of Freud or Jung, nor of John of the Cross or Benedict either, to name just a few authors cited. Each of these is a world in itself with its own nuances and inner development, and dealing with any one of these would expand this book far beyond its intended scope. To speak of them briefly, as I do here, necessitates a summary kind of treatment and what, at times, seems a superficiality of approach which I have had simply to accept. In one way, Freud suffers the most from a rather stereotypical presentation, but writing of Benedict, touching on Oriental thought in a few lines, is often equally unnuanced and insufficient. The whole should be seen as a series of spotlights showing up points of resemblance, similarities of theme. At times, in-depth study would bring out grave differences beneath these apparent similarities. This need not nullify the resemblances brought into focus by such "spotlighting." But it should be remembered throughout that the nuances and development of no writer's thought can be brought out within the scope of a work like this, which should rather serve as an introduction and an invitation to further reading and personal research.

Another point to note is that the progression of chapters is not accidental. There is, in the book, a certain movement from the beginning of spiritual life and psychological growth through various aspects of the middle stages toward the end. This progression is not rigid. One does not live what Chapter 5 discusses before beginning Chapter 6. But Chapter 2 is fundamental for early stages and Chapters 14 and 15 have to do with final ones. The earlier themes are presupposed in the later ones.

It appears that when Dom Bede Griffiths left for India, he said he was going to seek "the other half" of his soul[1] — and this, despite his profound commitment to Catholic Christianity. He has lived the Indian "half" of his commitment with equal depth, going far into the spirituality of that world so different from his beginnings. Perhaps psychology — and notably, though not at all exclusively, that of Jung — can also reveal to the Judeo-Christian world the other half of its psyche or soul. And then still other "halves" can be found in the East and elsewhere. Width and breadth in one's faith and thinking are not only signs of health, but they also open us to aspects of truth and reality we tend to lose without them. This book is an attempt to open to and reflect on some of these.

I owe thanks to many people whom I cannot list here for various insights that led to this book. I should like to mention only a few more recent helps.

My gratitude goes to my community for encouragement to publish what began as personal reflections: to Drs. Daveda Tenenbaum and Michael St Clair; Fathers Kieran Kavanaugh, O.C.D., and William Richardson, S.J.; Sisters Susan Campbell and Iona McLaughlin, R.S.C.J., for suggestions and criticisms to improve the manuscript; to Dom Sebastian Moore, O.S.B., for writing the Foreword; to Sister Ruth Richmond, N.S.C.J., for help with the technicalities; to Dr. Paul Sanderson and to the Jung Institute of Boston for seminars that greatly aided this reflection.

I am grateful for different sources of insight over the years and for the personal example of many who have reached the kind of integration discussed in this book. On another level, the silent example, encouragement, and prayer of those who live "hidden with Christ in God," in whatever way, but carry the needs of the world in their prayer and lives have spoken more loudly to me than words of the material in this book.

To all of the above, my thanks.

Feast of the Assumption, 1985

·1·

THE STRUCTURE OF
THE HUMAN PSYCHE

Through the centuries philosophers and early psychologists have had varying conceptions of the structure of the human psyche, many of which have been adopted by their contemporary spiritual theologians. We shall meet some of these below, in terms of spiritual writing, but for our present purposes the psychological theories of Freud and Jung seem a good beginning.

Let us follow Freud's thought first. Introducing one of Freud's final works, *The Ego and the Id*, the editor remarks that the fact or historical accident that psychoanalysis began with the study of hysteria led "at once to the hypothesis of repression" and "to a picture of the mind as including two portions, one repressed and the other repressing."[1] These were to be called the "Ego" and the "Id," and there follows immediately a history of the three terms that were to become the classical "topography" of the psyche in the Freudian tradition.

The term *'das Es'* [the Id] . . . in part replaced the ill-defined uses of the earlier term 'the unconscious' . . . and 'the systematic unconscious.'

The position in regard to *'das Ich'* [the Ego] is a good deal less clear. . . . It seems possible to detect two main uses: one in which the term distinguishes a person's self as a whole (including, perhaps, his body) from other people, and the other in which it denotes a particular part of the mind. . . . In some of his . . . works . . . the 'ego' seems to correspond rather to the 'self.'

There is one particular function . . . whose examination was to lead to momentous results—the self-critical faculty. . . . He then put forward the notion that there may be 'a special psychical

5

agency' whose task it is to watch the actual ego and measure it by the ideal ego or ego ideal. . . . It is as an equivalent to the 'ego-ideal' that *'das Über-Ich'* [the Superego] makes its first appearance.[2]

Depth psychology, in other words, needed to formulate a terminology to deal with its discoveries — first among which was the importance of the unconscious, and the notion that much in the unconscious is material we repress, for one or other reason. The above "topography," which passed through various stages of development before the final Freudian sense of the terms was set, was one result.

In still other words, and to speak developmentally, a baby emerges with time out of the unconscious inner world of instinct, drives, needs, desire into what we call the adult world. But we all still bear within us this original domain which affects the whole of our being constantly. And we revert to this world in different ways and at different times, notably in our dreams, according to Freud. This is the world governed by what he calls the pleasure principle, the desire for satisfaction apart from objective reality.

Out of this matrix, which is called the id, is born the ego. Freud writes:

> The ego seeks to bring the influence of the external world to bear upon the id and its tendencies, and endeavours to substitute the reality principle for the pleasure principle which reigns unrestrictedly in the id. . . . The ego represents what may be called reason and common sense, in contrast to the id, which contains the passions.[3]

What, then, is the third element, the superego, and what is its source?

> [Behind] the origin of the ego-ideal . . . there lies an individual's first and most important identification, his identification with the father in his own personal pre-history. . . . The object-choices belonging to the first sexual period and relating to the father and mother seem normally to find their outcome in an identification of this kind. . . .[4]

The small child needs to learn certain behavior patterns and values to live in society. These are learned from the parents, notably the father, and part of this learning has to do with punishment that follows infringement of the appropriate codes. With time this process becomes interiorized until the child has an inner mentor which continually reinforces these early dos and don'ts—and the result is a sense of guilt after infringement. What adults consider to be their conscious lives are far more affected than one always realizes by elements from the unconscious, which are repressed, and the self-criticism of this inner mentor which is always with us. Some people never become free of this inner self-criticism in the sense of being able to make truly personal choices concerning their principles and ideals. Total freedom is an unrealistic aim, but almost total unfreedom, especially when unrecognized, leads to psychological ill-health—whether that lack of freedom is a result of slavery to the unconscious or to the superego.

A discussion of Freudian thought, however brief, needs to include a few words on his theory of psychological development through the early years, for it is a rare adult who does not bear some marks of fixation at earlier stages. More, it is normal to have moments of return to the feelings of these earlier times.

Many of us associate babyhood with being "a child of the breast." Oral activity, then, is the first pleasure the baby knows, and it is the means by which food is received into the organism. This whole complexus of desire, need, pleasure, satisfaction forms a whole that remains operative in later years. The mouth remains an erogenous zone; the desires for food and sexual pleasure (even in this early form) remain strong, and there are many adult habits indicative of a certain centralization at this level of development. Oral satisfactions such as chewing, talking, eating, drinking are part of every life, but the need for more of these than is appropriate indicates a certain "orality" in one's developmental makeup. These processes may be carried on at other levels than the literal. Greed for information or knowledge, aggressive forms of language, feelings of dependency and inability to stand on one's own feet can all suggest that the developmental tasks of this stage of growth have not been sufficiently fulfilled, or that the needs of this psychological age have not been sufficiently met, for the person to grow beyond them to the next stage.

What Freud calls the "anal" stage, because it is characterized, in the lives of most children, by early toilet training and the feelings there aroused, involves tendencies even more recognizable for most adults. A perfectly normal human tendency and need, defecation, suddenly becomes for a small child a first area of conflict with the social world. He may not do what he wishes, when and where he wishes. Adults tell him when and where bowel movements are appropriate, and punishment follows disobedience. Trying to put oneself back into the mind of a small child makes understanding of this stage slightly easier. If messiness is excessively punished — according to the theory — the child will grow up compulsively neat, tidy, rigid, and possibly avaricious. Or, she will revolt and be deliberately messy and untidy, physically and emotionally. Temper tantrums, cruelty, destructiveness, aggression can result. The fundamental issue at this stage is one of control. The need to control everything and everyone around — or even everything in one's own life — relates to this stage of development. But also a healthy and balanced parental attitude, leading to the same in the child, can foster creativeness. Knowing that all one's activity is worthwhile to the surrounding world can begin here.

This stage is followed by the phallic, better known in terms of the Oedipus complex. The child becomes initially aware of himself or herself as attracted to a person of the opposite sex whom he or she would like to "marry." The parent of the opposite sex is the nearest and most familiar "object" of this type, and the wish for this union leads to rejection of the other parent as a rival. Perhaps it is unnecessary to say that the "pop psychology" notion that every boy wants to kill his father and marry his mother and every girl the opposite is an oversimplification. The issue in question is that of developing an embryonic sexual identity, which the same-sex parent normally models for the child and seems to impede. Both inner development and even the culture move the child in this way. It is normal that this development gropes obscurely toward what will later become adult sexual expression. The child rarely knows and even more rarely can feel what this might mean, but the groping is there and leads to the kind of activity we call "Oedipal." If this stage is not reached and gone through, an adult sexual identity can not be attained. Nor can the meaning of adult love be found. We do indeed learn from our parents — on the affective level more than in other ways. When reality points out to the small boy that he cannot "marry mommy," he slowly comes to realize that he can learn from daddy how to be a man and that he can befriend him rather than subconsciously fear him as a rival. But, in the Freudian scheme, much in this whole process involves both fear and shame, and so we repress what a simpler culture might make less traumatic.[5] This, to him, is the reason for much of our "forgetfulness" about early childhood. And pain in this stage of development, which most of us experience in some way, is the cause of much that emerges in later stages.

For some theorists, the father at this stage is the giver of both the child's identity and of his or her understanding of the "law," of ethics, of objective reality.[6] Later issues of identity, authority problems, questions of dealing with reality depend on the resolution of this developmental stage.

The final stage of development for Freud involves a further turning outward toward the real world and real people, where the earlier stages were more narcissistic. This ability for altruistic, even oblative, love is a characteristic of maturity. Such a person lives in the real world and gradually grows in freedom, both with regard to his or her inner determinisms and with regard to external power. He or she learns to choose more freely. To Freud, more of our lives than we realize will remain determined by factors we do not recognize and cannot control, but the mature personality knows more of what these are and faces them more honestly, so that they do not build up so much in the unconscious like waters too strongly dammed, which can then break their limiting walls. The means to prevent such a catastrophe is openness to the inner truth of what is really going on in our heart, psyche, and unconscious.

One of the early disciples of Freud, Carl Gustav Jung, broke away from the former painfully—after a time when they had worked together—partly but not wholly because of what has been called Freud's pansexualism. To Jung the field of the unconscious seemed far wider than that recognized by Freud—and far deeper as well.

Jung speaks as much as Freud about the ego and the unconscious, but the meaning of the terms differs. To Jung the ego is also the conscious "part" of the human psyche, but it is in a slightly different sense the center of awareness of the adult human person. The Jungian "personal unconscious" with its contents does not differ very much from the Freudian unconscious, but to Jung all this is just the tip of the iceberg. Deeper than the personal unconscious is the collective unconscious where the human person comes into contact with all that is part of the cultural, psychological, spiritual background of the whole human race—as well as, and more particularly, the parts of that heritage that are more specifically his or her own. Experiences, symbols, memories, predispositions, and much else besides are to be found in this storehouse of the whole human race's inner and outer being. Part of this world is what Jung calls the archetypes, or, as Whitmont calls them,[7] the "eternal images." These are what emerge in our dreams, fantasies, myths, fairy tales, in our art and culture. One could make an almost endless list, but there are a few basic ones central to human development. They will be discussed at considerable length in some of the following chapters, but they need a brief introduction here. The shadow can be briefly defined as "that part of the personality which has been repressed for the sake of the ego ideal."[8] It will be seen below, however, that there is a "bright" as well as a "dark" shadow, which some people find even harder to accept and integrate. For the facing and integration of the shadow is one of the basic tasks of the human journey, essential to the ones that must follow.

To Jung the stages of development do, indeed, form a journey. He speaks of the first half of life as a time when the human person needs to achieve something in life, to solidify the ego, so to speak; for a weak or insufficiently developed person on the human plane would not be able to undertake the "work" of the journey later life asks. For, to Jung, it is in the second half of life that the true human journey and development can begin. Externally stabilized by work and achievement, the human person can begin to get in touch with deeper values than the external—the values, notably, which contact with the unconscious world provides and which transform the personality, as in the Middle Ages alchemy worked to transform base metal into gold. As the following chapters will spell out in much greater detail, facing the shadow is the first stage in this process. The following stage involves the integration of the contrasexual element of the personality which, in order to develop a masculine or feminine identity, has so far been suppressed or repressed. The effect of this process of repression is the tendency to project onto others—mother, father, husband, wife, friends, enemies—the inner man or woman one has not allowed to emerge. This development of a sexual identity is a necessary process, but the time comes in human life when it needs to be complemented by a withdrawal of projections that have been put onto others. Thus one becomes a more whole and less onesided human being. The man who is so "macho" that he cannot be gentle; the woman who is so "feminine" that she fears her own strength are people who still need this stage of development, but in fact everyone does. It is interesting to see this stage as coming full circle after Freud's views on sexual identity.

Finally, the human person needs to come into contact with his or her true Self—a mysterious process involving not only all the processes already mentioned but openness to the archetype of the Self. In the process of ego development and of living in the world one sets up a persona—or many personas, ways in which we project ourselves on the stage of the social world. These are good to use upon occasion. They are deadly if we identify with them. The work of the second half of life involves this disidentification and the relating, instead, to this archetype of the Self which is the deepest of all. Trying to define the Self is running into risks Jung himself avoided. He did define, but in different ways in different places. While in one place he will speak of the Self as a totality comprising the unconscious and the conscious in the human person[9]—a definition extraordinarily poor unless one knows the full weight of Jung's word "unconscious"—in another he will speak of "something"

strange to us and yet so near, wholly ourselves and yet unknowable, a virtual centre of so mysterious a constitution that it can claim anything . . . the *self.* . . . It might equally well be called the "God within us." The beginning of our whole psychic life seems to be inextricably rooted in this point, and all our highest and ultimate purposes seem to be striving towards it.[10]

This process, even if some of the above terminology sounds religious, even mystical, is strictly psychological. Balance and integration are born of the readiness to deal with the contents of the unconscious, however demanding that process may be. One could say that Freud stressed more the healing of pathology and Jung more the development of the integrated personality, but Freudian principles can lead well onto the path of integration, and Jungian thought explains and works with the darkest places in the psyche. It seems better to do what Jung in fact did do—to use each of these systems of thought where it helps and seems appropriate and to do the same with any other psychological school or system. What helps one person or case may be no use in another.

At present, however, it seems important to lay beside these two theories another by a sixteenth-century spiritual theologian renowned for his own psychological insight, Juan de Yepes, known as St. John of the Cross. A Spaniard, he entered and helped reform the Carmelite order, after studies at Salamanca, a famous center of Thomistic thought. This latter was born of the efforts of Thomas Aquinas to apply Aristotelean principles to reflection on Christian faith. Aquinas, however, also drew heavily on Augustine of Hippo, and so on the Neo-Platonic tradition strong in early Christianity so that his work was born of a very rich and complex tradition. But his own philosopher of predilection was Aristotle, and this philosophical bent influenced both the theology and the psychology of his followers, as did the whole heritage on which he drew.

John of the Cross did not write psychology per se. His psychological principles emerge from his spiritual writing in which he deals, in considerable detail, with the journey of the soul or psyche from the period in which a person first develops some spiritual interests of sorts to the time of total transformation, which John considers to be rarely attained. Three guiding images inspire the three poems on which he wrote detailed commentaries—the dark night (which includes the motif of journey); a prolonged love-song of a bride, modelled on the biblical Song of Songs; and the living flame, which concerns more the later stages of development. Despite the poetic cast of his original writing, John can be extraordinarily realistic—and extraordinarily honest—in his commentaries and explanations.

The journey begins, for him, "on a dark night."[11] He discusses this darkness from both an active and a passive point of view. That is, there is a darkness one must choose in order to progress on the journey, and a darkness that is not chosen but just happens. The darkness one must choose involves the pleasure-seeking side of human nature, the appetites, as John calls them. He speaks of their power to blind, darken, sully the soul or psyche and says that only in controlling them can one find light, peace, strength. Then he goes one stage further and speaks of inner images, memories, desires, including religious ones and the desire for religious experiences on this level of the "inner senses." In all of this, he says, one must experience the darkness, night. Night is privation, and it is, of course, not privation in itself that purifies. It is, rather, love that purifies, and the faith and hope that deepen in this night. These are the essential. Again, it is not that desire in itself is harmful;

John is speaking of desire without control, balance, reason, or light. These are what "darken the soul," and with a darkness that is not that of God or of the purifying "night."

We have been speaking so far of the active level of purification as John describes it. On the passive he speaks of the fact that people who begin to enjoy prayer and spiritual things later lose this enjoyment and wonder what is wrong. They can even stop praying, thinking that it is going nowhere, and escape into activity. This is the early stage of "purification." In the later stage, it is faith itself that seems called into question—and, in fact, the whole relationship to God. Doubt, questioning, rebellion, temptations to blasphemy, a sense of rejection—all these fill this period with "deep darkness" and anguish. For John of the Cross there is no other way to transformation than this.

It is important to stress again that not every suffering or privation purifies. Suffering for its own sake is nowhere advocated in these writings—nor is privation of the good things of sense or spirit valuable in itself. What has value to John is the love and relationship to God that can make one choose a certain privation as more conducive to union with Him than the object renounced—or, again, the love and faith that can make it possible to undergo privation in a positive and purifying way. For to him the whole process is about growth in love, in relationship to God.

John based his thought on the Christian Scriptures as he lived and experienced them even more than on the philosophy he learned in Salamanca. While his writings appear austere to us today, it should be remembered that by the standards of his time they were, rather, moderate, balanced, and based firmly on the primacy not of penance but of love. The two nights of which he speaks are really two parts of a single purification in love and this centrality may perhaps make us reflect on some points of contact with Freud.

Rather than dealing in detail here with his other two main works, *The Spiritual Canticle* and *The Living Flame*, a look at his earlier two, *The Ascent of Mount Carmel* and *The Dark Night*, where this view of human development emerges is important.

* * *

Despite the fact that John is speaking of people seriously committed to a spiritual journey, his first major issue is the question of pleasure. At first blush, his point of view can seem diametrically opposed to that of Freud. The latter seems to believe that most major psychological deviations result from the repression of the sexual drive and therefore that greater openness in this domain would lead to greater psychological health. John of the Cross would seem to be saying, on the contrary, "Renounce all pleasure." Closer examination suggests, however, that the conflict may be more apparent than real. Freud does indeed believe that sexual repression — and repression in general — can be, in many cases, harmful to the human person. But he also characterizes human development as a growth from a stage of total unrealistic pleasure-seeking to one where the reality-principle is more important. Further, the person who has progressed through all the stages of development is one who has become capable of altruistic love and true relationship. His or her universe is no longer totally self- or pleasure-centered but related. This is a very different orientation from the early one.

For John of the Cross, the person beginning to live a "spiritual life" can be very much like Freud's baby — very oral, very desirous of talking to others (in this case, about spirituality), very desirous of pleasure, comfort, "consolation." To John all this is childishness — appropriate for a baby, inappropriate for the adult seeking God — and psychologically that makes perfect sense. While he does speak strongly about the renunciation of pleasure-seeking, he nowhere speaks of what we would call repression. In fact he remarks that some become obsessed with sexual images in prayer precisely because they fear this excessively.[12] John's renunciation of pleasure-seeking is about making other choices, about learning self-discipline and strength of purpose. Moreover, it is about obtaining a certain inner clarity that is born of being master in one's own house. This mastery is not born of castigating one's nature. (John's remarks on "the penance of brutes" will be discussed in a later chapter.) It is born of an appropriate dealing with one's instincts, needs, desires. The aim, once again, is personal growth toward relationship — in this case, with God.

Nonetheless, one must not fall into anachronism either. John of the Cross was not a contemporary psychologist and in his own life he carried penance further than many would think wise today. We cannot know what he would have thought, had he learned our present form of psychology. But we do know that he was capable of a gentleness and consideration many "penitents" did not know, and he did not see his orientation as primarily penitential nor advocate such a "way." His philosophy seems to have borne fruit in wisdom.

The next question concerns the sanjuanist attitude toward memory, imagination, religious experience. Once again, one would think at first sight that it was totally contrary not only to Freud's views on the necessity of remembering the past to be healed but even more to Jung's insistence on the importance of the world of symbols, myths, images. John seems much more a theorist of the "imageless"—and wordless—prayer to be discussed below. But this very statement reveals his paradox. This teacher of silent prayer was a great Spanish poet. His works are studied as literature. His awareness of the power of the image and symbol emerges in every line of his writings—prose as well as poetry. And, in his own life, his use of nature for prayer and formation; his sensitivity to pain and to relationships; his warmth with those he loved tell a different story from some theories that claim to come from him. In his thinking, memory and imagination are indeed to be disciplined. Rather than running wild, they are to be "emptied" to receive what is beyond either, faith. But faith—which, to him, is a personal revelation of God through Christ—is something alive and clothed in its own images, and it draws on some four thousand years of imagery already known. It draws, besides, on the imagery of nature and human relationship and love. John "reads" the world and human experience as speaking of this one great love of his life—the love of God. Is this attitude very different from Jung's concern that people be open to the wider world of the collective unconscious with its symbols which reveal to us depths we cannot find alone and in which the archetype of the Self becomes known and increasingly central to consciousness?

This brings us to consideration of John of the Cross's passive "night"; so far we have discussed only the active. The passive night contains two stages—the first involving lack of pleasure in spiritual pursuits; the second, darkness and anguish in the very relationship with God that is faith and prayer—though, as has been said, the two nights are in fact two moments of a single one. The lack of pleasure in the first is caused not by a real lack of desire (Jung would say Eros) but by the fact that something is emerging from a deeper level of consciousness without yet being truly experienced. (Later in these pages we shall find this same idea, again and again, in Jung.) In John of the Cross's terms the part of the psyche that is being "fed" is no longer "sense" but "spirit" so that the more super-ficial level of feeling, pleasure and sensation is left "dry."

> If in the beginning the soul does not experience this spiritual savor and delight, but darkness and distaste, it is because of the novelty involved in this exchange. . . . Since . . . its spiritual palate is neither purged nor accommodated for so subtle a taste, it is unable to experience the spiritual savor and good until gradually prepared by means of this dark and obscure night.[13]

> If those to whom this occurs know how to remain quiet . . . they will soon in that unconcern and idleness delicately experience the interior nourishment.[14]

These passages, as well as some on the more severe "second night," are interesting to compare with the following passage of Jung:

> [In this case which is one of depression] the unconscious has simply gained an unassailable ascendancy; it wields an attractive force that can invalidate all conscious contents—in other words, it can withdraw libido from the conscious world and thereby produce a "depression. . . ." But as a result of this we must, according to the law of energy, expect an accumulation of value —i.e. libido—in the unconscious. . . . The patient's conscious world has become cold, empty, and grey; but his unconscious is activated, powerful, and rich.[15]

Is it correct to identify Jung's unconscious with John's source of interior nourishment? John would say that this nourishment came from God. Jung might be less explicit. But to Jung, also, the uncon-scious is the place where one meets higher and deeper forces than one's own, and if the shadow is there, so is the Self. I do not believe this comparison is forced.

Finally, John of the Cross speaks of the "second night" with its terrible temptations, darkness, pain. Jung, in his turn, will say that transformation is possible only by going through the alchemical process of blackening (nigredo), as a log is blackened in fire, in order to be transformed into "gold." The log image is not alchemy's but that of John of the Cross. Once again, the process seems parallel.

But is Jung's "transformation" that of John of the Cross? Not explicitly. Jung does not speak of transforming union with God in those terms. But he does speak of the transformation of the human person, and he is not afraid to use the image of the *sequela Christi*, commenting that Western Christianity has failed by making this "following" external rather than transformative, as we shall see. One can hardly think that St. Paul, whom Jung often quotes, would disagree with this view. While one cannot identify the views of Jung and John of the Cross totally, there certainly seem to be points of convergence—notably on the level of experience, more than on that of theory, as the following chapters will show.

On a wider level, if one assumed that all three positions studied had their truth, what kind of general picture would emerge? It is tempting to begin with a statement of John of the Cross—that the first night subjects "sense to spirit" and the second night subjects the spirit, or the whole human person, to God—and compare it with Freud's remark that where the id was, the ego must come to be. While these two remarks—Freud's and the first part of John's —cannot be seen as saying exactly the same thing, they seem to speak of a similar dynamic. The immature person is a plaything of moods, feelings, impulses of which he or she is largely unconscious and yet they rule life to a large extent. John of the Cross will sometimes speak of desire and attachment as if the will alone could conquer these, but he also says, time and again, that a true "purification" needs its passive element as well. In more psychological terms, we may be aware to some extent of the passions and feelings that move us, but their unconscious roots go deeper than we realize and these cannot be dealt with by will power alone. As Jung would say, we need to become more conscious. As John would say, we need to be purified. And as Freud would say, we need to become more aware of repressed material and its effects on our lives, though his use of such material has a different finality than John's.

That is the first stage of the process for the average person. We are not speaking here of the gravely psychologically damaged. Nor is the issue here one of the primary stages of ego building which belong to the "first part of life." These stages will be discussed in later chapters, but both Jung and John of the Cross stress later stages more. When a greater level of "consciousness" has been achieved; when the human person is more in control of his or her instincts, more at peace in his or her own house; then, Jung would say, it is time for the salvific contact with the archetypes, the transforming symbols. The sanjuanist terminology would be that deeper contact with God will work a deeper purification. Once again, do these two sets of terms describe the same process? All proportion guarded, Jung's Archetype of the Self is the way in which one experiences God. He will stress again and again the importance of learning to surrender to a greater power than one's own in the living of a deeper life than the "unconscious" or ego-controlled life-style.[16] His care about naming this power should not blind us to what he really seems to be saying. "This step beyond science [in which one comes to recognize oneself as 'the object of an unknown and supraordinate subject'] is an unconditional requirement of the psychological development I have sought to depict."[17]

And Freud? Everyone is used to the idea that for Freud religion is an illusion, a projection of a superfather. It might be true to say, therefore, that Freud does not follow Jung or John of the Cross on what they describe as the second lap of the journey. But he depicts the intricacies of the early stages in such detail that Jung admitted his debt to and readiness to use the thought of his early mentor, and John of the Cross in many places seems to be analyzing some of the same phenomena Freud discussed. Awareness of the unconscious or subconscious per se may not have been present in the Renaissance, but its effects showed in people's lives and psyches, and John of the Cross was known for his practical realism in this regard. I find it difficult to believe that, had he lived today, he would not have made the most positive use of these discoveries. The following chapters can investigate some of the lines such use might take.

Before closing this chapter, a few words need to be said on a subject that would require a dissertation—and this, to avoid a lack of clarity or some real ambiguity below. The issue is: what is Jung's real position on religion? Is he a Christian? A pantheist? A vague sort of agnostic? Or what?

Anyone trying to answer this question briefly is foolish indeed, so the best solution seems to be to choose a few quotations from Jung himself, realizing that others in other places can balance these off and even say very different things. The reader is referred to Appendix 2 for some of these.

Immediately after a quotation on the Self given above, which allows us to call it "the God within us," Jung adds that this does not

imply a deification of man or a dethronement of God. What is beyond our understanding is in any case beyond its reach. When, therefore, we make use of the concept of a God we are simply formulating a definite psychological fact, namely the independence and sovereignty of certain psychic contents which express themselves by their power to thwart our will, to obsess our consciousness and to influence our moods and actions.[18]

What Jung is saying is that there is a power beyond our consciousness, which he sometimes calls the unconscious, which, if repressed, can only lead to harm. We need to come into contact with it and to know it is something in us but not subject to us. Surely, though, one could say, the unconscious is hardly the same thing as God.

The conception of God as an autonomous psychic content makes God into a moral problem—and that, admittedly, is very uncomfortable. But if this problem does not exist, God is not real, for nowhere can he touch our lives. . . .

If we leave the idea of "divinity" quite out of account and speak only of "autonomous contents," we maintain a position that is intellectually and empirically correct, but we silence a note which, psychologically, should not be missing.[19]

In other words, we are dealing with something mysterious, beyond our control and definition, but which cannot be adequately thought of without the inclusion of the note of "divinity." Theologians might find this definition inadequate for their purposes, but at least it suggests that, for Jung, the notion of a God intimately connected with the depths of human life, and with whom one must "connect" in order to live in any kind of healthy way, is essential. Further, "the individuated ego senses itself as the object of an unknown and supraordinate subject."[20] Individuation, then, or the process of coming to full psychological maturity, leads one to a deep relationship with this Other.

So, in terms of the above quotations: (1) there is within us something beyond our understanding and control which has a certain power over our consciousness and lives, with which we must "connect" in order to live in a healthy way; (2) this "something" cannot be adequately understood without the note of "divinity" being included; and (3) this "something" is able to relate to us as subject to object.

Jung adds elsewhere:

It is now quite possible that, instead of identifying with the mana-personality,[21] one will concretize it as an extramundane "Father in Heaven," complete with the attribute of absoluteness. . . . The logical result is that the only thing left behind here is a miserable, inferior, worthless and sinful little heap of humanity.[22]

He explains his terms:

"Absolute" means "cut off," "detached." To assert that God is absolute amounts to placing him outside all connection with mankind. . . . We can in fairness only speak of a God who is relative to man, as man is to God. The Christian idea of God as a "Father in Heaven" puts God's relativity in exquisite form. . . . This urge to regard God as "absolute" derives solely from the fear that God might become "psychological." . . . An absolute God . . . does not concern us in the least, whereas a "psychological" God would be *real.*[23]

How does the human person avoid becoming "miserable, inferior, worthless"? By the refusal to shift absolutely all value to the side of the divinity to the exclusion of the notion of human worth and dignity. The notion, for example, of the Christian as the child of God—in technical terms, the notion of created grace transforming the human psyche—is this kind of refusal, and one that any healthy theology will recognize. So Jung's position here is hardly unorthodox.

Jung is therefore adding to the above three points of his "theology" the notion that this "divine something" is related to us in all ways—is not, in other words, an eternal Watchmaker in the heavens. And being, in Christian terms, a "Father" to us—that is, deeply related—His "wish" would be that we be "daughters and sons," not worthless worms. And this is precisely the subject of the following chapter.

·2·

THE SHADOW

It has been said above that, to Jung, the dynamics of the human psyche involve a movement through an outer-directed "ego-building" phase, in which the human person establishes himself or herself as an adult and responsible member of society, into and through a phase Jung calls "the second half of life." This latter involves working through various stages of an inner journey or process toward the goal of true integration or individuation. The following chapters will discuss various stages of this process, and this chapter treats of an initial issue—facing and dealing with the shadow.

Freud, to all intents and purposes, would seem to be left behind here. Are not Freudian principles to be applied in building a sufficiently strong and healthy ego rather than in this second stage? But reflection on the meaning of "shadow" suggests otherwise. To Freud, mental illness is often born of the upsurge of instinctual forces no longer able to be contained by the conscious personality. And these instinctive forces which the ego represses as unacceptable are precisely the personal—if not the archetypal—shadow. It is this excessive repression of unconscious contents that is the cause of the "upsurge" in most cases. And, as Jung's quotations in the previous chapter show, one essential means to avoid this result is the bringing to consciousness of some of these contents—coming to terms with one's own darker side. This is the same basic process as Jung's facing of the shadow, though for Freud the issue remains one of the personal unconscious alone.

What, then, is the content of our shadow? To Jung, the shadow is everything in ourselves that we do not care to see, that we try to push back out of consciousness so that we can avoid owning it. And this includes, oddly enough, positive contents as well as negative. For some people it is harder to face their gifts, capabilities, positive desires than the negative in themselves. Nonetheless, it is important to take a long hard look at the negative.

First of all there is, as Freud continually pointed out, much concerning our sexual impulses that we fear to look at, face, name. This may seem less true today than in Freud's time, but there are nonetheless considerable areas for most people that they prefer to leave in darkness and that they express in euphemism if at all. (Four-letter words can, for some, be another form of euphemism.) One has only to think of the emotional reactions to some contemporary issues to notice this anew.

Beside sexual issues there are those concerning aggressivity, anger, narcissism. The present demand for classes in assertiveness indicates something about the repression of aggressivity people experience. Some fear that the open expression of anger will destroy all relationships; they fear to acknowledge the hate that so frequently accompanies love—as if expressing one would destroy the other. This leads to living with idealized parents, children, partners, rather than with real ones, while at the same time passing on very different messages at other levels where the real feelings emerge.

Deeper still is the tendency to set up an image of the ideal self and force into unconsciousness anything in us that opposes it. This unconscious content is, precisely, the shadow and is just what one most fears to see. But owning it is, paradoxically, the one way toward becoming one's true—and therefore much more "ideal" in the sense of whole or real—self.

All this is the personal shadow. It does not yet even begin to touch the wider areas of evil, sin, sickness, death, darkness, and one's reactions to this whole sphere. But that will emerge later if we begin by dealing with the personal shadow.

What does all the above mean in terms of ethics—let alone of religion or Christianity? Is it necessary to give free rein to what early writers called the "capital sins"—pride, covetousness, lust, anger, gluttony, envy, sloth—in order to reach integration? This, clearly, is not what Jung is saying. Knowing what one feels and is internally does not mean one acts on every impulse without reflection, for the powers of reflection and ethical judgment also form part of our psyche, if they are truly ours and the product of our own sincere and deliberate choices. But in order to reflect lucidly, one needs at least to know honestly what these inner feelings are. Denial only aggravates their power and cuts us off from our own truth.

Jung writes:

> This [the shadow] is now raised to consciousness and integrated with the ego, which means a move in the direction of wholeness. Wholeness is not so much perfection as completeness. Assimilation of the shadow gives a man body, so to speak; the animal sphere of instinct, as well as the primitive or archaic psyche, emerge into the zone of consciousness and can no longer be repressed by fictions and illusions. In this way man becomes for himself the difficult problem he really is. He must always remain conscious of the fact that he is such a problem if he wants to develop at all.[1]

One could ask: *why* get in touch with this "animal sphere"? Is it not better and wiser—to use a very appropriate image—to let sleeping dogs lie? Jung's position—and Freud's—is that trying to exclude the existence of these dogs from consciousness because they seem asleep does not remove their presence and, when they wake up, if we have not made friends with them, they can cause us very considerable trouble.

The human person, then, must recognize and come to terms with "the problem he really is." To build from here is to build from truth. And to begin anywhere else is to build from illusion. One could almost use this as a touchstone of the realism and value of different systems of thought and spirituality. For what denies the real builds without foundations.

> Recognition of the shadow is reason enough for humility, for genuine fear of the abysmal depths in man. This caution is most expedient, since the man without a shadow thinks himself harmless precisely because he is ignorant of his shadow.[2]

Facing the shadow, then, leads to humility as Jung understands it—genuine fear of the abysmal depths in the human person—to the knowledge of what one is capable of in terms of evil. This awareness makes it very difficult to indulge in the kind of moral smugness one finds among some religious people and of which we will find good descriptions in John of the Cross below. The person who sees him or herself as incapable of serious moral evil has not yet even inchoate awareness of his or her depths. This is the very first stage of growth or of the journey.

Jung was very aware, however, that this facing of the shadow is not simply a private luxury for the few with time and money to indulge in analysis. On the contrary, wherever this process does not occur, even the social effects of this repression are disastrous. For either the individual projects his repressed shadow on the people around him, with the effects on social intercourse and family life that one can imagine, or, on the collective level, countries go through the same process and then "the Enemy" is always outside and is universally evil—while we ourselves, of course, are good and the defenders of justice, democracy, or virtue in the world. The cosmic dimensions of this issue of facing the shadow make it of crucial importance on all levels of human life. Laurens van der Post writes in his biography of Jung:

> I knew Jung, alas, only in the last sixteen years of his life and when I first met him this problem of the universal shadow was his greatest concern. I clearly remember him saying to me that the individual who withdraws his shadow from his neighbour and finds it in himself and is reconciled to it as to an estranged brother is doing a task of great universal importance. He added quickly that the future of mankind depended on the speed and extent to which individuals learnt to withdraw their shadows from others and reintegrate them honourably within themselves.[3]

In each of our hearts, however, whether we strive to do this work alone or with another, there is a deep resistance to going through with this process. Speaking of her work as an analyst, June Singer writes:

> I let the analysand know from the beginning that he will face the dark, ugly, and tawdry aspects of his life which he has been avoiding and that since these contents are and have long been unacceptable to him, that something in him will take every possible means to frustrate their disclosure.[4]

"Every possible means" is a strong phrase. But experience does indeed show the varieties of techniques one learns to avoid this confrontation with one's depths. The literature of spirituality is full of these and that of psychology and psychoanalysis equally. One usual term for this phenomenon is "resistance" and we shall meet this again in the following chapter.

Finally, there is the issue of the "bright shadow." Some people find it even harder to admit their gifts, value, dignity than their vices. Jung's remarks on an "absolutized" God-conception that leaves the human person empty and miserable are very relevant here. Such people often fear that it is a kind of lèse-majesté toward God, or even toward other people, to admit what really is of good in themselves. One might be tempted to think, in the West, that this attitude is a result of a misunderstanding of the Christian message, particularly as regards humility, but then one discovers the Oriental notion of humility—and its travesties, no less damaging than those in the West—and one realizes that this is a human issue, not one of any specific religion. Greek drama with its meditations on the theme of *hubris,* pride, seems preoccupied with the same question. Perhaps the human awareness of personal limitation and powerlessness before certain natural forces which our ancestors placated by magic[5] is one root of this fear of personal dignity. And this whole question leads to study of the tradition of humility, especially in Western spirituality.

One could wonder about the sources of this latter tradition. Obviously, the Judeo-Christian heritage draws heavily upon Scripture, where the later Old Testament develops the notion of the *anawim,* the poor of Yahweh[6]—the simple and humble remnant of Israel that truly seeks God's will and "trembles at His word"[7] with the reverential fear so different from panic or distrust and yet so respectful of the numinous.[8]

Once one gets to the Gospels, there is the important presentation of the Beatitudes which one Scripture scholar called the "canonization of the *anawim.*"[9] When Jesus invites his followers to learn from him "for I am meek and humble [lowly] of heart,"[10] one can suppose the original term to have been *anaw.*

This tradition continues right through the literature of the Egyptian desert and through early monastic writings such as those of Cassian and Evagrius Ponticus into Benedict's *Rule for Monasteries* which was meant to be anything but an original document but rather a brief compendium of the earlier monastic tradition as applicable to monastic life in a specific place. It is worth considering this document briefly, then, to try to understand this thread of

Western spiritual tradition, though one could easily find the theme in other writers like Basil.

The spiritual centrality of Chapter 7 on humility in the Benedictine Rule is universally recognized in monastic circles. As the first seven chapters of this Rule are its spiritual kernel, that on humility is like the heart of the whole section. Research on the document shows, however, that almost the entire chapter is drawn from Cassian, who, in turn, claimed to be nothing but the transmitter of the doctrine of the desert. This notion of humility, then, is one that has been of great importance in the early Christian tradition.

What, however, is the meaning of this "humility"? From a twentieth-century vantage point one can think of Uriah Heep and shudder. But what lies behind the Dickensian portrayal—what original ideal and what perversions of it?

The Benedictine portrayal begins with the Gospel theme that "Whoever exalts himself shall be humbled and whoever humbles himself shall be exalted."[11] The conclusion is that present humility on earth prepares exaltation in heaven, and that humility involves both body and soul. There follows what could be characterized as a psychological description of the development of the attitude of humility through its several stages in the human person.

The first stage involves the kind of fear of God mentioned above in terms of Scripture—a constant remembrance of God's presence and commands and of the results of keeping or breaking these latter—one could say a kind of spiritual realism. In other words, the issue is one of awareness of the realities in which the Christian believes, rather than an attitude of forgetfulness and superficiality. The monk is invited to consciousness that his inmost thoughts and feelings are always open to God.[12] How foolish, then, to try to hide them from oneself: more, a later stage of humility will involve the owning of these thoughts and feelings before a spiritual guide.

There is also an invitation to avoid self-will. What does this concept mean? Self-will is contrasted with the divine will that brings God's Kingdom. One could conclude that the destructive tendencies in the human person that lead him or her to choose what interferes with not only personal growth but also the wider good of the community and the world are to be renounced. On a deeper level, life centered on oneself and one's desires rather than the Other who gives life is the issue.

But surely one has here in a nutshell precisely the attitude that both, in Jung's terms, empties the person and leads to the denial of negative desires?

There is no doubt that the misunderstanding of this exhortation as it has been passed down through many generations of religious people could read: *do* what you are commanded by any legitimate authority or law; *refuse* to let yourself desire or choose anything forbidden; preferably *deny* even such thoughts or desires as they arise within. This is not, however, what this document says—or means. For one thing, throughout this Rule come repeated warnings against external observance or action not born of the heart, not integrated and interiorized. The normal image, born of the book of Exodus, is that of "murmuring," even just in the heart—as the Jews in the desert murmured against Moses and even against God for bringing them away from the "fleshpots of Egypt" toward what was in fact their deeper, and originally chosen, destiny. The whole person must be behind whatever is done—not by violence but by the increasingly integrated choice of love. This cannot occur by sheer force of will: one's heart and feelings escape the determinations of sheer will. Only the in-depth purification that is the work of humility produces this result. So it is necessary to return to the examination of its stages.

The stages following the first involve not only the renunciation of self-will directly before God but also in terms of obedience to superiors, seen as a means to finding the will of God. In the tradition the superior was either a spiritual guide and teacher to whom the monk, particularly in the desert, committed himself to learn the ways of God—or the abbot who represented the common good of the entire *coenobium* and its needs, and God's will is found also in this community. Hence, these lines of the Rule speak of quietness of heart and steadiness before the suffering and contradiction that can ensue from the stance of obedience. There is nothing exalting or idealizing in the descriptions of this phase. "False brethren," the authority of other human persons imposed on the monk, blows and persecution expressed in scriptural imagery—all these are to be expected. So, in twentieth-century terms, what is being said? Basically, that the choice both to live realistically in terms of the universe seen in faith and to act realistically in terms of this belief will lead not only to recognition of the authority of others as well as our own—and to a greater authority of the part of some of these others—but also to suffering in the living out of these options. The humble person is one who lives in this reality without trying to escape from it—without even getting into an emotional state before what is, in our type of world, to be expected in the process.

The terminology of the later stages of humility sounds, again, like precisely what Jung had in mind when he spoke of emptying and becoming a worm. The monk is to be content with "the meanest and worst of everything," to consider himself a useless servant, and to recognize himself in his heart as "the last and vilest of all." What is this about?

For one thing, the scriptural reference to the useless servant is clear. There is no particular need for self-glorification for doing what needs to be done. Any other attitude smacks of narcissism, of which more below. If one needs the best of everything, is one's value in oneself or in possessions, convenience, comfort? Joan Chittister understands the readiness to see oneself as the last and vilest as readiness to accept criticism.[13] And this is an appropriate place to mention her concept of humility, for in conferences to her community she begins with a description of the narcissistic personality with its grandiosity, need for attention, inability to take criticism, lack of concern for others, seen as the opposite pole from the humble personality. For her, lack of humility involves precisely this personality disorder, to a greater or lesser degree.[14] Seeing oneself as "vile," then, can be a scriptural image for a realistic assessment of one's faith-place before God, others, and one's illusions about a personal perfection. One comes here very close to Jung's remarks on the acceptance of, and befriending of, the shadow. If I know my shadow, I know who I am, and I will not be surprised if others find me less than perfect or treat me accordingly. Nor will I want to be seen as the paragon of perfection I may want myself to be—or that others may want me to be.

Later "degrees of humility" may not, in fact, be "later," but may rather be the physical or external expressions of this inner attitude. Talkativeness, superficiality, inappropriate jocoseness, all are seen as reflecting life out of touch with one's reality and that of the world. One could say a life out of touch with the shadow, or a life of some degree of illusion.

The last paragraphs of this chapter on humility are the culmination of the whole section. First, there is the picture of the monk who has reached the final development of humility and who is always conscious of his sinfulness, showing this attitude even in his external deportment. And then there is the culminating explanation that the result of this process of growth in humility is the attainment of "that perfect love that casts out fear"[15]—an attainment that is not the result of intensive willed efforts but of the purification of the depths of the heart. The person who has reached this stage continues on a path begun out of a sense of obligation and in fear with a new and totally different attitude, for now he or she acts easily and without fear but out of love. This effect is seen as produced by God through the purification of the heart and soul.

To translate into twentieth-century terms including those of psychology, once the habit of denying one's negative tendencies and repressed material is over; once one has learned to live with the shadow; one is indeed in the truth of one's being—without illusion or pretense. And it is then, paradoxically, that one is freed from fear. The negatives have been faced and no longer threaten. One's own true face, both positive and negative, has been seen and acknowledged. In Christian terms, the need for divine mercy is recognized. And, receiving it, one knows there is no further need for fear. Salvation is not from one's own works and righteousness, as the Pharisee in the Gospel thought; rather, as the Publican knew, it is from God's love. And so, in one's humility—and only there—one emerges into freedom.

It is important to repeat that these reflections do not totally identify Benedict's thought with Jung's. The two came from different perspectives and wrote for different readers with at least partially different aims. But the convergence of their thought remains striking. The first step for any spiritual progress remains the recognition of the depths within—depths of evil as well as good—not exaggerating but not minimizing either. This recognition leads to a readiness for admitting this side of oneself, to a respect for others—both their value and their criticism—without this causing a loss of balance or grounding in oneself. The realities of the world, authority, God, and relationship are recognized without—or with minimal—projection and with awareness of one's own position in relation to them all. And the result of this process is deeper integration and freedom.

Recently, in response to a psychological study of Benedictine humility by Vergote,[16] an article appeared presenting this chapter of the Rule as a study of a progressive divine invasion taking place in the human psyche surrendered to God. Much in this article runs along the same lines as some Jungian themes, so a discussion of the article will be found in Appendix 1 of this book.

The Benedictine Rule is an early document. How do related concepts get expressed in later spirituality? A few passages from John of the Cross are enlightening.

This author gives a character-sketch of the beginner in the spiritual journey and his or her pride. This person is self-complacent in virtue, eager to instruct others, ready to condemn. "Some of these persons become so evil-minded that they do not want anyone except themselves to appear holy."[17] They will not listen to disagreement from their spiritual director or superior, but seek someone to tell them what they wish to hear. They want to be noticed for their spirituality, to appear well, to be freed of their imperfections and faults for the sake of their own peace rather than of God. They love praise.

By contrast, John says, those who are truly moving forward on the journey are not self-satisfied about their deeds but rather respect what others do. They are aware of their good deeds, but these only increase their sense of gratitude to God. They want to do much for God so that all they have done seems little, and they therefore want to be considered insignificant in this regard. They are ready to learn from anyone rather than to teach. They are also more ready to own their faults and sins than their virtues and live humbly, tranquilly, simply, truthfully, lovingly for others. When they "fall into imperfections they suffer this with humility, with docility of spirit, and with loving fear of God and hope in Him."[18] The whole mood is one of quiet and trust and respect for others. It is not one of neurotic self-depreciation but rather one of realism and readiness to relativize what they have done.

In other places in his works, John speaks at great length of the illusions into which one can fall for lack of this attitude of humility and realism. One can mistake the false for the true, the unimportant for the important, what is of the devil for what is of God. Reading these passages reminds one of passages in Jung on identification with the "mana-personality." Mana is the numinous quality, the "extraordinarily potent" energy found in the unconscious and in the archetypal themes of mythology and primitive religion. Identification with this mana-personality (priest, prophet, god, demon) leads to inflation. "The only defense is full confession of one's weakness."[19] The more one is in touch with the more-than-human, the greater the danger to anyone not anchored in this first foothold of truth, the attitude of humility. We shall return to this point again below, with Jung's discussion of inflation.

Meantime, Thomas Merton has some thought-provoking lines on this point:

> The Christ we find in ourselves is not identified with what we vainly seek to admire and idolize in ourselves—on the contrary, He has identified Himself with what we resent in ourselves, for He has taken upon Himself our wretchedness and our misery, our poverty and our sins. . . . We cannot attain to purity of heart unless first of all we accept the fact that our hearts are not pure and that there is in us no way of making them pure. . . . We must learn to listen to what goes on in our heart and interpret it correctly. We will never find peace if we listen to the voice of our own fatuous self-deception that tells us the conflict has ceased to exist. We will find peace when we can listen to the 'deathdance in our blood' not only with equanimity but with exultation because we hear within it the echoes of the victory of the risen saviour.[20]

Our discussion so far has dealt largely with the personal importance of dealing with and facing one's shadow—as well as, in Jung's terms, with the cosmic importance of the same process in order to avoid projecting the evil in oneself on other people or nations or ideologies. There is also a therapeutic effect of this process of self-recognition and self-knowledge, for freedom from illusion about oneself helps one to free others. One Jungian analyst writes:

> If the analyst has genuinely confronted her own shadow and learned to love the enemy, then the cornerstone which the builders rejected does become the cornerstone of the new building. . . . In Christian terms, as well as Jungian terms, the love of the enemy is not natural but *contra naturam,* not Eros but Agape. It is, as Jung described it, a form of grace arising from sacrifice, a resurrection coming out of death.[21]

Immediately after the above passage, Woodman speaks of an incident in which she referred to an obese woman's size in front of two others in the waiting room. The two were apparently horrified: the analysand herself came in laughing, yet close to tears. "Did you see their faces . . . when they were coerced to recognize me? For over a year I've been sitting invisibly in that room and when I was finally seen, nobody knew what to do with me. I was real."[22] Naming the shadows from which our culture tends to avert eyes, attention, and "naming" can liberate. But one can do this only when one has met and come to terms with the shadow oneself.

There is, finally, a related topic to which both Jungian literature and that of spirituality refer constantly and which was mentioned above—that of inflation. After speaking of the importance of getting in touch with the unconscious, Jung writes:

> The process of assimilating the unconscious leads to some very remarkable phenomena. It produces in some patients an unmistakable and often unpleasant increase of self-confidence and conceit: they are full of themselves, they know everything, they imagine themselves to be fully informed of everything concerning their unconscious, and are persuaded that they understand perfectly everything that comes out of it. . . . Overflowing with feelings of their own importance, [they] assume a responsibility for the unconscious that goes much too far, beyond all reasonable bounds.[23]

An opposite reaction is to become "crushed under the burden of the unconscious." Jung recognizes that he has here sketched two extremes usually met with in more mitigated form, but he adds that "every analysand starts by unconsciously misusing his newly won knowledge" until he or she has been healed of his or her symptoms. Jung relates this attitude to the "godlikeness, knowing good and evil" promised by the serpent in the book of Genesis— where one finds, in fact, in the Christian tradition, a description of the sin of pride. He finds the cause of this attitude in the obliteration of personal boundaries. In other words, the person forgets his or her own limits and limitations. Another form of this attitude, to be discussed later, is identification with one's business or titles.

In this context, John of the Cross's descriptions of the pride of beginners will be remembered. The resemblance is striking. Their complacency, readiness to instruct, wish to be noticed come in the same category of inflation. In an older tradition, one has, again

from the Benedictine Rule, the invitation to manifest one's faults
to one's spiritual father or mother seen as a desire coming naturally
with growth in humility, as well as the exhortation: "do not aspire
to be called holy before you really are; but first be holy, that you
may more truly be called so."[24]

In other words, both traditions—that of spirituality and that of
depth psychology—point to the same kind of deviation which mani-
fests itself in the same kinds of ways. Inflation or pride must be
healed by the purifying therapeutic process supplied by continuing
on the spiritual journey. One is also helped by honesty with significant others.

It seems appropriate to close with part of a scriptural poem:

Happy the man whose offence is forgiven,
whose sin is remitted.
O happy the man to whom the Lord
imputes no guilt,
in whose spirit is no guile.

I kept it secret and my frame was wasted.
I groaned all day long
for night and day your hand
was heavy upon me.
Indeed, my strength was dried up
as by the summer's heat.

But now I have acknowledged my sins;
my guilt I did not hide.
I said: 'I will confess
my offence to the Lord.'
And you, Lord, have forgiven
the guilt of my sin.

So let every good man pray to you
in the time of need.
The floods of water may reach high
but him they shall not reach.
You are my hiding place, O Lord;
you save me from distress.
(You surround me with cries of deliverance.)[25]

Here, the effects of hiding sin in the heart are described as the drying up of strength. Psychologically, this makes perfect sense: the effort demands considerable energy. On the contrary, the acknowledgement of truth before God, the acknowledgement of sin, brings the awareness of God as deliverer, and, with this, joy and freedom.

This psalm is known as the second penitential psalm and has been repeated as such through the centuries in the Christian spiritual tradition, as it was in the Hebrew. Saying that one needs to get to know the shadow, then, and to acknowledge it, has old roots indeed. One can wonder whether, when Jesus chose to make friends of publicans and prostitutes, this was because their readiness to admit their shadows made them more open to the real meaning of relationship and life with God.

·3·

WORK

"Work" in our contemporary vocabulary often refers to our means of livelihood, our employment, or often manual labor. The *Random House College Dictionary,* for example, gives as a first definition "exertion or effort directed to produce or accomplish something" and, as a third, "employment, as in some form of industry." Poets, artists, writers do indeed speak of their work—we distinguish pieces of music that way—but on hearing the word our first association is not usually in this field. It seems likely that there has been some modification of the understanding of this term in recent centuries—or at least a change of accent. In Greek and Roman times, the terms *labora, ergon, kopos* could mean heavy physical work. They could also, however, refer to an inner work or to what we would today rarely call "work." It is interesting, for example, that our term "liturgy" comes from the Greek words *leiton ergon,* the work of the people. In the sixth-century Rule of Benedict, again, the chapter on work is, in fact, also the chapter on *lectio divina,* on meditative reading, for this also was the monk's work. And earlier, in the Egyptian desert, the whole "active life" of moving toward purity of heart or contemplation by growth in the necessary ascesis and virtue was considered to be the "work" of the monk.[1]

In contemporary psychological circles, terms like "the work" and derivatives like "working through" are common, and they have filtered into many people's language by now. So what is the "work" involved, for example, in psychoanalysis or in the therapy connected with this tradition? A text written in the Freudian tradition remarks that psychoanalysis

35

makes the ego face its pathogenic conflicts in their full emotional value by undoing the opposing defensive forces, effective as "resistances." . . . [It] works by undoing resistances and interpreting transferences.[2]

It is not difficult to see, in such a context, why the word "work" should be appropriate. Shying away from facing conflict is a normal human reaction. Being forced to face it head on in its "full emotional value" is a battle in the deepest sense of the word. Obviously, the psyche sets up its defenses, its resistances, in an effort at self-protection. But what is protected is, in this case, not an area of health. The passage to wholeness requires the renunciation of this kind of self-defense, which takes great courage as well as time. When, in the Rule of Benedict, admitting one's secret thoughts to a spiritual father is described as a relatively high degree of humility, as well as a means thereto, this statement shows awareness of the human difficulty of such admission. The difficulty in analysis is not less.

There is further difficulty in the fact that this whole process interferes with already set patterns of behavior and thought, uncomfortable to call into question and far more uncomfortable to change. The analytic tradition speaks of a structural change in the personality resulting from analysis, and such statements terrify some who read or hear them. They fear being changed into a different kind of person, one that analysts would approve. But the fact is that the structural change in question is meant to help the individual come into touch with his or her deeper truth and reality—with what, in fact, is felt or desired, whether that is something considered "good" or "bad." Feeling hatred, for example, or wanting to kill someone is usually considered to be a "bad feeling," with the result that many people deny such feelings. Unfortunately, however, the feelings are as common as they are condemned and inner honesty requires that one admit them. The price of denial is the emotional energy required to keep building up defenses against this realization. Analysis aims at the removal of excessive defenses and the readiness to look at what one is in truth. Once this has begun to be achieved, one is more able to choose what, in fact, one wishes to be, in terms of what one truly is.

Another commentary, also in the Freudian tradition, speaks of the process of "working through" in these terms: it is "related to the time and energy required . . . to change his habitual patterns of instinctual discharge. . . . This implies coming to terms with (1) unconscious infantile conflicts . . . (2) ego control of drive cathexes . . . (3) a widening of the area of the ego's autonomy."[3] It results in an increase in the ego's control over its emotional investments, "in a domination of the pleasure principle by the reality principle" and in the types of thinking and discharging psychic energy characteristic of the mature rather than the immature ego.

In other words, most of us who are still leading "unexamined lives" have patterns of "instinctual discharge" which reflection or deeper self-knowledge and self-understanding might make us wish to change. Willing, however, is insufficient to achieve this end—as will be seen again in a later chapter. "Working through" is a slower process, but since it involves the whole person on all levels, it has somewhat more hope of achieving the end. In order to do this, it will be necessary to deal with conflicts born in infancy and of which one is still inadequately aware—loves, hates, needs, desires with the frustrations and struggle they involve. It will also be necessary to see where, at present, emotional energy is going and why, how freely the choices involved are made or, on the contrary, how determined they are. The fruit of the process is, however, meant to be greater maturity, autonomy, realism, freedom. For we are slaves of what remains in darkness for us: once it emerges into consciousness, we can be more free.

* * *

The above quotations come out of the Freudian tradition. The Jungian accents are rather different.

For one thing, Jung differentiates strongly between the work to be done in what he calls the first half of life and that of the second. His own field of predilection was the second, for which, in fact, he sees the first as preparation. His remarks on this point show what kind of "work" he believes the first stage requires:

> As soon as we speak of the collective unconscious we find ourselves in a sphere, and concerned with a problem, which is altogether precluded in the practical analysis of young people or of those who have remained infantile too long. Wherever the father and mother imagos have still to be overcome, wherever

there is a little bit of life still to be conquered, which is the
natural possession of the average man, then we had better make
no mention of the collective unconscious and the problem of
opposites.[4]

He goes on to say that once "parental transferences and the youthful
illusions" have been mastered, then it is time for the real work,
which is not concerned with external success or achievement but
rather with the meaning of life.

This passage gives one insight into Jung's views on this first
stage of life and its tasks. The human person must learn to take
his or her place in society; and must learn to achieve what is
"natural" for the "average man" to achieve. In other words, trying
to do in-depth analytical work with someone who has not yet
achieved adult stance in his or her world is likely to be illusory.
First things must come first, and achievement is part of the maturation process. So is the task of becoming free of one's family—not
just by an external departure from the home but more deeply, by
taking back into oneself the parental material one so easily projects
out onto others and by being able to make choices born of truly
personal rather than parental values. Everyone has met people
who seemed to be looking for another father or mother to marry,
for example—men who see their mother (overstrong, captivating,
seductive, or even perfect) in everything any woman says or does.
These attitudes again prevent realistic relating to the person who
actually exists. They are the task of the earlier stages of adult life,
though their completion may be a longer process. As these tasks
draw at least nearer to completion, the work of the second half of
life can begin. The work of the analyst, then, in the first half of life,
is "to clear away all the obstacles that hinder expansion and ascent."[5]
The second half, paradoxically, has to do with facing descent.

Jung distinguishes the "natural" (first) stage of life from the "cultural" (second), and he points out that what makes the process of
the second half of life so difficult, even traumatic, for some people,
is the fact that they continue to cling to the earlier values—youth,
health, beauty, children, the role of motherhood. He sees the transition to the second half of life as full of turbulence, like adolescence—another "dangerous age." When he begins to describe
the work, which one could truly characterize as struggle—agon-y, as
we have translated the Greek—of the second half, one understands.

The transition from morning to afternoon means a revaluation
of the earlier values. There comes the urgent need to appreciate
the value of the opposite of our former ideals, to perceive the
error in our former convictions, to recognize the untruth in our
former truth, and to feel how much antagonism and even hatred
lay in what, until now, had passed for love.[6]

This process alone would clearly be difficult and painful. But
Jung says still more is required. It is easy to pass from one opposite
to another, rejecting the first, in comparison with the struggle
required to embrace the second without rejecting or repressing the
first. If neurosis results from repression and denial, in this case
also neurosis will result if one simply represses the past—or if one
refuses to move into the future. The agony is to try to widen one's
horizons to accept the new without denying the old. Midlife crises
which jettison all parts of the old life to choose a new, are the
result—at least very frequently—of not having worked through
this process to the end. But balance and growth lie in this "working
through" alone.

The pain of this process of "exchanging the apparent security we
have so far enjoyed for a condition of insecurity, of internal divi-
sion, of contradictory convictions" can bring a crisis.

The practical necessities of treatment have therefore forced us
to look for ways and means that might lead out of this intolerable
situation. Whenever a man is confronted by an apparently in-
surmountable obstacle, he draws back: he makes what is techni-
cally called a regression. . . . But what helped in youth is no
use in age.[7]

Despair, at this point, can lead one to regress right back into
babyhood—in Freudian terms, into the oral stage—and beyond.
And it is at this point that the "work" of analysis in its truest sense
occurs. Deeper than the images of babyhood are those of the collective unconscious, the archetypes, and it is through contact with
these, Jung believes, that healing can come. This point will be
developed through several later chapters, but at this point it is
important to note that one chief road to contact with the archetypes
is through dreams. It is here that one main difference between
Freud and Jung emerges. While Freud sees dreams as "the royal
road to the unconscious," he sees the unconscious as the personal

unconscious and the dreams as giving coded signals from that realm—coded because of the need for censorship that our conscious mind imposes. Jung, on the other hand, sees the unconscious as a world widening out into infinity. Dreams, as symbolic messages from this wider world, not only help the dreamer become aware of his or her own inner store of images, associations, and inner movements, but they also serve as an introduction to a world common to the human race and rich in symbolism and energy.

Jung remarks:

> Certain kinds of psychic material mean next to nothing if simply broken down, but display a wealth of meaning if, instead of being broken down, that meaning is reinforced and extended by all the conscious means at our disposal—by the so-called method of amplification.[8]

He believes the psychoanalytic (Freudian) position on dreams can be reductive because it only analyzes, "breaks down." He proposes, on the contrary, what he calls a synthetic or constructive method which proceeds by the amplification mentioned above and tries to find all the wealth of connotation in a symbol rather than reducing it to a "code" revealing something the psyche is trying to censor. So the inner process or work involves coming into relation with this deeper world of significance that we bear within us and that opens us to wider horizons than our own. Jung remarks, in further explanation:

> The work involved in analytical treatment gives rise to experiences of an archetypal nature which require to be expressed and shaped.[9]

This "expressing and shaping" is, in turn, a further work which can continue at length.

These experiences can occur outside the limited field of analysis as well, and they do for most people, but analysis can further the contact with, and understanding of, such experiences. Everyone, however, needs the vivifying contact with the archetypes, the symbols that can transform life, in whatever form. Without this one cannot complete his or her search for meaning. But each person meets these archetypes in a different way. The unification and integration of the human psyche, its growing readiness to face the death that is both real and a new beginning, are the fruits of this "work." One could say that its aim is the true maturity of the human person.

Jung notes that it is possible to short-circuit this process of coming into touch with the archetypal world, with the unconscious. Speaking of the experience of the archetype, he says, "It is like a primordial experience of the non-ego, of an interior opponent who throws down a challenge to the understanding."[10] As a result, "we then look round for helpful parallels, and it happens all too easily that the original occurrence is interpreted in terms of derivative ideas." The issue is that it is both more comfortable and safer to try to find commonplace, recognized, or even traditional religious or cultural symbolism for what one experiences. For, as we shall see in a later chapter, solitude is frightening to many. The process of clothing inner experience in conventional rather than original language is, indeed, safe. It serves, however, to neutralize the experience and to "make men shadowy and unreal," putting "empty words in the place of living realities." The result is a "wan, two-dimensional, phantasmal world where everything vital and creative withers and dies."[11]

This issue can be illustrated by speaking of the religious field. A religious experience of contact with God can indeed have the force of a "meeting with an interior opponent." God by definition surpasses human powers of understanding. The history of religion is full of records of the lives of people who have tried to deal with this experience and their inability to express it in terms which suited those around them. Teresa of Avila's autobiography, with its history of misunderstanding, "trials" from those to whom she submitted her experiences, and her own inner anguish and doubt through it all, is a good illustration. But the level of religious art and culture in much of our society, the struggles of those seeking to express themselves authentically without shocking people, the inner temptation to find the easiest or least controversial words to clothe an experience—all of these show the difficulty of honest expression and the courage it requires.

Refusing the shortcut has its own dangers, however. The development of a mature personality involves the risk of becoming quite a nonconformist. For many years religions have found this to be a threat, as have many political positions as well. When one reflects, however, on positions such as Kohlberg's which portrays the moral consciousness as developing through stages of conformity and identification with the whole or the institution into a more prophetic mode where the individual is his or her own person and acts out of personal concern for value,[12] it seems that even our scientific research is beginning to bear out the need for a truer and more real development of the individual, no longer so identified with the whole.

In another set of passages, Jung speaks of the growing awareness within the psyche of the need for the integrative or analytical "work" and of the cost of going through this process.

> In by far the greater number, adaptation to external reality demands so much work that inner adaptation to the collective unconscious cannot be considered for a very long time. But when this inner adaptation becomes a problem, a strange, irresistible attraction proceeds from the unconscious and exerts a powerful influence on the conscious direction of life.[13]

This eruption of unconscious influences leads to a period of "psychic disequilibrium," which is, however, a necessary process on the road toward greater and deeper psychic health.

> I regard the loss of balance as purposive, since it replaces a defective consciousness by the automatic and instinctive activity of the unconscious, which is aiming all the time at the creation of a new balance and will moreover achieve this aim, provided that the conscious mind is capable of assimilating the contents produced by the unconscious, i.e. of understanding and digesting them.[14]

In other words, during the first stage of life we tend to set up a balance that is still as yet superficial and limited, though this is a necessary stage to enable us to perform the tasks of this early stage. There is, however, a period of transition into the second stage of life and into greater maturity and integration which requires the upsetting of this original balance in order for a deeper, richer, and more inclusive balance to emerge. This is the "work" of analysis and also of the individual human person. Not only of analysis, it will be seen, for this latter remains at present a process for the few. "Fate," suffering, the questions life throws upon our path lead many people to this time of questioning and "disequilibrium." Their path of integration is the same.

It is worth remembering in this whole area that John of the

Cross, speaking of the call to contemplation and then the increasing call to a deeper level of union, will use strikingly similar language about this interior drawing and about its psychological effects.

> This dark night is an inflow of God into the soul, which purges it of its habitual ignorances and imperfections. . . . Through this contemplation, God teaches the soul secretly and instructs it in the perfection of love without its doing anything nor understanding how this happens. . . . It prepares the soul for the union with God through love by both purging and illumining it. . . . his divine wisdom is [at first] not only night and darkness for the soul, but also affliction and torment.[15]

As John of the Cross speaks of the union resulting from the "night," so also Jung speaks of the effects of this inner "work" in the psyche:

> In this way there arises a consciousness which is no longer imprisoned in the petty, oversensitive, personal world of the ego, but participates freely in the wider world of objective interests. This widened consciousness is no longer that touchy, egotistical bundle of personal wishes, fears, hopes, and ambitions which always has to be compensated or corrected by unconscious counter-tendencies; instead, it is a function of relationship to the world of objects, bringing the individual into absolute, binding, and indissoluble community with the world at large.[16]

The matured personality, then, is wider, broader, freer, richer, more open to others as a result of its "work." These are the "tasks" life gives us to perform.

Having spoken, then, of the "work" of analysis; the "tasks" of each individual in the developmental process; the inner work that needs to be done to fulfill these tasks and to mature, whether in a therapeutic situation or simply by one's own inner process, what can we find in the early spiritual literature of Christianity that might be parallel to these outlooks?

*   *   *

In her translation of *The Sayings of the Desert Fathers,*[17] Benedicta Ward notes that the term "work" is "used in the Apophthegmata in two senses: either as manual labour, or as spiritual exertion. These two are seen as one, but the idea of interior 'work' predominates for the monk."[18] In other words, in the Egyptian desert where people went to live their search for God as totally as they knew how, their manual work was considered to be a part of this search and work, but their interior struggle was even more so. One could multiply quotations, but the similarity of this view with the psychological notion of inner work seems clear. A few illustrations may give the feeling of this early vocabulary:

> A brother came to Abba Theodore and began to converse with him about things which he had never yet put into practice. So the old man said to him, 'You have not yet found a ship nor put your cargo aboard it and before you have sailed, you have already arrived at the city. Do the work first; then you will have the speed you are making now.'[19]

> A brother asked Abba Poemen, 'Some brothers live with me; do you want me to be in charge of them?' The old man said to him, 'No, just work first and foremost, and if they want to live like you, they will see to it themselves.' The brother said to him, 'But it is they themselves, Father, who want me to be in charge of them.' The old man said to him, 'No, be their example, not their legislator.'[20]

> He [Silvanus] also said, 'Unhappy the man whose reputation is greater than his work.'[21]

In this context it becomes easy to see the relation between the notion of "work" in the early centuries and that of "active life" or *praktike,* ascesis. The term "active life" has come to mean today the work of the apostolate, as opposed to the contemplative life. As the following chapter will show, this kind of dichotomy is foreign to the early Church. For them, the active life or ascesis—outer and inner—was the work of acquiring the necessary virtues to prepare for contemplation or the contemplative life. Yet even this kind of phraseology is misleading, because our notion of "virtue" may be very different from theirs—as well as our understanding of contemplative life. We inherit, as regards the former, centuries of an increasingly voluntaristic position. For them, whether they realized it consciously or not, much of their thinking came from roots in the thought of philosophers like Plato and Aristotle. The latter wrote in his *Ethics*:

> If happiness is activity in accordance with virtue, it is reasonable that it should be in accordance with the highest virtue; and this will be that of the best thing in us. . . . That this activity is contemplative we have already said. . . . But such a life would be too high for man; for it is not in so far as he is man that he will live so, but in so far as something divine is present in him. . . . But . . . perfect happiness is a contemplative activity. . . . Happiness extends . . . just so far as contemplation does, and those to whom contemplation more fully belongs are more truly happy.[22]

To Aristotle other virtues prepare for this contemplative life, as one sees in all his preceding chapters. Virtues are good habits which, once habitual, become pleasurable.

Here, then, one has the whole notion of the contemplative life as the source of bliss and the happiness for which the human person is intended. Prudence, justice, fortitude, temperance—for both Plato and Aristotle—prepare for this. Is the end of human life, then, totally self-seeking? The answer lies in Plato's *Republic*, which preceded Aristotle. There, only the philosopher was fit to rule, for only he or she would rule wisely. For Plato contemplation is living in the sunlight of reality (spiritual reality) outside the cave of illusion where most people live, looking at the shadows of things rather than their real Essences or Forms. One who has gone out into the sunlight of contemplation will be blinded when he or she returns to the darkness of the cave, but it is necessary to return in order to help those inside to emerge. On the other hand, one who has not emerged is of little help to others.

The notion that the Essences or Forms of things in some eternal world are more real than their material existence around us has become foreign to our thinking—partly, through the influence of Aristotle who was more ready to see reality in the interpenetration of matter and form. This view became powerfully influential in Western Christianity and brought with it a tendency to value the material more than was done in the Platonic view. Yet Plato's conception of the importance of contemplating truth and of doing the necessary "work," both to attain this contemplation and to share it, has remained a strand of Western thought as well. All of this is what fed into the early notion of the active or ascetical life and its work.

This entire notion of work needs to be related to another strand which has been often misunderstood in recent times but which is central—and that is the idea of the "Work of God," the *opus Dei*. If one reads works written in the last two hundred years, particularly those discussing the monastic life, one often finds the term "Work of God" being used as a synonym for the Divine Office, the liturgical chant which is so much part of the life of the monk. It is clear that this is a narrower sense of the word "work" than the above, but also there is a considerable amount of misunderstanding connected with this whole issue. André Louf, for example, will say that the "true work" of the monk is "the battle with everything that would distract" from God.[23] This is the old meaning of the term. How, then, did it become synonymous with the Office?

In the early days of Christianity, the chanting of the psalms and readings characteristic of what became the Office was an activity of Christians in general, inherited from the Synagogue. From the early centuries until not very long ago—and in the Eastern Church even more than in the Western—the chanting of the Office was considered "the prayer of the Church" and, as such, of value for everyone and very far from being limited to the monasteries. (Witness the medieval Hour Books.) The monasteries did seem to specialize in the Office as the centuries wore on—at least in terms of the time and the importance they gave to this activity. But it was nonetheless something that belonged to the Church itself—religious, lay, and priestly. Vatican II has attempted to restore this perspective as productive of a healthier and more Scripture-oriented spirituality than some have known in the recent past.

How did the idea arise that the Office is primarily the work of the monk—that it is in fact the monk or nun who is delegated to pray this Liturgy of the Hours in the name of the Church? The truth is that it is the Canons Regular who have this as their charge and mission; the monastic office has another aim. An overview of the meaning of the term *opus Dei* in early Christian literature, following I. Hausherr,[24] will explain its evolution.

This author begins with a question on the grammatical sense of the word *Dei* in this context. Is it the "Work of God" because God does it? No, he concludes. The Work of God, in the terminology of Benedict, for example, is "not a work done *by* God but a work done *for* God." He then inquires into the Christian roots of the phrase. The Johannine literature comes to the fore. When Christ is asked how to do the works of God, he responds: "This is the work of God, that you believe in Him whom God has sent."[25] Hausherr concludes:

> *Our* "Opus Dei" is therefore above all, radically and essentially faith, the life of faith, the works informed by faith.[26]

No activity, he concludes, is more *opus Dei* than another.

He then passes from the study of Scripture to the Fathers. Origen, for example, writes that the most excellent work of God is the exegesis and the contemplation of truth which is best done "when the soul is calm through the peace which surpasses all understanding."[27] The influence of the Greek philosophers shows here, but Origen was a profound influence on the whole Christian world. He also writes: "Whatever comes from the commandments of God is called the work of God."[28] Justice, meekness, patience, piety are examples given elsewhere in his work. For Athanasius virginity is a "work of God" requiring all that is necessary to maintain this state as a kind of marriage to Christ.[29] In going over Greek Christian literature, Hausherr concludes that *to ergon tou theou* never means the liturgy; rather, as we have seen, it refers to the ascetical life. In the Latin literature, he cites a text from Abba Ampo: "An old man said: 'Wherever the bee goes, it makes honey: wherever the monk goes, he accomplishes the work of God.'"

Later, the term "work of God" came to refer to the Greek Synaxis or liturgy, for example, in Latin translations of the *Vitae Patrum*. It is Pelagius, probably Pope Pelagius, who gave the term *opus Dei* the meaning often used later, that of the Office. Nonetheless, the other translation remained as well. "The hardest work is the *ponos kardias* (the work of the heart) of which a Saint Barsanuphius and an Abbot Isaiah among others speak insistently," says Hausherr.[30] The work of God remains the work of the heart. And the aim of all this work remains "the perfection of prayer" in a direct line from the desert through Cassian to Benedict. This "perfection" is not a passing spiritual experience but a union with God that remains. It is also the perfection of charity. This is the Work of God par excellence, the aim of the monastic life or the life of the desert. So one can conclude from Hausherr's work and the reading of the tradition that the Work of God, the *opus Dei,* is the work we have seen described throughout the desert literature, the search for God, the ascesis that moves toward union. And later centuries were to continue to use the term thus. John of the Cross was to say: "That which is wanting . . . [is] silence and work."[31] He adds elsewhere: "To love is to labor to divest and deprive oneself for God of all that is not God."[32] Later, speaking of the higher stages of the spiritual life, he says that here "A man's activities, once human, now become divine."[33] He explains how this can be so:

> . . . All the operations of the memory and other faculties in this state are divine. God now possesses the faculties as their complete lord, because of their transformation in Him. And consequently it is He who divinely moves and commands them according to His spirit and will. As a result, the operations are not different from those of God; but those the soul performs are of God and are divine operations. Since the one who is united with God is one spirit with Him, as St. Paul says [I Cor. 6:17], the operations of the soul united with God are of the divine Spirit and are divine.[34]

Still more: "The soul will participate in God Himself by performing in Him, in company with Him, the work of the Most Blessed Trinity."[35] This is, for John of the Cross, the point toward which life with God tends.

We shall find these thoughts again in the last chapter below. Meanwhile, one can conclude that the human person moves toward human and spiritual meaning through effort, work, struggle—spiritual writers would say, toward "divinization." The traditions of spirituality and psychology agree on the first levels, and some psychology begins, as we shall see, to point to the later ones as well.

Can one summarize the points of convergence in both traditions? First of all, in both there is the notion of an inner work to be done—a work that is demanding and that can require the reorganization of deeply entrenched manners of being, thinking, relating. In both there is a tradition of another person who is able to facilitate this process for the one "working." This point will be the subject of a later chapter. But for both the main "worker" is the actual person, though the work is not done by ego alone.

One could say that in the Freudian position, the aim of the working process is psychological health and maturity. For Jung, the same process is visualized as going much deeper—beyond the issues of the personal individual psyche and into those of its relationships with a wider and more spiritual world. But this aspect of the Jungian view does not make it possible to neglect the aspects pointed out by Freud and which are an essential first stage, whether they take place by means of an analysis or by the process of working through to an appropriate maturity simply by dealing reflectively and seriously with the issues of life. The view of Christian spirituality is exemplified, above all, in its early stages in dealing with the human person's relationship with God. But such a relationship does not take place in a vacuum. Relating to others with charity, selflessness, humility is the theme of story after story from the desert. So also is relating to oneself with equal lucidity. While one could not say that the psychological "work" is a requirement for the spiritual work—for there have been people who were psychologically ill and yet lived deeply spiritual lives—nonetheless one can say that the psychological work is not ignored with impunity anywhere in the spiritual domain. If one tries to "seek God" with an immature or unbalanced psyche, this immaturity and imbalance will exist in the relationship with God as well. Grace builds on nature. Perhaps it is truer to say that there is a work incumbent on every human being on earth—one which involves all relationships including those with self, God, others, and the world around us. One could laze through life out of fear of, or dislike for, work. But the message of the two disciplines we have looked at is the same. As the baby needs to act and use his or her muscles and abilities in order to grow, so the older human person needs to use not only outer but inner abilities and deal with far more serious struggles. This struggle, this work, is only over with life. But the image of athletics is not false. Practice and effort bring skill. Work produces an effect in us as well as outside of us. Both fields, psychology and spirituality, proclaim an equal invitation to this work, an equal challenge to grow toward the stature to which we are called.

·4·

DICHOTOMY

One aspect of the "work" we have discussed must deal with the issue of dichotomies born of a tendency deep in the psyche and to which Jung referred in the previous chapter. The words "What God has united let no man put asunder" apply to more than human marriage. For, as we have seen, "putting asunder" or away from the psyche any aspect of reality—inner or outer—brings its own inbuilt penalty to human life. And yet, paradoxically, there is a way in which one must "put away" some things and choose others at certain stages of life to avoid living forever in a formless and chaotic muddle of unconsciousness. This paradox is the subject of the present chapter.

Jung describes the process of human and psychological growth in terms of some of these choices. For one thing, in speaking not of the individual psyche but of the dawn of consciousness for the human race, he often refers to the passages in the book of Genesis on what has come to be called "original sin." He remarks that, in fact, the eating of the forbidden fruit was "the act of becoming conscious"[1] as opposed to living in an undifferentiated union with nature as did the primitives, but this coming to consciousness was achieved by infringing a taboo "as though knowledge meant that a sacrosanct barrier had been impiously overstepped."[2]

This may sound as if Jung approved this eating of the fruit —whatever that symbolizes—and he is hardly a partisan of remaining in the state of unconsciousness or what he calls "participation mystique," this undifferentiated union. On the other hand, he remarks that this eating of the fruit is a Promethean exploit which can bear within it its own punishment; and the risk of inflation which comes with new knowledge can indeed "turn the head" of the person involved.

> I think that Genesis is right in so far as every step towards greater consciousness is a kind of Promethian guilt: through knowledge, the gods are as it were robbed of their fire, that is, something that was the property of the unconscious powers is torn out of its natural context and subordinated to the whims of the conscious mind. The man who has usurped the new knowledge suffers, however, a transformation or enlargement of consciousness which no longer resembles that of his fellow men.[3]

There is, then, a "bad thing," a risk—that the conscious mind will misuse its new power—and a "good (but also dangerous) thing," an enlargement of consciousness. But all this means not only risk but paradox. In order to move toward greater consciousness, it was necessary to "infringe the taboo," to seek the forbidden knowledge. (Did God really mean to forbid this? Or was the prohibition in this *mythos* meant to be, like the pedagogy of the Old Testament Law, a training in awareness that one did not move into this domain of knowledge—or freedom—without risk?) But having made this choice to move toward greater human maturity, the human person runs the risk of inflation or pride, of misuse (even internal, as inflation is internal) of the knowledge acquired. It is important to come into contact with the unconscious. But if the conscious mind lacks the wisdom to deal appropriately with what it experiences and learns, it is playing with fire.

The act of becoming conscious is, in one sense, the choice of one side of a dichotomy. It is the choosing of light, of knowledge, of clarity—or of passing beyond the taboos into the unknown. This "one-sided" choice is necessary or the personality remains in unconsciousness. But if this one-sidedness is maintained or if the person is too wedded to the brightness of the light and too disrespectful of the darkness of the unconscious to remain in touch with its rhythm and its indications, the result is catastrophic. The same result occurs if the person tries to become totally one with this newly experienced unconscious world. Both these forms of inflation are, in fact, one-sided. Both lead to harm. In other words, dichotomy is necessary—and dichotomy can lead to doom.

The same process is involved in the growth of each individual child toward adulthood. In order to take one's place in the human world, one has to choose to be one way rather than another, to do one work rather than another, to marry one person rather than another. All these choices move toward the formation of the human psyche. They are part of the first stage of life. To refuse to make them on the grounds that the other choices are equally good, or that the unconscious is as important as the conscious, is to fail to fulfill the tasks of this first stage. One can, for a concrete example, choose to do six types of work. The choice may be valid, but for most people it precludes becoming truly proficient in one of the six. Again, a twenty-year-old may decide that his or her main occupation will be becoming conscious of dreams and unconscious contents. But if this is truly a "main occupation," it will preclude involvement in the formative tasks and work that lead to the development of a truly adult personality. Again, one must choose one side of a "dichotomy" if one is to move with strength.

For Jung, however, the growth into true maturity is the task of the second stage of life, and this is precisely the moment when one becomes aware of the need for the "other" choice from the one previously made. Whether this stage is to end in catastrophe or growth will depend on the person's ability to make the new choice without abandoning the old. The point has been discussed in the previous chapter and need not be repeated here. But Jung goes farther:

> Old Heraclitus, who was indeed a very great sage, discovered the most marvellous of all psychological laws: the regulative function of opposites. He called it *enantiodromia*, a running contrariwise, by which he meant that sooner or later everything runs into its opposite. . . . Thus the rational attitude of culture necessarily runs into its opposite, namely the irrational devastation of culture. . . . The irrational cannot be and must not be extirpated. The gods cannot and must not die.[4]

Jung seems here to be speaking of something very close to Hegel's dialectic. Our culture often claims to be based on reason, and eventually irrationality takes its toll for being repressed and submerges the Western world—the world which most claims to be rational. This, as Jung notes, was something he wrote before the Second World War which seems to have brought ample confirmation. And yet, this occurs because the irrational has been repressed, something which must not be. "The gods cannot and must not die"—the gods in the sense Jung gives above.

Jung describes what happens when the psyche allows itself to center too exclusively on any one thing:

> The ego is drawn into this focus of energy so powerfully that it identifies with it and thinks it desires and needs nothing further. In this way, a craze develops, a monomania or possession, an acute one-sidedness which most seriously imperils the psychic equilibrium.[5]

He adds that this monomania is the secret of success and so is furthered in our society, but "the passion, the piling up of energy in these monomanias is what the ancients called a 'god.'" In religious terms one could say that these gods become our idols and become the causes of our inability for true worship. In psychological terms they become blinding with the results mentioned above.

> The only person who escapes the grim law of enantiodromia is the man who knows how to separate himself from the unconscious, not by repressing it—for then it simply attacks him from the rear—but by putting it clearly before him as *that which he is not.*[6]

But this is a process of which only a person who has done the work of the first half of life appropriately, someone who is "a viable member of the community," is capable. Again, the first stage is choice and the stage of maturity is that of embracing both sides.

Jung describes the mature personality as one which has attained its "mid-point"—"the point of new equilibrium, a new centering of the total personality, a virtual centre which, on account of its focal position between conscious and unconscious, ensures for the personality a new and more solid foundation."[7]

The attainment of this stage is the purpose of the whole maturation process, as it is the purpose of analysis when this is undertaken. The blocking of such development is an indication that it would be important to have help to continue the movement of growth, to locate the obstacles. Jung calls this "mid-point" the "transcendent function, the transformation of personality through the blending and fusion of the noble with the base components, of the differentiated with the inferior functions, of the conscious with the unconscious."[8]

This definition in itself can give one pause. One would have thought that the purpose of personality growth was the exclusion of the base. But it is just this issue that the discovery of the unconscious and the whole field of psychoanalysis brought to the fore as had the ancient tradition about humility. Once again here, the "base" is present in us and needs to be recognized. Only thus can one grow.

On the deepest level, this whole question leads to a point much discussed in spirituality. Speaking of the dream of someone coming to this stage, Jung makes two observations. One is that his reason for using dreams so much in analysis is their ability to make a person aware of unconscious processes in a quite unique way. And this awareness is a sine qua non. Secondly, speaking of the individual involved, he says:

> Through her active participation the patient merges herself in the unconscious processes, and she gains possession of them by allowing them to possess her.[9]

What is involved here is a surrender. And yet, again, the surrender is not—under pain of false mysticism in the psychological sphere—a total letting go of rationality.[10] It is a maintenance of both personality and surrender, of both reason and the surrender to the unconscious. It is both poles of the dichotomy.

This inner "work" not only has effects in the wider social world of relationships and even of cultures, but the lack of it can lead to tragedy in these wider domains. Jung speaks of the "mass psyche" born of a more dehumanized culture than in the past when stronger emphasis on "brotherly love" and organized brotherhoods and groupings fulfilled functions that "increasing internationalism and the weakening of religion have largely abolished . . . only to create an amorphous mass." The result, in our culture, is a condition of chaos only painfully held in check and "for this there is but one remedy: the inner consolidation of the individual, who is otherwise threatened with inevitable stultification and dissolution in the mass psyche."[11] The inner consolidation involves "the union of the divided components of the personality, on the psychic level, . . . [and] would form a counterbalance to the progressive dichotomy and psychic dissociation of collective man."[12]

What is being said here involves the inner chaos of our culture insofar as this is born of dichotomizing and alienation. Only by the unification of individual psyches and the more harmonious relationships that can result from this can one hope for a healthier national and international culture. Jung died before the atomic threat reached its most acute level. One can wonder, however, if his comments today would be very different. He continues with an analysis of the phenomenon of mass-mindedness and its roots that is worth more than passing reflection:

> It is of supreme importance that this process [of inner consolidation] should take place *consciously,* otherwise the psychic consequences of mass-mindedness will harden and become permanent. For, if the inner consolidation of the individual is not a conscious achievement, it will occur spontaneously and will then take the well-known form of that incredible hard-heartedness which collective man displays towards his fellow men. He becomes a soulless herd animal governed only by panic and lust: his soul, which can live only in and from human relationships, is irretrievably lost. But the conscious achievement of inner unity clings to human relationships as to an indispensable condition, for without the conscious acknowledgement and acceptance of our fellowship with those around us there can be no synthesis of personality. . . . The inner consolidation of the individual is not just the hardness of collective man on a higher plane, in the form of spiritual aloofness and inaccessibility: it emphatically includes our fellow man.[13]

This brings us to the issue of convergences of such thought with spirituality. For one thing, the above quotation shows the effect of individual and collective or communal hardening against relationship. Yet from the days of the Crusaders shouting "God wills it," as they brandished their swords and set fire to buildings, right into the present manifestations of religion-based fanaticisms, we see demonstrations of what happens when hearts are hardened to others, most especially in the name of an ideal. Even justice suffers, without speaking of love, and yet through the centuries this remains a pattern among many religious people and institutions, as well as on the political level. Even individually, ideals and laws can be put before persons. It would seem that Jesus had much to say in this regard.

On another and very different level, the contemplative-active dichotomy which has plagued people trying to live a spiritual life—and notably religious as individuals and as communities—is another example of the harmfulness of dichotomizing, and that on many planes. For one thing, if truly "the conscious achievement of inner unity clings to human relationships as to an indispensable condition," what is to be thought of efforts to become deeply contemplative by cutting off relationships as a matter of principle rather than inner drawing? It would seem truer to believe that what hampers my relationships to others will exist equally in my relationship to God and so it would behoove me to learn to relate.

On the other hand, Jung himself will insist that there is no union with others without unification within the self, which requires solitude. Commenting on the recent translation of Luke 17:21 as saying that the Kingdom of God is "among you" instead of "within you," he says:

> This shows the modern tendency to replace man's inner cohesion by outward community, as though anyone who had no communion with himself would be capable of any fellowship at all! It is this deplorable tendency that paves the way for mass-mindedness.[14]

In Christian circles one often hears that all things can be judged by one's fraternal love in action without any consideration of the quality of such love as opposed to merely "do-goodism." But the recipients of this kind of "love" recognize the difference. Once again, dichotomy leads to doom. Contemplation without relationship; attempts to love others without sufficient centering in oneself, these and other such onesidednesses become sterile.

Dom John Main, a monk with extensive experience of Eastern thought and spirituality, wrote:

> All matter, all creation, too, is drawn into the cosmic movement towards unity that will be the realization of the Divine harmony. . . . No unique beauty will be lost in this great unification. . . . Only in union do we know fully who we are. . . .
> Putting this from the point of view where most of us start, it means going beyond all dualism, all dividedness within ourselves and beyond the alienation separating us from others. . . . It is dualism . . . that creates for each of us the impossible, unrea-

listic 'either-ors' that cause so much unnecessary anguish: God or man, love of self or love of neighbour, cloister or market place.[15]

This writer continues by saying that he is in no way denying that some are called to a contemplative life of silence and solitude: his point is that the call to the Absolute lived radically, in one way, by these is still present for every human person and sometimes it is not answered out of fear that everything material or "ordinary" in life dilutes this call. On the contrary, as Merton unceasingly pointed out, nothing is more "ordinary" than the daily living of the monastic or contemplative life with its daily routine of housework or field-work, material duties, chores, and each one's work and reading. This life can relate deeply to any human life—if, once again, the contemplative element is integrated as part of being human.

How is this to be done? Thomas Merton speaks of a common error in this effort and its results:

> One's inner life simply becomes a desert which lacks all interest whatsoever. This may no doubt be explained as a passing trial (the "night of the senses") but we must face the fact that it is often more serious than that. It may be the result of a wrong start, in which (due to the familiar jargon of books on prayer and the ascetic life) a cleavage has appeared, dividing the "inner life" from the rest of one's existence. . . . This is bad theology and bad asceticism. . . . Very often, the inertia and repugnance which characterize the so-called "spiritual life" of many Christians could perhaps be cured by a simple respect for the concrete realities of everyday life, for nature, for the body, for one's work, one's friends, one's surroundings, etc. . . . Meditation has no point and no reality unless it is firmly rooted in *life*.[16]

Elsewhere he writes:

> . . . It is often impossible to be recollected when one has shut his eyes and 'excluded' all sensible things. Yet it is quite easy to be recollected when, in tranquillity and peace, one gazes at some innocent and neutral thing—a tree, a picture, a flower, a ray of light, a landscape, a corner of the sky.[17]

In other words, it is not the world around us, nor is it others, who are the obstacles to contemplation. Rather, it is the attitude with which one approaches all this that makes a thing help or hindrance. Fear and negativism can cause as much harm as attachment. On the other hand, however, this contemplative attitude to things and people is not born of pure immersion in these things and people but rather of something that has become a tradition, for example, in Japan and that is well worth Western reflection. Despite their habitual courtesy, more than one Japanese will speak unenthusiastically of Western flower arrangement, gardens, and the like. "You push a whole lot of flowers together into a bowl and one cannot see the individuality of any one of them." This principle permeates not only Japanese flower arrangement and gardens, but also the tea ceremony, furnishings, poetry, and many other aspects of life. Interestingly, some Japanese trace a relationship between the tea ceremony, with its Buddhist roots, and the ritual and rubrics for the celebration of the Eucharist, as these were known in Japan when the tea ceremony originated. Each gesture and object here is valued and reverenced — an important way toward becoming contemplative and one difficult to ignore if one seeks a truly contemplative attitude. Daisetz Suzuki speaks along the same lines:

> The Western mind has been coarsened by the techniques of exact analysis, whereas the Eastern mind is pre-eminently mystical and concerns itself with the so-called mystery of existence.
>
> In a certain sense, life is art. However long or short life may be, no matter under what conditions we have to live it, we all want to make the best of it — the best not only in the technique of living, but also in understanding its meaning. But that implies apprehending a glimmer of its mystery. From this standpoint the Japanese consider every art to be a form of schooling which grants insight into life's beauty, for beauty transcends all rationality and utility thinking, it is the mystery itself. In this sense Zen has close affinities with the arts, with painting, tea drinking, flower arrangement, fencing, archery, and such-like.[18]

Thus each detail of daily life in its concreteness can become a return to the center, to unity, nonalienation. This center is not a cutting off of the periphery but their integration.

This same reverence is an integral part of the Western contemplative tradition. The Benedictine Rule is characterized by it and speaks of using utensils in the house as if they were "sacred vessels of the altar."[19] A culture full of advertising, noise, consumerism, throw-away goods can be more harmful for the development of such an attitude than we realize.

If the same issue of active-contemplative dichotomy is taken onto a wider level, it turns into a distinction of religious communities: into "contemplative" or "active" or "apostolic." Such distinction was foreign to the early Church and remains so in Orthodoxy. While clarity is necessary for self-definition, especially in early stages, it can be ultimately harmful for any kind of mature synthesis. The Orthodox position sees the spiritual life as coming out of a single tradition, shared by all Christians, lay and religious (and the religious life, whatever its orientation, is seen as monastic). Each religious community has its own characteristics and tradition, its own "color." Nonetheless, Orthodoxy has not even felt a need to regulate the religious life in terms of any canon law. This may reflect a more unified conception of the religious life than the Western one, with its tendency to categorize and fragment.

One finds this same view, but here unified in terms of contemplation, in the writings of an Indian religious we shall be quoting again in later chapters. Writing of life in an ashram, which should be "a place where people come to experience God," she says:

> Everything should be either a means or an overflow of contemplation. . . . When an ashram has a work or an apostolate, be it a school, dispensary, leper asylum or whatever, a good criterion by which to judge its service value is this: when the work becomes so 'big,' either in its reality or in the ashramites' hearts, that it is no longer either a means towards or an overflow of contemplative prayer, it should be considered as being outside the vocation of that ashram.
>
> This criterion seems to me a good one to use in tackling the basic problem of the integration of prayer and work. For if we consider why hindu ashrams flourish today, and why the fewer christian ones do not, one important answer is that we Christians seem to consider contemplative prayer as something rare to be practised by only a few of our brethren. But surely all . . . are called to it. In religious life, the novice should be introduced to it from the beginning.[20]

Deeper than all these questions lies the issue not of phases of life, but of unification of life. Is it not essential for each individual to find the optimal fulfillment of what his or her individual nature and call demand? And that, in itself, can vary with the times and seasons of a human life. Whether one is speaking of a lay person or a religious, or a member of whatever community however classified, the basic call would seem to be both contemplative on a very deep level and also expressive of brotherly and sisterly love. It would seem truly difficult to legislate the roads to such an end, for anyone. Perhaps our Western tendency to categorize needs to find another solution than dichotomizing.

To sum up, psychology as well as spirituality speaks of the need for choice to enable the individual to reach a stage of adult identity and strength. Both, however, show the unilaterial maintenance of these choices as becoming, later, damaging for the person, society, and the life of union with God. Especially in our Western culture with its tendency to emphasize the rational and the organized, we need to beware, even in our life with God and with others, of setting up dichotomies that can ultimately force choices damaging to reality, truth, and life—and to the very values in which we wish to grow.

·5·

DESCENT TO THE HEART—
AND DEFENSES

In discussing the structure of the psyche, mention was made of the Freudian understanding of the id or the instinctual area of the human person as something that could be experienced as a source of danger, as something that could overrun the tidier realm created by the ego and superego. Anxiety—that is, the fear that this will occur—can take both healthy and pathological forms and, in either case, there is a set of defenses normally recognized in psychology which the ego sets up for its protection. It is unnecessary here to give an exhaustive list of these defenses, even if that were possible, but it can be of interest to look at a few which most directly concern the purposes of this book.

Repression has already been discussed. If one simply erases from consciousness any offending material, life apparently becomes considerably simpler. Thus one meets religious people who, for example, will announce that they experience no difficulties at all dealing with issues concerning sex and anger. Considering that these are probably the two strongest and most normal passions of the human person, one can certainly wonder what process a person has used to experience no difficulty in these areas. A related defense in such a situation is denial. The impulse simply does not exist in this person's heart. The hope is, of course, that saying it is not there will make it go away—even from consciousness. And the same process can be used concerning unpleasant external realities. Projection is another commonly mentioned defense, but it will be discussed more at length in later chapters.

Two defenses that are of most concern for the purposes of this chapter are intellectualization and rationalization. The latter is a familiar term in daily language: the former is perhaps even more common than we realize and can be even more pernicious. Intellectualization "transplants all conflicts to the realm of secondary process thinking and talking. Whatever contributes to the emergence of anxiety is repressed."[1] It is not particularly difficult to see what this does to the psyche. The person becomes split into two separate zones—the intellectual, where all the thinking, talking, and reasoning take place; and the emotional, which is well blocked off and not dealt with properly. People who prefer this defense are often very aware of their strong emotions—though, in some cases, these may also be pushed to a realm well under the surface of true consciousness—but they choose not to get into this untidy and explosive domain because they sense very accurately that it will turn out to be beyond their powers to control. So they continue to think, reason, talk, and avoid expressing or even dealing with this area of ebullition. This process, of course, eventually increases their—largely repressed—anxiety, because the more emotional material piles up undealt with, the more threatening that whole area becomes. Firm suppression or repression becomes the only solution. Obviously, for religious people, and religious organizations as well, this process can be a great temptation if they do not wish to deal with the murky world of shadow material. It is easier to have an answer for everything, a theory about everything, an easy word out of one's head for everything.

The trouble, of course, is that thus one becomes divorced from one's heart. The heart, as a symbol, tends to be used rather more in spiritual than in psychological writing. The term "center," however, is used in both. Interestingly, this concept of "center" and "centering" has come to be even a business issue, in that people begin to realize that human performance is impeded by the inability to center. In the NTL catalogue for 1983, for example, one finds the following caption: "Centering for personal and professional development." The explanation follows:

> "Centering" is the process of finding one's own physical and mental point of equilibrium. Once recognized, that balance becomes the source of more effective interaction with others in groups and organizations and within the self.
>
> While group interaction is an essential part of this Laboratory, the journey is very much a personal one for each individual to take in seeking out his or her own unique center.

Our goal in "Centering" is greater clarity about the self in relation to the human and physical environment. Thus, in organizational life, a centered self is able to be decisive and to act clearly and appropriately. When the self is clear, then others are seen more clearly and their motivations and behavior can be observed more objectively.

A variety of techniques are used, many of which are particularly useful for stress reduction: guided imagery and fantasy, graphic imagery, sensory awareness work, meditation and physical activity.[2]

It will be noted that the techniques chosen to work toward "centering" are techniques involving sensory awareness and imagery—in other words, techniques moving the person away from pure "head trips." (One is reminded of Fritz Perls's adage about the need to lose one's mind in order to come to one's senses.)

The implication of the above passage is that balance can only really be obtained from this position of "centering," equilibrium. Given the points already mentioned about the effects of intellectualization and denial, this is hardly surprising. It is important to note, also, that it is from this centered position that better relationships with others become possible. But, however organizationally and socially important the result of this process, the journey toward this goal must be made alone. No one can do it for us. Not even any technique—though technique can help to some extent. Head techniques can be learned without the engaging of the rest of the psyche. But real centering involves more than just technique.

Not only relationships but intellectual clarity result from this process. Is this simply a matter of advertising? It would seem rather that there is a relationship with the issues discussed in the last chapter: the unified psyche sees each individual thing and person in a new and clearer way. This is not simply a spiritual issue: it is a psychological fact. NTL describes itself as "a pioneer known since 1947 for excellence and reliability in human relations training and consultation," and its services are used by a large number of "big businesses"—for clearly pragmatic reasons. In Japan, also, meditation is furthered in some large businesses for the same reasons.

Meditation can, however, be as much a "head trip," a technique isolated from the heart, as any other. Some techniques simply aim at a form of relaxation otherwise obtainable by a glass of wine. Done in this form, they are not necessarily profoundly helpful toward deep balance or serious human development, though relaxation is preferable to tension.

In some of his Journal Workshops, Ira Progoff speaks of meditation and journal techniques that are, indeed, to involve the entire psyche. Following in the Jungian—and, in this respect, the Freudian —tradition, he instructs his readers or participants to write whatever comes to their minds, once they have established themselves in a basic centeredness and stillness. They are not to censor or command the unconscious but rather to allow it to express itself fully through and to them. The result is an increasing awareness of the "inner well" or stream within each person which, despite its depth, is paradoxically the point at which each person most deeply meets others.[3] In other words, this is a movement away from pure intellect, away from defensiveness, and into an integrated position open to the movements of the unconscious. This is a "centeredness" that bears fruit socially because it bears fruit personally and spiritually.

In an interesting passage on a specifically religious topic, Jung shows in forceful language the effects of externalization and objectivization, which intellect divorced from heart or depth can produce:

> The demand made by the *imitatio Christi*—that we should follow the ideal and seek to become like it—ought logically to have the result of developing and exalting the inner man. In actual fact, however, the ideal has been turned by superficial and formalistically-minded believers into an external object of worship, and it is precisely this veneration for the object that prevents it from reaching down into the depths of the psyche and giving the latter a wholeness in keeping with the ideal. Accordingly the divine mediator stands outside as an image, while man remains fragmentary and untouched in the deepest part of him. . . . It is not a question of an imitation that leaves a man unchanged and makes him into a mere artifact, but of realizing the ideal on one's own account—*Deo concedente*—in one's individual life.[4]

It is easier to think about, theologize about, talk about Christ than to surrender oneself to a transforming action that makes serious demands. Even the readiness to be open to the unconscious requires a courage many find difficult. Yet it is a first step. I do not believe that the above passage need imply that reverence for Christ as an "object of worship" is harmful. If that "object," however, is wholly external—is something to think or talk about, rather than risking a "plunge into the fire"—then, indeed, what is said above holds. Externalization protects one from truly entering into contact. And this is the risk of intellectualization—one risk. The atrophy of the heart and the splitting of the person are others.

Jung's attitude, as traced by Barbara Hannah, came from his own disillusionment with the church his father seemed to represent and which spoke of doctrine and value rather than of experience.[5] The young Jung felt alone in his inner experience and came to fear the mental constructs divorced from life. Different early contacts might have made a big difference, but the fact remains that the above quotation speaks of a mature assessment of what Christians can live.

Awareness of the dangers of this intellectualizing tendency is old in the Christian tradition. The Orthodox spiritual masters, for example, consider the very beginning of the process of prayer to require "putting the mind into the heart."[6] John Main writes:

> The truly religious understanding of man is not found in terms of reward and punishment, but in terms of wholeness and division. The supreme religious insight in East and West is that all our alienations are resolved, and all our thinking and feeling powers united, in the heart. One of the *Upanishads* says that the mind must be kept in the heart. St Paul proclaims the same vision of unity in man when he gives love the supremacy over every other dimension and activity. The holy men of the Orthodox Church see the essential task of the Christian life as being to restore this unity to man with a mind and heart integrated through prayer.[7]

In a contemporary book on prayer which, however, draws on the very earliest sources, André Louf speaks of the present crisis about prayer and refers to it as a blessing. Is not reeling off set formulas often formalism? he asks. Is not much "interior prayer" simply the introvert's search for tranquillity? How much of our prayer, especially before this crisis, was simply sentiment—or intellectualism? To be freed from all this is to be freed from illusion, and that is the purpose of his book. He will speak there of a prayer prayed by the Spirit in us and to which we must become attuned.

This is a reality one can live only at the level of the heart, which he calls the "organ" of prayer:

> The heart, in the ancient sense of the word, is not the discursive intelligence with which we reason, nor the 'feelings' with which we respond to another person, nor yet the superficial emotion we call sentimentality. The heart is something that lies much deeper within us, the innermost core of our being, the root of our existence or, conversely, our summit, what the French mystics call 'the very peak of the soul.' . . . In our everyday life our heart is usually concealed. It hardly reaches the surface of our consciousness. We much prefer to stay put in our outward senses, in our impressions and feelings, in all that attracts or repels us. And should we opt to live at a deeper level of our personal being, then we usually land up in abstraction: we reflect, we combine, we compare, we draw logical conclusions. But all this time our heart will be asleep.[8]

To Louf, the only real prayer is that of the heart beginning to awaken and come in touch with the movement of the Spirit within. And from this place in us, too, come our only truly deep relationships. Away from this center the human person is alienated from self, from the depths — and even from others. The whole process of learning to pray is, then, one of "surprising one's heart" which is already at prayer, of becoming conscious of the grace already given. God does not "pray," but the Spirit of God in our hearts speaks what we know not of prayer and relationship, and entering into this movement of the Spirit is our entry into the Trinitarian movement and life. This, to Louf, is prayer — and such a summary can not do justice to the richness of his treatment which needs study in itself. For him, true prayer begins only at the level of the heart. It continues there as well. Speaking of the moment when a word of God strikes the heart, awakening it to life, he says:

> Of course, we must again take good care at this point not to wander off into an intellectual analysis of some truth or other concerning God. At this moment any attempt at rational thinking would not only serve as a distraction but would be a death-blow to the new life that was on the point of being born. The fact is that we are standing here at the very base, the very springs of our heart and of our existence, with our defenses down, exposed

to the love of God, to the power of the Spirit and to the consuming omnipotence of his Word.[9]

Centuries earlier Augustine describes the conclusion of his own years of struggle and effort to find God:

> Behold, you were within me, while I was outside: it was there that I sought you, and, a deformed creature, rushed headlong upon these things of beauty which you have made. You were with me, but I was not with you.[10]

Applying a commentary on the Prodigal Son to St. Benedict, Gregory the Great makes the same kind of remark:

> Had the prodigal son been with himself, whence then should he have returned to himself? Conversely, I might say of this venerable man (Benedict) that he dwelt with himself (*habitare secum*) for watching constantly over himself he remained always in the presence of his Creator.[11]

The notion of "watching constantly over oneself" may not sound like the heart-level we are talking about, but there is a calm vigilance and awareness of the heart — Louf would say "awakenedness" — that is indeed the present question.

What all this is about is alienation. It seems that in the spiritual as in the psychological life there is no happy ground of mediocrity. Refusal to choose the depths, the center, the heart condemns one to wandering forever in a domain of superficiality where both one's life with God and one's human relationships become only a fraction of what they could be. And perhaps this is a case where indeed "the last shall be first," for it is often those simple and poor in what our culture and world value who find it easier to live on the level of the heart — often, or more often at least, than those who seem more gifted by fortune. But not always, for in our culture even the poor are surrounded by means of alienation. Life in front of a television screen does not help awareness of the heart and of those we meet by this awareness — God, others, our self. Yet it remains true that it is the simple, the humble, the uncomplicated (should one say, the not overdefended?) who can find this way the most easily — though one finds such people in any class of society. The reverence mentioned in the last chapter also helps. For "inside" and "out" are, of course,

images. A true and reverent openness to any reality can bring one
to the heart.

Speaking of prayer, John of the Cross has an interesting psychological analysis of what can occur. Commenting on the stanza of the
"Spiritual Canticle" which reads:

> You girls of Judea,
> While among flowers and roses
> The amber spreads its perfume,
> Stay away, there on the outskirts:
> Do not so much as seek to touch our thresholds

he remarks that "the pleasant sensory operations and movements"
of the imagination and the affections "try to draw it [the soul] out
of its interior to a desire for the exterior things which they crave."[12]
This author's first two books stress unceasingly that it is not things
but inappropriate *desire* for things that is an obstacle to spiritual
growth. "They [these operations] also endeavor to move and attract
the intellect that it may be wed to them in their base way of feeling,
and they strive to bring the rational part into conformity and union
with the sensory."[13]

As has been said, the sanjuanist psychology of the spiritual life
speaks of a first stage in which the sensory part of the personality is
made subject to the spiritual, and a second period when both
become subject to God. In other words, a scattered and disunified
personality led in every direction by sense impulses not integrated
with the deeper tendencies of the person has the whole battle still
to fight. Once this first stage of integration has been achieved and
the personality seems more unified, it still remains necessary for
this more unified personality to surrender to God in a relationship
that opens one to a wider world than one's own. John's remarks
here about the attempts of the senses to mislead the intellect refer,
then, to a dynamic opposed to healthy spiritual growth.

He continues:

> The outskirts of Judea (and Judea . . . refers to the lower or
> sensory part of the soul) are the interior senses (memory, phan-
> tasy, and imagination) in which the forms, images, and phan-
> tasms of the objects gather and reside. . . . When they are quiet
> and tranquil, the appetites are also asleep. These images enter

the outskirts, the interior senses, through the gates of the exterior senses. . . . They do so in such a way that we can call both the interior and exterior sense faculties "outskirts," for they are the districts outside the walls of the city. That part of the soul called the city is the innermost part, the rational portion, which is capable of communion with God; its operations are contrary to those of the sensory part.

Yet because there is a natural communication between the people . . . dwelling in these outskirts of the sensory part with the superior part or city, this communication is of such a kind that what occurs in this lower part is usually felt in the interior part, and consequently distracts and deprives it of the peace it has from its spiritual activity and attentiveness to God. As a result she tells those dwelling in the outskirts . . . to remain quiet.[14]

This quotation shows the reasons for a whole long spiritual tradition in both East and West concerning the need for quieting and disciplining the senses. Many techniques of Zen and Yoga, for example, serve this need. But these same techniques also quiet the intellect, which the Zen koan deliberately means to disconcert. John's "rational part" in the above quotation is not the discursive intellect. Rather, it is the "high" or "deep" part of the soul of which Louf speaks. And if he speaks of the need to quiet the senses, the intellect is just as much "outskirts" compared to the heart.

What is one to conclude from reading such passages? Some mistaken readings would lead one to try to deaden or deny one's senses totally. A careful reading not only of John of the Cross's works but also of his life shows that this is far from his meaning. His poetry is hardly that of someone dead to the senses! The issue, once more, is that of integration against alienation. Where the "outer and inner senses" work in harmony with the deeper faculties, they serve integration. Where they lead the whole human personality without rational or heart control, they lead in all directions at once and the result is inner chaos. But the intellect, in its own way, leads to the desert of sterile speculation as well, if it is separated from the heart.

Another writer who has developed this same tradition beautifully is Teresa of Avila. Her *Interior Castle* discusses the whole theology and experience of growth in prayer and union with God in terms of a single main image. The soul is seen as a mansion or set of mansions/rooms, with God in the innermost and central place. Growth in union is movement toward this central place where God is. From there He is a source of light and radiance, and Teresa remarks on the error or illusion involved in seeing one's soul as something dark. On the contrary, "the King of Glory and Light" lives there, and, from thence, irradiates the whole building. In the outer rooms one finds disorder: animals and reptiles roam around, for the person living here has not yet chosen a life for God and willed free from sin. And one can always return to these outer rooms. On the contrary, the innermost room is not reached by most people in this life, but one can approach—at least for moments.

Teresa remarks, as did Jung in the first chapter above, on the dangers of spiritual pusillanimity and fearfulness.[15] This, to her, is not a fruit of true self-knowledge but of an illusion of the devil. A bit later in the book she states that it would be absurd to think one could enter heaven hereafter if, in this life, one had not troubled to enter one's own soul.[16] On the subject of intellectualization, notably in prayer, her position is strong: what is needed in prayer is not to think much but to love much.[17] For this is the meaning of prayer. She continues at some length on the subject of what Benedict calls "bitter zeal"—the desire to reform everyone around one. Since the only aim of the life her readers have chosen is love, she asks them to leave reforming others alone as fruitless.[18] Finally, in an interesting passage, she remarks that the true center of the soul is deeper than the heart:

> A verse which I have already quoted *Dilatasti cor meum* . . . speaks of the heart's being enlarged. I do not think that this happiness has its source in the heart at all. It arises in a much more interior part, like something of which the springs are very deep; I think this must be the centre of the soul, as I have since realized. . . .[19]

While this text may point to the changing of the meaning of the term "heart" toward the more romantic and superficial sense it has taken in the last centuries, it also points to the fact that the "center" of which Teresa speaks needs to be something deeper than that of which the advertisement quoted at the beginning of this chapter spoke. For ultimately, in Christian theology among many others, the human soul opens out into God. This is the true center one finds by first "going in" and then "through" oneself—out of self and into the selflessness that finds a deeper love and a deeper self as well.

One last point needs to be made on the subject of this chapter, and it is one less frequently made than one would think—and one that balances the need for discipline mentioned above. The preconciliar teaching that many Catholics learned was that "feelings do not count." If one wills to forgive another, the essential has been dealt with. (And occasionally this even meant it was not necessary to deal with what anger remained as it was "only a feeling"!) In prayer, also, the principle was that one prayed for God's glory, not one's own satisfaction, and so persevering through years of dryness was praised. The hagiography of the period shows this well.

An Orthodox text, however, shows the older tradition of both East and West:

> Fulfilling the rule zealously, preserve sobriety of mind and warmth of heart. If the latter begins to diminish, hasten to warm it, being convinced that its disappearance will mean that you have withdrawn more than half way from God.[20]

This quotation is not meant to be an encouragement to the seeking of "good feelings" in the sense of what used to be called "sensible consolation" in prayer, as the context shows:

> It is not for sweetness that prayer is practised, but because it is our duty to serve God in this way, although sweetness goes of necessity with true service.[21]

Why this relating of sweetness or warmth and true service? The notion fits with one already discussed, the relation of mind and heart. To try to serve God, pray, or relate with a splintered-off portion of one's psychic anatomy, with the mind divorced from the heart, for example, is to move away from any possibility of true prayer and true relating, which require at least the attempt at unified being. The sign is, precisely, this lack of warmth, for when the personality is unified, it is more normal than not that what brings peace to the heart would overflow into the senses. That this is not always the case we all know. And that there are periods of transition and conflict where for a long time this may not be the case also. Nonetheless, the "normal" situation would seem to be that described above, and the Orthodox tradition seems sufficiently convinced of this to say that such a lack of "warmth" requires attention.[22]

This chapter can best be summarized by a few thoughts from the writings of an author who has done much of late to further the knowledge of "centering prayer" in this country. Beginning with the observation that God is all around us and in us, as the air we breathe, as the water around a fish in the sea, he remarks that to experience this reality, one way is centering prayer.

> By turning off the ordinary flow of thoughts, which reinforces one's habitual way of looking at the world, one's world begins to change. It is like turning a radio from long wave to short wave. . . . As you go to a deeper level of reality, you begin to pick up vibrations that were there all the time but not perceived. This broadened perspective gives you a chance to know both yourself and God in a new way.[23]

He continues by analyzing all the different types of thoughts that can come to mind during the process of centering prayer, some of them very deep and apparently crucially important. His advice on all of them is: leave them. They can be reflected on later. "While in this prayer, dedicate the time to interior silence." While the fruit of this prayer is peace and tranquillity, Keating remarks on the psychotherapeutic effects of the experience as well: things long hidden in the depths of the psyche will emerge and can be disturbing. They, too, must be dealt with like all the rest: their emergence will do its work notwithstanding.

In other words, the findings of psychology and spirituality come together here again though the domains they discuss are not totally coextensive. Intellectualization, rationalization, superficiality, externalism—all these defeat the need of the human person for unity, integration, and peace. The intellect is a power of great importance —and the senses, also, can be vehicles of real enjoyment and beauty —but to live one's whole life in either domain or to allow any of these powers to guide everything in life is to lose touch with one's center or heart, the place where one meets God. It is to lose touch, also, with the possibility of relating in truth.

Abba Poemen said, 'Teach your mouth to say that which you have in your heart.'[24]

Abba Pambo said, 'If you have a heart, you can be saved.[25]

* * *

A brief corollary to this chapter needs to be mentioned, and that concerns the relations of concepts like "cell" and "cloister" with the material just covered. Much ink was spilled around the time of Vatican II on the validity or not of the various types of cloister for various types of religious, and the theologies behind the reflections varied considerably. In Benedictine circles, questions have also been asked about what thought lay behind the conception that a monastery should be self-sufficient so that monks need not go out "beause this is not at all good for their souls."[26] The reflections that follow will, however, be phenomenological rather than historico-theological.

As is well known, the Buddhist tradition about *zazen* which we often refer to when speaking of "Zen Buddhism" is about "sitting." That is, in one sense, all that is involved—just sitting. The sitting is, however, maintained in a specific posture of stillness and is accompanied by an internal procedure intended equally to still and center the mind. It is well known in Japan that people who experience the need for a certain quieting and pacification may well go even for a day to a Zen monastery to participate in the sessions of sitting quietly: they often return refreshed and renewed.

This concept of "sitting" is reminiscent of a famous story from the desert. A young desert-dweller went to an ancient, an "Abba," and asked for help in temptation. He was told, "Go, eat, drink, sleep, do no work, only do not leave your cell."[27] Other texts on the cell abound:

The most important thing for the solitary is to be a solitary, to "sit in his cell" because the cell will "teach him all things."[28]

The cell of the hermit is the furnace of Babylon in which the three children found the Son of God and the Pillar of cloud in which God spoke to Moses.[29]

What is all this tradition about? It is certainly the ancestor of the remark from the Benedictine Rule.

What is being said is that roaming is scattering. What is one looking for outside that cannot be found within? Our culture today is a wholly different world from the one in which these texts were written. Few communities—religious or sociological—are self-contained as in the past. People experience more complex needs and obligations. Mobility seems the order of the day. And this is contemporary *reality*. It need not, however, blind us to the psychological effects of such mobility because it is our realism in this regard that will make it possible to deal with these situations appropriately. We are not pure spirits. Everything our entire body-person does or undergoes affects our whole psychological mechanism. It is wise for us to understand how.

In "Confessions of a Lay Contemplative" and coming out of a Franciscan tradition, Carol Carstens writes:

> No lay contemplative can overcome the distractions of secular life without a centered approach to living. The key to a centered lifestyle is economy and simplicity. Work, home, and worship should be integrated as much as possible. Ideally, the workplace should be within walking distance of the home with worship occurring within the same work/home community. A kind of secular monastery is the university environment where one can reside, work, and worship within a defined community. Housewives can integrate work, neighborhood, and parish in the same way. . . . The Benedictine maxim "ora et labora" is clearly applicable outside the monastic environment.[30]

One can suppose that this is written out of the kind of experience just mentioned.

Nothing should be absolutized. Catherine of Siena wrote of the "interior cell" she carried with her on her journeys. And no amount of exterior cell or cloister can replace this interior cell. But nonetheless, the positive meaning and psychologico-phenomenological sources of some of these older traditions need to be taken into account as we try to understand the dynamics of both human living and the attempt to grow in spiritual depth. When we seek our center, our heart, this centripetal movement is in the opposite direction from what I have called "roaming." Roaming, too, can be centered. There were saints in the early Church whose whole life was roaming, following Him who had no place to lay His head. But this is a roaming very free of external attachment. The roaming of the heart and desires and attention is another phenomenon, and it is against this that the external centering of cell and cloister was an intended aid. To know this is to be abler to make intelligent use of whatever means are appropriate. For this means—like all others —finds value only in terms of the end.

·6·

PERSONA, EGO, AND SELF

The material discussed in the last chapter leads to a deeper reflection on issues already broached, particularly as they emerge in the writings of Jung. As has been said, to Jung one of the main tasks of the first half of life is the establishment of an adult identity in the world; the fulfilling of the tasks incumbent upon every human person in terms of work, responsibility, action. All these are the work of the ego and they in turn build up and reinforce the ego. They also involve what Jung calls the "persona."

The term "persona" in its origins referred to the mask used in Greek drama to indicate the role and mood of the actors. One finds the same custom at present in Japanese theater. As a result of some misunderstood popularizations, the persona has come to be denigrated in some circles, as if acting out of it was a failure to be one's "real self." This was not true in early drama, nor is it Jung's thought. There is a persona appropriate to, for example, a school teacher that would not be appropriate for the same person at home; if she were to act in a primary school classroom as she would with her husband at the breakfast table, the need for the persona would soon become evident. And so in many other domains. The persona is something through which we act and project what we choose to project, and it is interesting to realize that it is often symbolized in dreams by clothing. The symbol is worth reflecting on, for the clothing we choose to wear expresses very clear choices and self-understandings, as well as ways we choose to relate to our environment. This is not always fully conscious, but it is nonetheless real, both in us and in its effects around us. Reflection on this can be illuminating.

On the other hand, Jung remarks:

> The construction of a collectively suitable persona means a for-
> midable concession to the external world, a genuine self-sacrifice
> which drives the ego straight into identification with the persona,
> so that people really do exist who believe they are what they
> pretend to be. The "soullessness" of such an attitude is, however,
> only apparent for under no circumstances will the unconscious
> tolerate this shifting of the center of gravity.[1]

The unconscious will struggle—and, ultimately, revolt. This is
the cause of the malaise felt by so many who seem to be living in
the world very "appropriately." It can result in a neurosis, or a
midlife crisis—and, in both cases, this is growth rather than di-
minishment, for the result is meant to be deeper awareness and
integration.

Jung points out another aspect of the persona, however, for while
it is "a mask that *feigns individuality*," it is also "a role through which
the collective psyche speaks."[2] It is

> a compromise between individual and society as to what a man
> should appear to be. He takes a name, earns a title, exercises a
> function, he is this or that. In a certain sense all this is real, yet
> in relation to the essential individuality of the person concerned
> it is only a secondary reality, a compromise formation, in making
> which others often have a greater share than he.[3]

In other words, to some extent—whether the person involved
realizes it or not—the persona is something imposed on him or her
from without, from societal expectations or customs. This factor
explains the inner confusion and restlessness that result as the
individual grows in awareness of personal identity. The persona
that was previously experienced as part of oneself or even, perhaps,
as oneself, now begins to be perceived as something external to the
true self, imposed, and perhaps undesirable. The result of this
increase in consciousness may be the effort to shed the persona, but
if one is to live in society, it soon turns out that the persona is as
necessary as one's clothing. It serves a purpose. The difference lies,
however, in the ability no longer to be identified with the persona.

What faculty is it in the human persona that can make this disidentification? This is what Jung calls the "ego":

If the ego identifies with the persona, the subject's center of gravity lies in the unconscious. It is then practically identical with the collective unconscious, because the whole personality is collective. In these cases there is a strong pull towards the unconscious and, at the same time, violent resistance to it on the part of consciousness because the destruction of conscious ideals is feared.[4]

Such a person, then, is or tries to be wholly what society asks, but because the whole world of the unconscious is unknown to him or her, its power is both doubled and experienced as frightening. One can wonder, for example, at the terror of some people at the suggestion or very idea of therapy. (Some even surround psychologists with a kind of uncanny aura: "What might they know?") Is this not basically a fear of what might be found if one looked at the unconscious and its contents—a fear, also, that the structure of "conscious ideals" and standards one has set up might not withstand this experience? It is as if the world of "civilization" and perhaps faith were conceived as a fragile structure that could be destroyed by any freeing of what might be in the depths of the human heart. But were that the case, both civilization and faith or religion would be based on so partial an aspect of the personality as to be worth very little. One would hope, rather, that it would be the whole human person who could be involved in culture and religion. The only cure for this kind of identification with the persona, of which Jung speaks, is at least some growth in consciousness.

When this occurs, there is a freeing of the ego, or at least there can be. For Jung speaks of another risk in the opposite direction from the above. Besides identifying with the persona, the ego can also identify with the unconscious, the anima for a man, the animus for a woman. (These will be discussed more at length below.) When this occurs, there is such identification with the unconscious that "adaptation to reality is severely compromised."[5] Here, too, the ego has not appropriately come into its own.

In other words, the ego with its tasks is the conscious part of the personality, the part that takes responsibility in the adult world— not merely in the way that society and the collective dictate but in the way that the individual chooses.

Jungian psychology can seem to be ambivalent about the ego. In one sense the importance of the ego is stressed, specifically in the context given above and in terms of the first half of life. But what distinguishes Jungian from, for example, Freudian thought is the concept that remaining on this level of development characteristic of active adulthood can, in later stages of life, be still another fixation. For the human person is called to move beyond simply the level of the ego, and, if it does not, the ego itself will stagnate, though Jung fully recognizes that not everyone is called to the same level of consciousness.

But there are other ways in which the ego might not come into its own. Looking at the first can help toward understanding the way the persona and the ego act in relation to each other. For example, Jung speaks of one possible way of reacting to adversity in human life. He says that what analysis can do for the few who seek it for greater integration of the unconscious and individuation, the trials and sorrows and even tragedies of life can do for others who do not seek analysis. Ability to deal positively with adversity, then, brings deeper integration. But one way of reacting which is harmful rather than helpful for growth Jung calls "regressive restoration of the persona." If, after becoming bankrupt, a businessman

> goes to pieces, abjures all further risks, and laboriously tries to patch up his social reputation within the confines of a much more limited personality, doing inferior work with the mentality of a scared child, in a post far below him . . . he will as a result of his fright have slipped back to an earlier phase of his personality.[6]

He has, then, regressed into his persona, and a more limited one than is appropriate. A stronger ego would respond by not allowing

> himself to be discouraged by this depressing experience, but, undismayed . . . [to keep] his former daring, perhaps with a little salutary caution added.[7]

In this case, the trial has served its purpose in his life.

On the other hand, the ego can also identify either with the personal unconscious (the animus or anima, in this case) or with the collective unconscious. "This would amount to an acceptance of inflation but now exalted into a system."[8]

> The dissolution of the person in the collective psyche positively invites one to wed oneself with the abyss and blot out all memory in its embrace.[9]

The quasi-religious fervor of some Nazi groups during World War II is an excellent illustration, particularly when this movement drew on ancient German myths. But there is an alternative, which begins with the healthy development of the ego:

> There is a destination, a possible goal, beyond the alternatives dealt with in our last chapter. That is the way of individuation. Individuation means becoming an "in-dividual," and insofar as "individuality" embraces our innermost, last, and incomparable uniqueness, it also implies becoming one's own self.[10]

Not the ego, then, but the self is the true goal of development.

The notion of the self is hotly contested among Jung's followers. Even the fact that some feel the word should always be capitalized and others not is indicative. The discussion of the self in Chapter 1 would give some idea why this might be so. The self is our own "innermost, last uniqueness"; it is also that by which we become able to say, "I live now, not I but Christ lives in me."

> The aim of individuation is nothing less than to divest the self of the false wrappings of the persona on the one hand, and of the suggestive power of primordial images on the other.[11]

The unconscious processes rise within the psyche and can be responsible for conversions as well as for psychoses, depending on the ability to deal with them. Growth in self-knowledge and awareness widens the person's horizons until "there arises a consciousness which is no longer imprisoned in the petty, oversensitive, personal world of the ego, but participates freely in the wider world of objective interests."[12] The individual comes into "absolute, binding, and indissoluble communion with the world at large."[13] In other words, a transformation of the personality occurs which Jung likes to compare with the work of alchemy in the Middle Ages. He is not afraid to say that this is "the primitive Christian ideal of the Kingdom of Heaven which 'is within you.'"[14] And this is Jung's obvious point of connection with spiritual theology. As a bridge toward this subject, it would be good to look at a quotation from the *Upanishads*, which Barbara Hannah considers a source for Jung's use of the term "Self":

He who dwells in the seed, and within the seed, whom the seed
does not know, whose body the seed is, and who pulls (rules) the
seed within, he is the Self, the puller (ruler) within, the immortal;
unseen, but seeing; unheard, but hearing; unperceived, but per-
ceiving; unknown, but knowing. There is no other seer but he,
there is no other hearer but he, there is no other perceiver but
he, there is no other knower but he. This is thy Self, the ruler
within, the immortal. Everything else is of evil.[15]

In spiritual theology, the issues mentioned around the persons
have a double parallel. There is, in the first place, the "spiritual
person" or "saint" or ideal that beginners in the spiritual life can
set out to be and which serves as a spiritual persona. On a deeper
level, there is what one really is, in one's ego, but without yet
having lived either transformation or the docility to the Other, to
the Spirit, that, in itself, transforms, as the chapter on obedience
will show.

As regards the first case, two examples of the teaching of past
centuries have already been given—the remark from the Benedictine Rule that reads: "Do not aspire to be called holy before you
really are: but first be holy, that you may more truly be called so"[16]
and John of the Cross's remarks about beginners who do not want
anyone but themselves to appear holy and who want badly to be
well thought of by those who direct them, as well as others.[17] The
whole issue can, however, be taken to a deeper level. Conceptuali-
zation about what a holy person, or—sometimes—a religious or
even a Christian can and should be like can lead to refusal to act
otherwise than in terms of these self-understood norms, as well as
to refusal to admit that one feels and wants to act quite otherwise.
As has already been said, this saps the very foundations of both the
spiritual and the psychological processes where truth, humility,
and facing the shadow are the only way. God tends to disconcert
our preconceived ideas, and refusal to let Him do so leads to a
spirituality where the human rather than the divine is the norm.
The life of Jesus is a prime example, for He clashed time and again
with human rules set up for holiness and which could not contain
Him. Among His many protests comes the remark that John the
Baptist came fasting and was accused of having a devil while Jesus
was accused of being a glutton and a wine-bibber. "But wisdom is
justified by all her children."[18] In this context, Francis of Assisi

asking for cookies on his deathbed and Teresa of Avila's "When I fast I fast, and when I eat partridge I eat partridge" make supreme sense. The saints were not measuring up to others' norms. That may be an essential criterion of sanctity.

Where the whole discussion leads is to the issue of "wisdom's children." Thomas Aquinas, in the part of the *Summa* which deals most explicitly with spiritual theology,[19] speaks of the development of the habits or virtues that form the Christian life. He sees this life in terms of relationship with God, with others, with oneself, with the things around one. Following Aristotle, he sees the moral life in terms of justice which gives others their due; fortitude and temperance which regulate human passion as it relates to things, people, events; and prudence, which, as right judgment, rules all of these. Virtue, in all these fields, tends to lie in the mean between two extremes—and here, again, this continues the Greek tradition.

Relationship with God, however, is a matter of what we call—for want of a better term—the "theological virtues." For these there is no "mean." One cannot love God too much or believe too much (though one can indeed love or believe wrong). In other words, these "virtues" open onto the infinite which cannot be regulated by human norms.

But even this is only a beginning. For these "virtues" themselves are what open us, no longer to our activity but to God's activity in us—to the world of "Gifts of the Holy Spirit." The Fathers of the Church spoke of these, following Scripture, as a wind which, by blowing into the sails of a boat, moves it infinitely faster than the human activity of rowing. The only human activity here is openness, surrender, docility. In a conference I heard in Rome in 1960, Father M.M. Philippon, following in the tradition of Aquinas, spoke of the choice before each human person to be a "barnyard fowl," living according to human norms and understanding, or to be ready to fly on the wind, past the confines of the barnyard, as an eagle does. But this means abandoning the security of having everything humanly clear. Once again, God is not subject to human norms.

How does all this relate to the persona/ego/self complexus? The persona involves the world of social expectations and the ego that of human understanding and effort. Christian spirituality, like the thought of Jung, points out that to stop at this level is to lead a truncated life. More is offered to one who has the courage to go beyond the merely human and reasonable—into what Jung called the world of the archetypes, the Self, and what Christianity spells out as the world of the Kingdom.

> Abba Lot went to see Abba Joseph and said to him, 'Abba, as far as I can I say my little office, I fast a little, I pray and meditate, I live in peace and as far as I can, I purify my thoughts. What else can I do?' Then the old man stood up and stretched his hands towards heaven. His fingers became like ten lamps of fire and he said to him, 'If you will, you can become all flame.'[20]

This word from the desert finds expression in a later text from the same tradition:

> Through this love, all that he [the monk] once performed with dread, he will now begin to observe without effort, as though naturally, from habit, no longer out of fear of hell, but out of love for Christ, good habit and delight in virtue. All this the Lord will by the Holy Spirit graciously manifest in his workman now cleansed of vices and sins.[21]

> As we progress in this way of life and in faith, we shall run on the path of God's commandments, our hearts overflowing with the inexpressible delight of love.[22]

And finally, a passage that could in itself be a commentary on "become fire":

> The soul now feels that it is all inflamed in the divine union, and that its palate is all bathed in glory and love, that in the most intimate part of its substance it is flooded with no less than rivers of glory, abounding in delights. . . . And the soul sees that every time that delicate flame of love, burning within, assails it, it does so as though glorifying it with gentle and powerful glory.[23]

Human life, then, is not meant to be limited by its own horizons but to open to something infinitely wider. Jung did not claim to spell out what this could mean. Thomas Aquinas, having seen more than he wrote, looked back on his writing and found it "all straw." And John of the Cross found silence more expressive than language. But at least it is possible to know that while words fail and are meant to fail, there is a reality beyond our thoughts and words which can enkindle us with its fire. But always, with us as with Mary, this will require that we say: "Yes."

·7·

THE FACES OF ANIMUS AND ANIMA

The unconscious of a woman is masculine and that of a man, feminine, writes Irene Claremont de Castillejo[1] after Jung. What does such a remark mean? And how does this whole question relate to the development we have just been studying? To deal first with the first of these two questions, we are all familiar with references to the soul as "she," especially in some early spiritual literature. What can be the source of such a way of speaking? Various spiritual writers speak of the soul as necessarily "feminine to God" in the sense that, if one compares the activity of God and of the human person in mutual relationship, it is God who is the primary "Actor" and the human person who is more passive. In Bernard of Clairvaux's commentary on the Song of Songs, as well as in those before him, it is the human person—whether woman or man—who is "the Bride." All of this gives us one clue to Castillejo's meaning.

Is this only a question for religion? In Jungian thought, when a man falls in love or dreams of a beautiful woman, he is seeing outside himself a projection of his inner "anima," his soul, the part of himself he needs to meet and relate to in order to make the journey toward transformation and individuation.

Woman, with her very dissimilar psychology, is and always has been a source of information about things for which a man has no eyes. She can be his inspiration; her intuitive capacity, often superior to man's, can give him timely warning, and her feeling, always directed towards the personal, can show him ways which his own less personally accented feeling would never have discovered. . . . Here, without a doubt, is one of the main sources of the feminine quality of the soul. But it does not seem to be the

85

only source. No man is so entirely masculine that he has nothing feminine in him. The fact is, rather, that very masculine men have—carefully guarded and hidden—a very soft emotional life, often incorrectly described as "feminine." . . . The repression of feminine traits and inclinations naturally causes these contra-sexual demands to accumulate in the unconscious.[2]

In other words, the "soul" of a man contains all those elements which, in order to establish his masculine identity, he has pushed back into the unconscious. He is—often vaguely—aware that these same qualities can be natural to woman and so, rather than recognizing them in himself, he sees them in her and, as a result, can idealize her. This projection can occur in imagery or with a real woman: in the latter case it is called "falling in love." But the essential in either case is for the man to come into contact with this feminine within himself which is his own richness, which can nuance a too hard or categorical way of looking at things or living, and which can help him to relate in a more nuanced and sensitive way. A man who does this is on the way to a more "androgynous" and thus more balanced and mature existence. What happens to a man who does not?

The reflection that opened this chapter may shed some light. If the unconscious of a man is feminine and he is out of touch with that unconscious, it can play the kind of tricks on him that all the preceding chapters have discussed. Separated from relationship with consciousness it can go wild and act exactly like a woman gone wild. The reverse side of all the good qualities mentioned above appears—moodiness, witchlike behavior, irrationality. A man is conscious of these moods, of course: in fact, they seem to control him. And that is why such a state is called "anima-possession." But what is the solution? Only the process mentioned before—the effort to come into touch with what one really is and with what really happens on the levels deeper than consciousness. This task can be accomplished by openness to dreams, to imagery, to strong feelings (particularly those one would want to repress), to themes in literature (fairy tales, poetry, novels) and art that attract and "speak to" one. One's own artistic expression is important, too. All this can help one to come into touch with the deeper levels of the personality where they begin to touch the collective unconscious as well. A man who does this will find his own sensitivity and intuition —or whatever is the content of his own particular anima—and be able to relate to others from this deeper realm. And so, what could have turned into unregulated moodiness becomes instead a source of awareness and gentleness. The "dream woman" is no longer projected outside a man—so that he rages when his merely human wife cannot measure up to his dreamed ideal—but is recognized as showing her face inside him, as inspiration and spiritual or emotional strength. To Jung this is, after dealing with the shadow, an essential step in the process of integration.

What does this same process look like for a woman? As a man represses certain aspects of his personality in order to develop his masculine identity, so does she with the feminine. Recent literature is full of comments on the way women have felt the need to repress all signs or even feelings of authority, power, intelligence, organizational ability as "too masculine."[3] Not too long ago they were encouraged by the whole culture to let men take the stage on all these fronts even where their personal gifts surpassed those of the men around them. And, on the other hand, there was the stereotype of the "career woman"—hard, mannish, successful but out of touch with the richer values of the feminine ideal. All of us have known women who combined full careers with a flowering of their feminine gifts, but they were not "career women" in the stereotypical sense of the term. What constituted the difference? Even in the common folklore these women remained in touch with their own souls, their own femininity, sensitivity, "softness." And yet they also manifested the ability, power, gifts of men—but in a way very different from men. This was their way of being "androgynous." Is the soul of a woman, then, feminine, too? Jungians argue on this.[4] The point is that a woman cannot lose her femininity without losing her "soul," but femininity is no more enough than pure masculinity is for a man. She needs to get in touch with the power and lucidity that live in her unconscious and that have perhaps been projected onto various men. Castillejo points out that the animus is multiple and one must be able to speak to all his aspects— cowboy, priest, "mealy-mouthed boy," devil or criminal, sycophant, professor or teacher.[5] Terrifying dreams of rapists or murderers as well as dreams of companions, lovers, sources of intelligence or wisdom, all reveal him. Jung wrote in a relatively early text:

> The animus corresponds to the paternal Logos just as the anima corresponds to the maternal Eros. But I do not wish or intend to give these two intuitive concepts too specific a definition. I use

Eros and Logos merely as conceptual aids to describe the fact that woman's consciousness is characterized more by the connective quality of Eros than by the discrimination and cognition associated with Logos.[6]

It is this quality of Logos which symbolizes the elements in herself with which woman needs to come into touch in order not only to stop projecting onto others but also to find her own inner harmony. The failure to perform this task leads to much one would recognize in the "career woman" stereotype, or, on the contrary, to the falsely "feminine" stereotype instead, but to other things besides — not only the hardness of the successful whose success is bought by heartlessness but even more seriously to the opinionated stance that can seem true stupidity. Castillejo speaks of "irrelevance," pointing out that where a woman is in touch with both her soul and her animus, her opinions will not betray her feelings. When, on the other hand, she comes out in slogans, generalities, remarks ever so slightly beside the mark, somehow, somewhere, she has lost touch.[7] Her task seems rather more complex than a man's in this light, but ultimately, the movement is the same — away from superficiality, away from sheer intellectualization, centering into a position where the heart and the unconscious in general can speak and be recognized, where the deepest part of the personality is free. In still deeper language, it is the Self that emerges when this work of unification is done.

Some myths like that of Amor and Psyche have been used to illustrate this task of woman and the ways in which it must be worked out.[8] The tasks Aphrodite gives Psyche are seen as symbols of what woman needs to learn on the road to integration or individuation. This issue is important today when a head-centered education has become the sine qua non for most professional work. What a man can undergo without violation of his deeper ways of proceeding and integrating, a woman cannot live without far greater damage. If she must continue to stuff away knowledge unintegrated by the heart, she loses the specific kind of insight and lucidity that is hers. The world of pure Logos is not a natural home for her so that the result, instead of being androgynous, is simply sterile. A rather good case could be made for a specifically feminine type of education, as, indeed, for any kind of education that allows the individual as such to grow and integrate in terms of who he or she is. Mass production is hardly the answer.

It is precisely at this point that the convergence between all this teaching and that of spirituality becomes clearest. Speaking of Psyche's tasks in the myth, Johnson remarks:

> The myth tells us that the feminine need only obtain a bit of the fleece—the hem, not the whole garment—to have enough for her purposes, to be made whole.
>
> When we talk of a woman's acquiring the fleece, or masculinity, we must understand that we are not striving for an equal amount of masculinity and femininity within ourselves. . . . One must be a woman with masculinity backing her up, or one must be a man with femininity backing him up. . . . The woman who understands this can go into the business world and use her objective masculinity. She brings, along with a focused consciousness, her quietness, her touch with the source, her quality of reminding those around her of the Grail castle.[9]

Speaking of the next task—filling a goblet with water from the Styx—he writes:

> Almost every woman I know is too busy. She is into this, studying that . . . working hard on some big project, racing around until she is ragged. She needs to be quiet, to approach the vastness of life's responsibilities in a more orderly manner, to do one thing, take one crystal goblet at a time, concentrate on it, and do it well. Then she may move on to other things.[10]

One may find the tone of this last a trifle patronizing, but the two quotations together point in what seems an important direction. Woman—in herself and as anima—represents a contemplative dimension of life without which sterility ensues. This is a direction often in contradiction with the movement of our culture. The early spirituality of the *fuga mundi,* the flight from the world and the depreciation of its values, is often frowned upon today as negative. But one could present quite a case for the urgent need for a *fuga mundi,* a flight from the values our contemporary culture espouses, right in the heart of the world. For our culture seems bent on destroying itself and the planet. The contemplative dimension of the human soul can only be furthered by radically different choices which fly in the face of the culture.

One of these choices is about being rather than doing. The choice of heart over intellectualization has already been discussed and is a

choice specifically concerned with the furthering of the feminine—
in man or woman. The need to do the deeds of love would seem to
be obvious in the Judeo-Christian perspective and is not denied
here. But what is forgotten, as an equally profound religious value,
is the importance of being, of contemplation, of what Joseph Pieper
speaks of as "leisure."[11] As one might expect, this is a frequent
theme in spiritual writing.

John of the Cross deals with this issue again and again, and especially when speaking of the duties of a spiritual director. He
applies this teaching especially to the field of prayer. At the beginning of the spiritual life, when a person has begun to move
away from an active form of prayer to a more contemplative and
passive or God-given form, both the person involved and an in-
experienced or ignorant director will be unable to understand what
is happening. An individual who has been able to meditate and
"act" in prayer suddenly neither wants to nor can. If he or she is
the kind of person for whom doing or achieving is of great importance, this will be a bridge that may never be passed. Methods
of meditation have proliferated through the centuries and especially since the recent developments of the Society of Jesus. Now
various Eastern methods, too, increase, but they are often different
in purpose. Nonetheless, finding oneself before God naked, useless,
action-less is more than many people can handle. What is worse,
however, is when someone might be able to handle it and the
director is not.

> Since God, then, as the giver communes which him through a
> simple, loving knowledge, the individual also, as the receiver,
> communes with God, through a simple and loving knowledge
> or attention. . . . It is obvious that if a person does not lay aside
> his natural active manner, he will not receive that good except
> in a natural manner, and thus he will not receive it but will
> remain with his natural act. . . . If a person should, then, desire
> to act on his own through an attitude different from the passive
> loving attention we mentioned . . . he would utterly hinder the
> goods God communicates supernaturally to him. . . . If he wants
> to receive it [this loving knowledge] a person . . . should be very
> annihilated in his natural operations, unhampered, idle, quiet,
> peaceful, and serene, according to the mode of God.[12]

And this last state is even deeper than the "loving attention" mentioned above which, even itself, is too "active" for this deep silence in God. But

> because of the refined quality and purity of these delicate and sublime anointings and shadings of the Holy Spirit, neither the soul nor its director understands them. . . . Although this damage is beyond anything imaginable, it is so common and frequent that scarcely any spiritual director will be found who does not cause it in souls God is beginning to recollect in this manner of contemplation. How often is God anointing a contemplative with some very delicate unguent of loving knowledge, serene, peaceful, solitary, and far withdrawn from the senses and what is imaginable . . . when a spiritual director will happen along who, like a blacksmith, knows no more than how to hammer and pound with the faculties. . . . He will say, "Come, now, lay aside these rest periods . . . meditate . . . this other method is the way of illusions and typical of fools."[13]

The blacksmith image in an apt one. Precisely the kind of hammering and pounding born of a lack of reverence for the receptive, silent, feminine, result from this kind of direction. Yet it is still today far more common than one would think. And one finds people aspiring to be spiritual directors in increasing numbers which, inevitably, raises the question of their motivation and of readiness in terms of personal experience and deep spiritual learning. Barring these last, what could possibly qualify a person? And what could prevent the risk of being a "blacksmith"? Or the opposite risk of false mysticism if one has not the experience or learning to discern well?

But John of the Cross carries his thinking on this point still further:

> It should be noted that until the soul reaches this state of union of love, she should practise love in both the active and contemplative life. Yet once she arrives, she should not become involved in other works . . . even though the work be of great service to God. For a little of this pure love is more precious to God and the soul and more beneficial to the Church . . . than all these other works put together. . . .
> Great wrong would be done to a person who possesses some degree of this solitary love, as well as to the Church, if we should urge him to become occupied in exterior or active things, even

if the works are important and demand only a short time. . . .
After all, this love is the end for which we were created.

Let those, then, who are singularly active, who think they can
win the world with their preaching and exterior works, observe
here that they would profit the Church and please God much
more, not to mention the good example they would give, were
they to spend at least half of this time with God in prayer. . . .
They would then certainly accomplish more, and with less labor,
by one work than they otherwise would by a thousand. . . .
Without prayer, they would do a great deal of hammering but
accomplish little, and sometimes nothing, and even at times
cause harm.

This quotation gives a principle essential to sanjuanist thought.
And it is interesting to note again the imagery of hammering. Yet,
lest one think this is a purely personal theory, one can find the
following in the documents of Vatican II:

Members of those communities which are totally dedicated to
contemplation give themselves to God alone in solitude and
silence and through constant prayer and ready penance. . . . No
matter how urgent may be the needs of the active apostolate,
such communities will always have a distinguished part to play
in Christ's Mystical Body where "all members have not the same
function" (Rom. 12:4). For they offer God a choice sacrifice of
praise.[15]

The problem is, of course, that in the document here quoted the
masculine spirit of categorization is very strong and so the above
remark is made of only one category of person, rather than, as in
the case of John of the Cross, of anyone to whom God gives a
deeper call to contemplation. This can occur in the case of a house-
wife, an active religious, a priest, a business man. Obviously in
some of these cases, all work cannot be abandoned. Nor did John of
the Cross himself leave his duties. But there is an issue of daily
choices that is very much the domain of the contemplative, the
feminine, the anima, the "soul." Inability to make this choice—to
the degree to which, for each individual with each individual's
makeup, it is important—bears its own penalty.

John of the Cross is relatively late in the tradition that passed on
such teaching. Bernard of Clairvaux writes, in his twelfth-century

commentary on the Song of Songs, an even more forceful castigation of the absence of the feminine or contemplative attitude where it is needed:

> My brethren, if you be wise, you will make yourselves to be reservoirs rather than conduits. The difference betweeen a conduit and a reservoir is this, that whereas the former discharges all its waters almost as soon as received, the latter waits until it is full to the brim, and only communicates what is superfluous, what it can give away without loss to itself. Remember that a curse has been pronounced on him who deteriorates the lot which has been transmitted to him. . . . Yet we have in the Church today many conduits but very few reservoirs. So great is the charity of those through whom the celestial streams of knowledge are communicated to us, that they want to give away before they have received. They are more willing to speak than to listen. They are forward to teach what they have not learned. Although unable to govern themselves, they gladly undertake to rule others. . . . Charity . . . wishes to abound first unto herself, that she may also abound unto others. . . . My brother . . . thy charity . . . [is so great] that, not content with what is of precept, it inclines thee to go beyond and to love thy neighbour even more than thyself; whilst at the same time, it is so little, that contrary to what is commanded, it dissolves in consolation, faints under fear, loses its peace in sadness, is contracted by greed, distracted by ambition . . . inflated with honour, consumed with envy. Then, by what strange madness, I ask, dost thou, perceiving thyself to be such, desire or consent to be the director of others?[16]

This tradition, however strong its language, goes back through the centuries. Evagrius Ponticus wrote in a work that was to be like a theology of the desert, a description of temptation to leave contemplative leisure and prayer:

> When the devils see that you are really fervent in your prayer they suggest certain matters to your mind, giving you the impression that there are pressing concerns demanding attention. In a little while they stir up your memory of these matters and move your mind to search into them. Then when it meets with failure it becomes saddened and loses heart.[17]

Hausherr comments that these "certain matters" or "pressing concerns" would be food, drink, reputation, having something to give the poor, concern for one's family.[18] (One must remember, on this last point, the context of the desert where this was written.)

The balance for this apparent harshness must be seen later in Evagrius's work:

> Happy is the monk who considers all men as god—after God. . . .
>
> A monk is a man who is separated from all and who is united to all.[19]

This is the other side of the same tradition. The ability to value being more than doing, silence more than words, contemplation more than action when it is appropriate to choose in this way results in a deeper love for and union with others. A word from such a person can bring more healing than endless conversation with another. And those in the desert knew the healing value of their silence.

> The same Abba Theophilus, the archbishop, came to Scetis one day. The brethren who were assembled said to Abba Pambo, 'Say something to the archbishop, so that he may be edified.' The old man said to them, 'If he is not edified by my silence, he will not be edified by my speech.'[20]

One finds this kind of quotation in the East as well as in the West and can only conclude that it belongs to a tradition of wisdom. It also belongs to a tradition of respect for the feminine values, as well as for the Logos in its deepest sense, that leads to a unified and deepened personality. The fruit of this unity will be discussed in the chapter on the "holy marriage." For the present, suffice it to say that both aspects of the human—masculine and feminine—have their place and importance. The way to the depths passes here.

·8·

SOLITUDE, DISCRETION, VIRTUE

In his *Life Together*[1] — a book on the subject of community life, Dietrich Bonhoeffer wrote that, whatever else happens we answer God's call alone and we die alone. This makes sense. No one can do these things for us; no one, in any essential sense, can even be much help. A friend or director can be with us as we reflect. Loved ones can surround a deathbed. But the ultimate journey is made alone. And Bonhoeffer adds that one who cannot be alone should beware of being in community just as one who cannot live in community should beware of being alone.

The inner journey toward integration or union with God—this, too, is made alone. No one else can reach into the deep levels of our conscience and consciousness. What happens there is solitary—before God or before the ultimate values we choose; and even if we decide without realizing it to slide along and not choose, that, too, is a choice.

Through the ages some people have chosen lives of greater solitude in order to look lucidly at these choices and values, to live undistracted by the *divertissements*[2] or distractions many people seek—sometimes in the hope of avoiding the seriousness, even the fearfulness, of solitude and final responsibility. The literature of solitude is long in both Eastern and Western spirituality.

But one of the things that becomes immediately apparent for those living any depth of solitude is the need for discernment, or, as the literature of the desert calls it, discretion. The history of the solitaries there is full of stories of hermits trying to outdo all others with their ascetical feats—to the detriment not only of their spiritual lives but even of their sanity. Cenobitic monasticism came partly

from the growing understanding that training was needed for solitude.[3] Even if one takes the issue out of the religious sphere, what
does a person in solitary confinement do to keep his or her sanity?
There are stories of the way people occupied their time and their
minds for such a purpose. And the mere fact that solitary confinement is considered such a punishment shows us the dangers and
fear of solitude. Yet without some solitude no truly human life is
possible. Here, again, discernment, discretion, is needed. How
much is the appropriate amount of solitude and how should it
be lived?

But there is another aspect to solitude as well. Lovers seek to be
alone together. Artists, poets, researchers seek solitude in order to
be able to give full attention to what they do. Solitude is the "place"
for undivided attention—to a person or creation, to reflection or
study. This solitude may seem pure joy. But, as every married
person knows, there are moments in a marriage when time alone
together can be torment. And so can moments of creation or research. This solitude, too, has its struggles and its purgative aspects,
and one must know when the solitude is too much and must be
broken; when it is purifying and must be faced, and much besides.
Once more, discernment is needed.

But there is still another aspect of this question of solitude. If one
lacks the appropriate inner attitudes, any solitude can become
poison. A lack of trust, a lack of ability to love or believe in love—
these can make it impossible to sustain a marriage, a relationship,
even a creative or scientific or certainly a religio-spiritual work. In
this case, it is not the other or the work that is the problem: it is
one's own inner world. And this leads one into the domain of
psychology.

Erik Erikson, in a study of human development that has become
famous, described the first psychological task of the child as development of "basic trust."[4] We shall follow his study at more length
in order to see the core attitudes of human psychological health as
they develop, for without these it is impossible to live either relationship or solitude.

Basic trust shows in ease of eating, depth of sleep, relaxation of
the bowels. The child becomes aware of familiarity with surroundings and life patterns, a feeling of comfort and security, a sense of
inner goodness. It then becomes possible to let one's mother go out
of sight without anxiety, knowing she will return and care for the

child. Erikson sees in these early experiences the dawn of a primitive ego identity. He calls this state "basic trust," remarking that
the lack of this experience shows in people who withdraw into
schizoid and depressive states. Projection and introjection are born
at this stage:

> In introjection we feel and act as if an outer goodness had become
> an inner certainty. In projection, we experience an inner harm
> as an outer one. . . . These two mechanisms, then . . . are assumed
> to be modeled after whatever goes on in infants when they
> would like to externalize pain and internalize pleasure, an intent
> which must yield to the testimony of the maturing senses and
> ultimately of reason. These mechanisms are, more or less nor-
> mally, reinstated in acute crises of love, trust, and faith in
> adulthood.[5]

We shall be meeting these phenomena of introjection and projection often again in these reflections. What we introject as infants
affects our whole lives, and this is a fundamental principle behind
psychoanalytic treatment. The habit of projecting inner pain—or,
for that matter, inner dreams and energies—is also an issue that
must be dealt with at length if we are to "come into our own" psychologically, humanly, and even if we are to relate to reality as
it is.

Another interesting thing about this passage, however, is the
juxtaposition of love, trust, and faith. These will be recognized as
the same terms used by St. Paul to characterize relationship with
God.[6] In other words, there seem to be certain basic attitudes essential to any relationship—human or divine—essential even to
one's own psychological health and well-being. The lack of these,
from the very beginning of one's babyhood, is a serious obstacle
and one that needs healing if one is to fulfill this very first basic
task, the development of trust. Erikson sees organized religion as
an institutional safeguard for "the parental faith which supports
the trust emerging in the newborn," though he also remarks that
the same religion can be trust's greatest enemy. Each age, he says,
must find its appropriate religious expression, but "The clinician
can only observe that many are proud to be without religion whose
children cannot afford their being without it."[7] Without this basic

attitude of trust, then, the psychological health either for solitude or for relationship is undermined.

Erikson continues his reflections by saying that as the child grows, experimentation with the surrounding world increases. As this occurs, outer control must be such that the basic trust now acquired "will not be jeopardized by this about-face of his, this sudden violent wish to have a choice."[8] Encouragement to "stand on one's own feet" must be accompanied by protection from excessive experience of shame and doubt. Where this protection is absent, a person develops obsessiveness as a means of control, "a tendency to govern by the letter." Or what develops is excessive shame—feeling small, dirty, evil, not wanting to be looked at . . . or the defiance which is a reaction to shame. Doubt relates to fear of being attacked from behind.

Once again, these are issues of basic attitudes of faith. Erikson relates them to law and order in society, as in the early family. They relate to solitude and discernment as well. The obsessive compulsive tendency prevents free, reasonable, responsible discernment needed to live and choose alone, as, on the deepest level, we all must. The inability to believe in an ordered world and in Providence makes solitude frightening and relationship threatening. For some, failure to fulfill the tasks of this stage makes the later development of intimacy impossible. The choice of solitude begins at this early stage when the child begins to stand alone, to experience life in terms of personal choice—however small the first choices are.

Erikson's third stage involves the development of initiative versus guilt. During this crisis, the child "must turn from an exclusive, pregenital attachment to his parents to the slow process of becoming a parent, a carrier of tradition."[9] For some it is very hard to stop being parented, to take an adult or parenting role in one's turn. Again, in Freudian terms, the superego develops here, with all the issues of true and false conscience that can result—all the issues, too, of the parents as true or false carriers of moral codes. This, then, is the moment of "leaving home," psychologically if not physically, of being one stage more ready for inner solitude. In Jungian terms, it is a departure from the incestuous ambiance the family involves, for to Jung refusal to face the outside world at the appropriate time is, precisely, what constitutes living "incestuously."[10] It is what the incest taboo is set up to avoid.

Not only is this a stage of greater solitude. It is also the stage where the possibility for later responsible discernment is born. For the task of development of conscience in later life is that of moving from pure superego control to rational, personal reflection on values and choices.[11]

Erikson's fourth stage involves the development of industry versus inferiority. We need not stop over this stage here, except to note the importance, again, of an attitude of confidence, as against inferiority.

The fifth stage involves identity versus role confusion, and it corresponds with adolescence. Ego identity, once established, can express itself in choice of a career, as well as in the other choices of life. Confusions over, for example, sexual identity can lead to crises at this stage, as can problems about career choice. Then there is falling in love:

> To a considerable extent adolescent love is an attempt to arrive at a definition of one's identity by projecting one's diffused ego image on another and by seeing it thus reflected and gradually clarified. This is why so much of young love is conversation.[12]

In the earlier stage, faith and trust were imporant. Now they begin to flower into love. It is still rather a self-centered love; it is oneself that one projects onto the other, rather than loving that other for him or herself, and this point will recall all that was said in the previous chapter. Nonetheless, the center is moving outward, away from self-centeredness and toward the other—without losing the essential nature of the inner search for identity. This process continues in the next stage which involves intimacy versus isolation.

Erikson defines intimacy as "the capacity to commit himself to concrete affiliations and partnerships and to develop the ethical strength to abide by such commitments, even though they may call for significant sacrifices and compromises."[13] He continues:

> Body and ego must now be masters of the organ modes and of the nuclear conflicts, in order to be able to face the fear of ego loss in situations which call for self-abandon: in the solidarity of close affiliations, in orgasms and sexual unions, in close friend-ships and in physical combat, in experiences of inspiration by

teachers and of intuition from the recesses of the self. The avoidance of such experiences because of a fear of ego loss may lead to a deep sense of isolation and consequent self-absorption.[14]

In one sense, we are here on the outer edge of solitude, for isolation is solitude gone awry, poisoned. There is no one who can protect us or be with us as we risk the loss of self in such experiences, as we go out beyond the safety of rules, norms, human securities. Deep friendship, sexual experience, readiness to be "inspired" from without or guided from within beyond previous boundaries — all these demand solitude even from self. There is a sense in which we are here also beyond the domain of discretion. Reason and judgment belong on a previous plane where we decide our readiness for such commitments. But we do not abandon here an increasingly deep need for the attitudes of trust, belief, love. Without them, balance can be lost.

And if we refuse these risks? Then, says Erikson, we go into isolation and ego-absorption. It is a sterile life — rather close to the way Dante describes hell. So this stage is the one of most serious choice. But only in terms of the previous stages can one be ready for it, for readiness to lose oneself in a healthy way can only come when one has found oneself. Only then is one free for the risk.

Maturity brings the choice of generativity versus stagnation, and this involves creativity of any kind. And then age involves the choice of ego identity versus despair — ego identity being seen as the fruit of all the previous stages. It involves the full acceptance of one's "one and only life cycle," the "owning" of all that one is. To Erikson the sign that one has failed in this task is despair — the fear of death, or the wish that things were or had been otherwise. This is deliberately seen as off-setting the first stage of trust. For to Erikson this early and healthy trust flowers in the final integrity that does not fear death. "Ego integrity . . . implies an emotional integration which permits participation by followership as well as acceptance of the responsibility of leadership."[15] The world has truly grown greater for the fully adult person.

How should these last passages of psychological insight be summarized? I believe they point to an increasing individuality and so solitude of the human person — but a solitude that is able to lose itself in intimate relationship as well. They point to the fact that no healthy living can take place without belief, trust, love, and show the maturation through which these must pass. And they also show that, where these are lacking, the human person cramps him or herself into rules, regulations, rituals for control, rather than learning to discern with a free choice of value. We shall see that these same themes recur throughout the literature of spirituality. Finally, they characterize the adult who has sufficiently performed past tasks as: trustful, free, self-motivated, industrious, in possession of personal identity yet able to risk it in intimacy, and, finally, as creative and serene, a person of faith, confidence, love.

Erikson comes from a Freudian perspective—or, more precisely, that of Ego-psychology. To Jung, one of the main issues of discernment is the ability to recognize the source of an inner message or impulse. Is it from the head or the heart, from the ego or the self? Is it from the animus (or anima) and, if so, which one? And ultimately, one needs to distinguish all of these from oneself. Learning discernment is a long process. This type of discernment will be discussed again in Chapter 11 below.

If one shifts from the tradition of psychology to that of spirituality, what does one learn? One early text that has been used through the centuries as a central symbol of this whole theme of solitude is the Gospel story of Christ in the desert. Before beginning his preaching career, the Gospel presents him as "driven by the Spirit into the desert."[16] Both symbolically and humanly this is a question of the need for solitude before a serious engagement or beginning. One thinks of the all-night vigils of medieval squires before they were knighted, of the Christian custom of vigils before great feasts. This notion of vigil came quite literally from this kind of source—as well as from the many Gospel exhortations to "watch."

What is happening in this solitude? There is mention of wild beasts, and of "angels ministering to him." What does this mean?

The imagery of wild beasts classically has been the imagery of temptation. The passions, thoughts, feelings one struggles with in solitude are often portrayed as beasts. Athanasius's life of Anthony, the first hermit—and its pictorial rendering by Jerome Bosch are one example. Teresa of Avila's *Interior Castle* with the animals moving around in the outer mansions is another. The wildest beasts are within, as psychology certainly points out.

The counterpoise to this is the angels. John of the Cross speaks much of the fact that God can reveal himself to people through angels—which, it goes without saying, refers to spiritual intelligent

beings rather than the pictures of angels seen in paintings!—though
the sanjuanist thrust is more toward an im-mediate union. ("Do
not send me any more messengers."[17]) But throughout Scripture
angels are seen as messengers, comforters, guides, sometimes healers.
They mediate God. To say, then, that Christ was with beasts and
angels is to say that he was living the solitary combat with the inner
forces emerging in each human life—and *a fortiori*, in his; and that
this struggle had to come before the external ministry. The temptation scenes which follow are an externalization, an explicitation, of
what was already said in the opening images. One goes into solitude, then, to face the struggle with evil—and first, the evil in one's
own heart.

Christ responds to these temptations with words of Scripture.
But they are words spoken out of his own assessment of the real
meaning of the situation and temptation. This, for the Christian, is
the first example of discernment. Christ looked at what was being
said and responded out of his own depths and choice of his Father,
a choice born of his own trust and love. Anything that happened to
the hermits in the desert was seen in terms of this one great paradigm. And there is no Christian, no seeker of God whatever, who
does not go through his or her desert, surrounded by beasts and
angels.

An extraordinarily rich and deep treatment of this theme as
inherited from the whole desert tradition can be found in Louf.
This author begins by linking solitude and prayer. Only as the
Christian prays, "can he make solitude something viable and transform a desert into a luxuriant paradise."[18] This theme of the
return to paradise is the one frequently found in the Cistercian
writers, and Louf links it deeply with the Paschal Mystery. For
solitude is not only an experience in refreshment from the noise of
the world. It is an experience of poverty, emptiness, often desola-
tion, inner death.

> This experience is in the literal sense of the expression 'dreadful.'
> Solitude shuts a man off from everything else and takes him
> back to his own nothingness. . . . Every superficial prop, every
> distraction, has gone. A person stands naked and defenseless
> before God, that is to say, in that poverty and weakness which
> are his only asset. Before solitude brings him to the encounter
> with God, it first teaches him his limitation, his abysmal in-
> significance.[19]

The desert, he adds, is a place of temptation, a place to find one's own inner sin and frailty. "In a sense the effect of solitude is a secularizing one: it gives release from many false ideas and illusions, from myth. . . . It teaches one how to be an ordinary human being, frail and in need of help."[20] In Jungian terms, it cures inflation.

Why should anyone go through such an experience? And how? The answer to the first question has already been given in germ. Solitude is the place where one faces ultimate values and choices, the ultimate test. And what is its fruit?

> Each and every solitude throws us back upon ourselves and God, on our extreme poverty and God's immense love and merciful kindness. In this being made to rely exclusively on God's saving entry into the solitude, the faith in our hearts is burrowed out and an unsuspected depth of our being is laid bare: that core of ourself where prayer is already given to us. It was in the wilderness, surely, that water flowed from the rock (Exod. 17:6), that rock which is Jesus Himself (I Cor. 10:4).[21]

This text shows, once again, the essential nature of the attitudes of trust and faith. The desert is stark. Our poverty seems total. Yet, in this poverty, faith knows of God's love: trust can rest in this knowledge, despite all feeling. Without these basic attitudes of both psychological and spiritual health, this experience of poverty can be destructive. Solitude tests the very depths of a person and it is because of the nature of this testing that some cannot bear solitude. Yet, when solitude is unbearable, the answer would seem to be not flight but rather examination of the reasons for this unbearableness, for they lie in our own hearts and our own need for faith. Not all are called to solitude. This call is a gift and doubtless a rare one. But some solitude is asked of—and given to—us all. If we cannot bear it, we need to look at the reasons for they will tell us much that we need to know, and to hear.

If one can only persevere in this desert, says Louf, "the depth of our being is laid bare." Prayer can begin to flow freely from that depth where it is given, as the Spirit is given to us. If we have overlaid the solitude of our hearts with endless clutter, some form of separation from it all becomes the condition for the awakening of prayer. The grave tests of life can throw us into solitude. But the desert image in itself speaks of what needs to be said.

The world of solitude gave Jesus room to be tempted. As it
turned out, it had a part also in His victory. Angels came down
and ministered to the Lord (Mk. 1:13). Only at this point did the
world become completely itself. From being a world-of-tempta-
tion it became paradise on earth and indeed already a new
heaven too—for where Jesus is present, the earthly and the
heavenly paradise are one.[22]

How can Louf use such language? Is it not hyperbole? If one
truly follows his text, which brevity here forbids, one sees that this
is not so. If the going into solitude and temptation and through
this into victory was for Jesus the foretaste of his paschal struggle,
then the beginning of his resurrection lay in this first victory. In
another text, Louf speaks of the paschal birthpangs of creation,
adding, "But soon the whole world will explode into resurrection
and new life."[23] The reference is, of course, to the eighth chapter of
the Letter to the Romans. But one can also see, in much that he has
written here, the thirty-fifth chapter of Isaiah. The promises of a
transfigured desert there foreshadowed the new creation of Paul.
And this whole struggle takes place first in human hearts—first of
all in the heart of the "Firstborn" of this new creation, but his
struggle (his agony and temptation) does not dispense us from
ours. Once again, we are born and die—and we must struggle
—alone. But into that solitude comes the help of knowing we are
loved as he was, and the ability to receive that love with trust. As
this process deepens, the desert can indeed flower and—on a more
cosmic level—the creation can begin to take on the true meaning
for which it was created and toward which it struggles in the human
heart. Our external misuse of our surroundings, like all other
misuse, is born in the heart. And the transformed person uses the
world in a new way. Solitude, then, does not separate from the
world but heals it. The Christian call into solitude, in the wake of
Christ, is a call toward this transfiguration.

Louf treats of the stages of this experience of solitude:

> Solitude is an easy thing only for the beginner who is still tho-
> roughly sick and tired of the noise and pressure of the modern
> world. . . . But the desert is not only a place of relaxation, even if
> God is being sought there. In next to no time it begins to weigh
> like lead. . . . It fairly quickly presents itself as both inhospitable

and uninhabitable. . . . This temptation we can only withstand in the power of the Holy Spirit.

This is certainly not a question of willpower and human staying-power. Much more the opposite. They would soon put too heavy a strain on the solitary and even endanger his psychic equilibrium. It is in the first place a question of interior quiet, of freedom from all constraint, of equanimity, of a natural flexibility and of loving surrender to a peace that we carry hidden deep within us, but which can only break through into our consciousness in a fragmentary fashion. The slightest personal interpositioning, the smallest idle, ineffectual tension could be too much at this moment and could prevent the very thing that was just about to happen.[24]

There is much in this passage that bears serious reflection. For one thing, the solitude of which Louf is speaking is not the few days or weeks that supply a rest from strenuous activity. To say one seeks solitude at such a moment is to speak of a rather different reality, though a related one. For while rest from noise and agitation is needed, the true testing power of solitude comes when it is prolonged beyond this point where it is "rest." And it is through this testing that the real victory — or breakthrough — occurs. Louf stresses that no human effort is of value here, and the lesson is crucial. There are many spiritual fads at the moment which seem to offer the spiritual equivalent of multivitamins. But the action being sought in the experience Louf describes is not human, but God's. The consciousness being sought is a consciousness of something already given but from which our insensitivity and distraction remove us. One can live in the way Louf describes only if one truly believes in an action other than the human, and a presence other as well. Faith is truly tested at the moment when one is asked to leave all human means — believing that there are others. John of the Cross will call this "dark night," and not for nothing. And it is the passage through this night that "has united the lover with his beloved."[25]

Anyone who thus embraces solitude has made himself unreservedly free for the dialogue with God. But to this God cannot immediately respond. Or rather, because He does not reach us satisfactorily at the level where he would naturally tend to look for Him, He must first try to divert our attention and draw it towards the deeper regions of the heart . . . where He Himself awaits us. . . . If we take care to ensure that this solitude is at all times a real solitude . . . we shall intuitively, as it were, follow a path into the presence of the Lord who dwells there deep within us.[26]

This passage sounds as if solitude were bliss. In fact, Louf points out, it leads straight into a very contemporary experience, that of the absence of God. This is the other side of the coin—and one from which there is no escape. But this is the meaning of the paschal nature of solitude. The experience of presence requires that of absence. In fact, the new form of presence born of solitude can come into being only out of absence. And that, too, is part of the single death-resurrection dynamic. Where Jesus went alone, each single person who chooses him must follow, equally alone. And that path through solitude is the way to victory and to a new and glorified world.

·9·

PROJECTION AND
THE PENANCE OF BEASTS

The notion of projection has recurred frequently in the preceding pages, notably in its definition by Erikson, and it is closely related to the concept of transference. There are some domains where reflections on these concepts can be quite extraordinarily enlightening, and certainly essential if one is to journey in terms of reality rather than illusion.

The original idea of transference comes from the psychoanalytic setting where, normally, the analyst sits out of view of the analysand who is using a couch and free-associating. (This framework is typically Freudian: the Jungian differs in its arrangements.) Given the relative silence and invisiblity of the analyst, one can suppose without much risk of error that a good part of the client's feelings about the analyst and suppositions of what the analyst must be thinking, feeling, wanting, expecting is likely to be a function of the client's own inner world of associations and memories. Family background also plays a large role here. Getting in touch with what one projects onto others and recognizing this, at least, as projection rather than reality forms a large part of the process of psychoanalysis as therapy. It remains possible, however, in less structured settings, to become aware nonetheless of one's own processes along these lines, and this is the price to be paid for realistic relationships.

In *The Future of an Illusion* Freud speaks of religion as a great projection.[1] This notion bears serious reflection. While those of us who have some form of religious faith do believe that there is a real being "whom all call God," nonetheless it is worth considering where our thoughts and feelings about God find their real roots. Are these latter in some revelation? Or do they come from personal experiences, perhaps from very early childhood, which we "project" out onto this being we call God?[2] For God is frequently as silent and invisible in our lives as is the classical psychoanalyst. If, then, we reflect on the content of our God-image—as well as that of others—we learn some interesting things about our own projections. What are all the "notes"—or knowable parts—of this image, the positive and the negative? What, once more, is their source? Faith and its teachings? The Church? Parental training? Early fears? Aside from thoughts about God, what are our feelings—all of them? And, again, what are their sources? Entirely aside from the religious aspects of this kind of questioning, and entirely aside from the faith or lack of it in the questioner, this process of reflection can show us much for, within the Christian context, anything in this God-image that is not consonant with the God revealed by Jesus Christ as his Father has to be the result of some sort of projection. Or, at least, one needs to inquire as to its source. Surely it was awareness of how frequently this is the case that led a John of the Cross to insist so strongly on the need of a purification of faith. Policemen-gods, bogeymen-gods, mathematician-gods who chalk up successes and failures carefully or have recording angels do it for them, vengeful gods, soft-soapy gods, and the endless list of other possibilities—none of these is the Christian God or anything like Him. Nor is the pale Galilean who turns the world grey with his breath the figure one finds in the Gospel. If that is what the churches seem to have made him, then that process, too, is well worth analyzing from the point of view of projection. What have church people found it necessary to put onto Him—and to say He requires of others—and why? What are the roots in themselves?

One could find other recipients of projected material than God for such examination. But God lends Himself very well to this kind of investigation because invisibility and silence lend themselves to a projection in rather purer form than cases where the recipient of projection is visible and speaks.

One can, of course, say that God does speak—through Scripture, for example, and through inspiration of varying kinds. Through others, as well. The question then becomes, as with any communication, what the receiver does with it. One can, for example, take a communication literally without inquiring as to what was really meant. If a frustrated child hits his or her mother and says, "I hate you," and the mother withdraws forever without trying to understand where the child is coming from and what caused such words, what does this say about the mother's emotional situation, rather than about the child? And yet God's word does not necessarily come from a simpler place to understand. Again, one can take a communication in terms of what someone else says about it. "She told me she had no use for you." If I proceed from that point without questioning the information and its source and truth, what, again, does that say about my own process? Yet "God will judge and condemn you for that" is not too different a communication from the one just quoted. Once again, the position — emotional and intellectual — of the speaker, his or her ability to convey truly what God's "position" might be, and, ultimately, that "position" itself remain the real issues if one is seeking the truth of the relationship. That is, if one is sufficiently free interiorly to seek that truth despite such intermediary messages. Once again, the issue involves our own inner past history. And our conception of what God is relates to our understanding of what He asks.

Over four hundred years ago, John of the Cross was to remark that the penance of some people he knew was "a penance of beasts"[3]: it was unenlightened and did only harm. Today, we think, such issues are dead. One rarely hears of a tendency to extreme penance or ascetical exploits, in Christian circles at any rate. And yet psychologists and therapists meet today's equivalents of these phenomena at every turn.

When Freud developed his theories which some consider to be pansexualist, he was dealing with something we all recognize in the Victorian world — the fear of even mentioning sexuality in any of its manifestations. Had Freud lived in a less recently repressed world, in that sense, his thinking might have been very different. One wonders what turn his thoughts might have taken today. But it is a fact, whatever one thinks of his conclusions, that he ran into case upon case whose problems were rooted in this particular repression. The French proverb reads: *"Qui veut faire l'ange, fait la bête"*: wanting to act the angel makes one act the beast. If we try to force ourselves into a mold that is not ours — like the supposed angelic — the result will be that the instinctual force we have dammed up will explode in some way in the end. One need not always act the beast: there are other "outs" — becoming ill, neurotic, psychotic, manipulative, to name just a few. But the intensity of all of these comes from the repression.

What are the repressions in today's world and people which lead to our own forms of the "penance of beasts"? It would be foolish to believe that, because our society seems so permissive, they are lacking. Hearing people share their problems makes one aware, for example, that repression in the sexual sphere is far from absent today, particularly among religious people and perhaps even more among women. The younger generation may be freer, but that still remains to be seen. Doing what one wishes is not always an indication of freedom. And certainly there are people who after years and decades of marriage have not yet become reconciled to their sexuality nor able to live it in a full and positive way. That this is stunting in their lives they are aware, and yet freedom seems difficult to attain. One wonders why so difficult, if we are as free as we think we are today.

Again, the process of becoming one's own person rather than fulfilling the expectations of one's parents, gang, culture, peers —rather than living according to norms that are not one's own but rather collective—is another great struggle. This is part of the process of becoming adult, we believe. And yet, when one encounters the persistence and deep-rootedness of some of the blocks in people's hearts and psyches, one realizes how deeply certain cultural and familial imprints mark each person and how hard it is to become free. The unnecessary "penance" we accept from these sources can be a real burden.

What, then, is the place of the "discretion" discussed above and the consequent decisions? Or, in other terms, what is the place of adult freedom, mature judgment? Many in the Judeo-Christian tradition grew up for years with a series of quite rigid, and apparently clear, norms about conduct. Certain things were to be done and others to be avoided—and this, it seemed, was the way of salvation. Salvation was, to Christians, a gift from Christ, but nonetheless one was expected to toe the line. God would judge those who did not. And it seemed the judgment would be in terms of external actions.

In ascetical and religious literature, all the more, one reads injunctions to give up one's will, to struggle with one's passions, to resist temptation (and/or the devil). The issue in question is, however: what, precisely, *is* a temptation and what is a suggestion from one's deeper self that should be followed? How does one make this judgment? Is the norm for answering this question an external rule? It has seemed to many that the norms were indeed to be found externally and that they were clear enough. Anything that goes along with the guidelines of religious morality is from a good source: anything that does not is not.

That looks very simple—and blissfully clear. Unfortunately, things are not so easy. If I am rigid, compulsive, and narrow, notably in the ways mentioned by Erikson above, my interpretation of the meaning of my faith and its moral dictates will tell me that all sorts of things come from the devil or temptation when in fact they perhaps come simply from human nature and may even be necessary for me to live humanly. The issue of anger is a case in point. How many generations of Christians have repressed anger and feelings of hate or desire for revenge as un-Christian, wrong, sinful? And yet, is the human—or the truly Christian—way to deal with anger really repression—or even suppression? Is it not rather an honest facing and "working through" of the issues so that the problem concerned is dealt with in depth and what purification occurs happens at the level of the heart? Can true love of any kind survive if anger is not also looked in the face? Short-circuiting this process out of terror at one's "passions" can twist the whole psyche out of shape, as can any major refusal of truth. As one's body has to move out of its natural position if it is determined to avoid a certain movement become painful, so one's psyche can be forced into all sorts of contortions if one is (even unconsciously) bent on avoiding a certain truth or part of one's being at all costs. And, of course, under these circumstances there can never be any question of coming into touch with one's shadow nor of learning the true meaning of humility. And one continues to find ascetical writing with just such suggestions.

Another result of a mistaken understanding of the Christian position concerning anger is the issue of guilt and remorse. Teaching about mutual love can be interpreted by some to mean that in any case where there is a conflict with another, the person who either seems to cause the conflict or who allows it to continue by refusing to appease the other is guilty of a lack of love, even a sin against love. Taken to its extremes, such a position can not only further a doormat stance in its holder—or the tendency to say one thing and think or feel another—but it can also lead to a situation where one is totally a prey to manipulation and not only develops into more of a manipulator oneself but furthers this attitude in the other.

Hardly a fruit of love! In this view, all direct communication that could include a touch of confrontation becomes a cause of feelings of guilt and so is studiously avoided. Appeasement becomes the necessary order of the day—and the unexpressed anger that results does the kind of work we have already seen in the unconscious. It is tempting to believe that the source of this issue is a misunderstanding of Christianity. But one finds in the Oriental avoidance of confrontation, and need to protect the other's "face," a situation whose dynamics are not very different from the above and which can lead to equal feelings of guilt.

Rather than continuing with such a position, it would seem important to understand that anger, like other emotions, is healthy in itself and serves a purpose in the human psyche. Misused, it becomes a danger to the one expressing and the one receiving the anger, but the issue is to know when there is misuse. Only "discretion," discernment, judgment can help here, rather than external norms which serve rather as signposts than as infallible laws.

The feeling of guilt is another case in point. It is easy to believe that feeling guilty is a sign that one has offended God, justice, or morality and needs therefore to do whatever is necessary to remove the feeling. It has long been known that this judgment is untrue for the scrupulous, and even for those whose conscience is not yet correctly formed. But how often is it basically untrue for others until a serious examination of what causes the feelings of guilt reveals their true source? The understanding—as far as possible—of who God is and what is truly commanded may indeed cause feelings about choices out of harmony with this. But it is crucial to distinguish true from neurotic guilt and to explore what the feelings really mean and why, to see what is actually commanded and why as well.

Ana-Maria Rizzuto cites a passage from Freud that was one of her four guiding quotations for her work on the development of the God-image in people's lives:

It is a remarkable thing that the super-ego often displays a severity for which no model has been provided by the real parents, and moreover that it calls the ego to account not only for its deeds, but for its thoughts and unexecuted intentions, of which the super-ego seems to have knowledge.[4]

We have a hard interior taskmaster, and one whose commands and judgments need serious examination if a truly personal morality and judgment, a sense of guilt or innocence according to what God or our personal conscience really is are to result. Our "guilt feelings" are not necessarily a safe guide to a mature morality, nor are they to be identified with our conscience. This latter is concerned with free moral judgments which come from a very different place in the psyche.

One ends, then, with a paradox. Discretion is possible only when one has achieved a certain measure of inner freedom and wisdom. And inner freedom and wisdom are possible only if one learns discretion. What is the key to this paradox?

One possible key lies in learning from others. Thomas Aquinas remarks somewhere that if one wants to learn good judgment, one important way is to ask the opinions of others who have it. The Benedictine Rule asks the abbot to consult even the youngest. The same principle holds spiritually and psychologically. The determination to walk entirely alone is likely to lead to a serious impasse where there is no one present to unmask one's illusions. Hence the insistence, in all religious traditions, on the need for a spiritual guide, and the questions, in psychological circles, about self-analysis. But, even aside from such a guide, a certain amount of open-minded reading and consulting can be most enlightening. If I am almost alone in holding a certain conviction, I may be a prophet— but I may also be wrong. On the other hand, consultation may, at a certain stage, become a cover for dependence or lack of courage to go on alone. The ultimate choices cannot be made for us—nor the ultimate moral decisions. Clinging to rules is another way to avoid this solitary responsibility.

One rarely hears people, especially young people, say that their aim on their journey is to become people of discretion. Of courage, generosity, love, hope, yes. But discretion seems so dull. Yet the person who has managed to reach a certain level of discretion is capable of a degree of freedom and maturity quite impossible without this single light. Freedom from one's inner compulsions and crampings, from one's projections and tendencies to perform "the penance of beasts," is a necessary step toward a journey that would be truly one's own and unique. Our culture does not put a premium on wisdom. But if it does upon freedom, we may learn with time that the two cannot be separated.

·10·

THE OBJECTIVITY OF THE PSYCHE

In her study of the life of Jung, and specifically of his period of "confrontation with the unconscious," Barbara Hannah remarks on one essential discovery of these central years:

> The main thing Philemon taught him [Jung], which really gave him the key to his whole psychology, was the *reality of the psyche.* He did this in a very plastic way. He told him that he (Jung) regarded his own thoughts as if he had made them himself (which is indeed the usual Western prejudice). But Philemon said that to him thoughts were much more like animals in the forest or people in a room and added: "If you should see people in a room, you would not think that you had made those people, or that you were responsible for them." It was through Philemon that Jung learned the objectivity and reality of the psyche, its absolutely independent existence. . . . Investigations of the unconscious are exactly like any other science: *you can investigate only what is there.*[1]

This discovery and conception are of central importance. Later in the same book, Hannah illustrates it another way. For Jung, the discovery of "the mandala as an expression of the Self" was "what was for him the ultimate reality,"[2] but this remained for him a purely personal discovery until he came upon an old Chinese text which, to him, proved just that point and became empirical proof that his discovery "had collective and not just subjective value." Hannah remarks: "Most people find it difficult to realize that psychology is no invention, but an *empirical science*. It becomes easier when they can see the same symbol in totally different empirical material."[3] The convergences of findings of other traditions and cultures begin to point to a common human experience—both in the psychological and in the spiritual fields. And this, in Jung's terms, points to an empirical reality.

The fact that psychology is, in many ways, still in its scientific babyhood helps further the conception that its theories are vague and unreal suppositions about an equally vague and perhaps unreal interior world. Yet, if one thinks more deeply, is there any reason to believe that this is so? Because we can touch the material things about us, it is easy to speak of empirical science in their regard. But is the fact that something cannot be touched with the hands or seen by the eyes or that its study is still young proof of its unreality — especially in an age where natural science itself needs to speak of the unseen? Sometimes psychological effects can be so clear and so recognizable that they become parts of common parlance. Few people, for example, believe today in purely physical causes for an ulcer. There is little reason to see other factors in the psychological realm as less real. Yet it is not entirely easy to know what to do with this knowledge. Understanding the sources of our present attitudes can help.

Some of our skeptical thinking is the result of post-Enlightenment mental habits. Medieval theology and spirituality, for example, were very conscious of operating out of a single, though varied, tradition. They spoke of a *philosophia perennis*. This tradition had many sources—some of which differed so much as to be contradictory in places: one thinks, for example, of some views of Plato and Aristotle concerning the reality of the material world. Yet the tradition was wide enough to hold contradictions and yet become a single stream of knowledge that was part of the education of the time. Thomas Aquinas, for example, would draw upon Augustine, the early Church Fathers, Aristotle, Plato, Jewish and Arab sources, agreeing with some and disagreeing with others. But they were part of his world. There was an awareness of the difference between theory and fact, but there was also a sense that there was an objective spiritual reality independent of the knower, which the latter came to know in truth by becoming aware internally of the varying "notes" of the real. We shall see below that whole currents of Oriental thought shared this conviction of the reality of the spiritual or psychic world. An interesting study could be done on the question of whether post-Enlightenment Western culture is not unique in its denial.

These cultures had their own share of conflicts and difficulties, but their thinkers tended to share these convictions. Understanding such mentalities can help us to understand and, perhaps, relativize ours. However young our psychology, the reality of which it speaks may be as real as the world about us—or as the God in whom we say we believe.

This last is the crucial issue. If the unconscious is real—and today it would seem difficult to doubt this—then one essential way to God passes there and helps us find Him there, where He dwells. To limit religion or faith to the realm of consciousness would be to give God rights only to the tip of the iceberg, and the writings of the mystics through the centuries show the impossibility of such a stance. This view would also condemn prayer to great superficiality. If, on the contrary, the unconscious and its processes are real, then our relationship with God, ourselves, and others comes to fruition only in terms of this deeper realm, by our learning to relate to it and operate out of it more deeply.

Where would such a conclusion lead us? To return to the author with whom we began this chapter, one place would be the awareness of whether one is "out of oneself" or not and when—an awareness she mentions more than once as being a preoccupation of Jung's in very concrete circumstances. Such a conception implies being "conscious" of what is going on within and around one, not being divorced from one's true inner reality nor from one's inner and centered perception of what is going on outside. This issue of being truly "conscious" and lucid is illustrated by a story much loved by Jung. It concerns a Chinese village struck by drought:

> Everything had been done to put an end to it, and every kind of prayer and charm had been used, but all to no avail. So the elders of the village told Wilhelm that the only thing to do was to send for a rainmaker from a distance. . . . He came in a covered cart, a small, wizened old man. He got out of the cart, sniffed the air in distaste, then asked for a cottage on the outskirts of the village. He made the condition that no one should disturb him and that his food should be put down outside the door. Nothing was heard of him for three days, and then everyone woke up to a downpour of rain.

Wilhelm asked him in wonder: "So you can make rain?" The
old man scoffed at the very idea and said *of course* he could not.
"But there was the most persistent drought until you came . . .
and then—within three days—it rains?" "Oh," replied the old
man, "that was something quite different. You see, I come from
a region where everything is in order, it rains when it should
and is fine when that is needed, and the people also are in order
and in themselves. But that was not the case with the people
here, they were all out of Tao and out of themselves. I was at
once infected when I arrived, so I had to be quite alone until I
was once more in Tao and then naturally in rained!"[4]

Being "in oneself" then implies being in harmony with everything else—and it bears fruit for everyone else. The implication is
that there are laws of the universe—inner and outer—with which
one can be in touch. Once again, one has the feeling of an objective
reality that measures humans, rather than the other way around.
Perhaps we are due for another Copernican revolution.

These reflections can be taken one step further. An earlier chapter quoted Augustine's remarks that he had foolishly sought God
outside until he realized that God was within and that he, Augustine,
was "without." Perhaps it was this kind of experience that led to his
famous maxim that to know himself would be to know God. For in
truth, if I do not know myself—in the experiential sense in which
the word "know" is used in Scripture—how am I to know God who
dwells in me? It is through the center of our own being that we
emerge into God. This is not to deny God's total "otherness." But
transcendence complements immanence. In that objective world
that is my own psyche and the collective psyche, there is also the
objective reality of God. Asked whether he believed in God Jung
made the now famous statement: "I don't believe, I know." (Though
the second appendix to this book is necessary to reflect on what
might be some of the content of that knowledge.) Aquinas felt that
for the truly reasonable person it would be natural to know this.
Jung's inner journey of "confrontation with the unconscious," then,
meant a journey into contact with something more than the purely
personal. Those who have the courage to follow him on this journey
to the end will normally find the same Reality opened to them,
under whatever name.

Esther Harding treats of this developing consciousness of the
reality of the psyche in terms of the Tantric Yoga system. There

the development of consciousness is studied in terms of the personification of "the libido of these intense instinctive emotions . . . in the symbol of the Kundalini serpent that lies coiled up at the base of the spine."[5] She remarks that individual growth in consciousness parallels that in history and culture, and insists that this growth—on the level she is discussing—is a matter not of intellectual knowledge but of experience, enabling one "to recognize this 'doer,' this superior power within the psyche."

> We have to learn not only *that* our intense affects are due to projections, but we have also to discover *what* it is that is projected—for only then can we begin to discern the "doer" within.[6]

In other words, when we are strongly moved emotionally—more than the exterior situation warrants—we may well be projecting out of our own inner experience. When we learn to stop projecting outward both the negative and the positive elements of this inner world of ours, a deeper experience of our inner reality, and even of its nature, becomes possible. The projections themselves, as seen in the last chapter, give us much information. But that growth is a long process. Harding, following Jung, traces its stages.

> There are three channels by which Kundalini can rise, represented by the intestinal or ego-power route, the genito-urinary or erotic route, and lastly by the little known channel that runs through the middle of the spinal cord, the psychic route that alone represents the road to transformation of the not-personal, instinctive life of the individual.[7]

If the serpent takes the first two routes, the individual remains unconscious, and it is basically these two ways that are represented in the theories of Adler and Freud. The gods of a nation will also show the projections corresponding to the chakra being lighted up by Kundalini.

When a particular chakra has not been pierced, the individual (or nation) is not able to master the powerful instincts threatening his or its consciousness, but "When Kundalini *has* pierced a particular chakra, the individual is enabled to recognize that the emotion he feels is not due to the impact of the object but comes from a projection to the object of some aspect of the inner unknown deity within himself."[8] This, then, is the beginning of awareness of what kind of deity that might be.

This process of becoming conscious, however, cannot simply be willed. It must be given. "Unless something happens that arouses the sleeping Kundalini and forces her to rise by the central path, nothing more than an intellectual knowledge of the reality of the psyche is possible."[9] Harding quotes Jung: for this awakening to occur there must be "a purified spirit, a right attitude"[10]; "Something in you must lead you to it . . . a leading spark, some incentive, that forces you on through the water (of the unconscious) and towards the next center."[11] Frustration, conflict, suffering can serve this purpose: energy begins to flow, no longer outward but in this central, psychic direction. In earlier stages "the energy of the objective psyche is experienced only in its projections"[12]—the free flow of life carries one along, the intensity of passion and emotionality. Only in the next stage does "feeling for the object as such and recognition of the spirit become possible."[13] This achievement is symbolized by "an inner light by which the world without can be seen in its true perspective and the images from the inner world can be recognized as symbols instead of being projected. . . ."[14] This stage of development is a crisis, a transition.

One stage further, "not only is there a light but . . . one first becomes aware of the inner presence of a person, a center of consciousness separate from the ego."[15] This view is seen as equivalent to the Christian teaching about "the Christ within, a personified symbol of the Self."[16] A rebirth of the personality is involved in passing to this stage, and Harding describes it in terms a Christian could only call paschal:

> The new consciousness requires a rebirth of the personality. . . .
> In the experience of modern persons this *transitus* is very frequently symbolized by the death of the ego . . . in which he loses all initiative, all the elan and fullness of life he was possessed by in the former state leave him and he feels himself empty. And, indeed, he is emptied; the daimon has gone out of him and for the first time he is in a position to realize the reality of the objective psyche. . . . Should this *transitus* be achieved . . . there occurs the birth of the hero-child, one possessed by greatly increased energy and creative power. . . .[17]

One must go through this death as regards the previous unconscious projecting way of living, and the rebirth is hard. There is still, says Harding, one final stage to come, a stage where one truly *experiences* the objective reality of the psyche, even of God. "Intellectual knowledge of psychic matters is empty, only experience convinces of the reality of the psyche."[18]

Harding applies this whole question to the area of world issues. Wars result from the unconsciousness of those who cause them, moved by compulsions in themselves that they do not understand. Once the reality of the psyche is truly understood, however, this kind of unconsciousness has been left behind to a great degree. Growth in consciousness is not a luxury for the few who are sensitized to this need. Its absence is paid for on all levels of our culture and society.

To summarize Harding's stages once more: in the very lowest chakra the reality of the world is experienced, through the senses. In the next comes abstract thought and psychic recognition, and the outwardly real becomes experienced as inwardly real. The third stage sees the psyche in terms of the indwelling Lord, but it remains necessary to experience "in the instinctive *Urgrund*" of one's being the reality of the psyche and the world it contains. One can never be sure of being free of projections: there is always more to learn. But the experience of which she speaks, says Harding, remains important for those who can live it. What Harding says here—and Jung as well—complements the preceding chapter. As we learn to recognize and withdraw projections, the inner reality becomes more clear and more real in our lives.

We have followed Harding's line of argument very closely, for it contains both her own—and Jung's—thought and an Eastern tradition that sheds much light on human spiritual evolution. Finding further religious parallels to this view seems unnecessary. The whole of what people traditionally call the spiritual life has been directed toward the experience of and union with God. Writers like John of the Cross and Teresa of Avila amid so many others try to describe this experience, but they repeat unceasingly that words betray that whereof they speak.

Psychology does not replace spirituality—any more than spirituality can replace psychology. But if the two speak of a common experience, however much their understandings of it differ, then what each can learn from the other can only be of benefit to both.

·11·

LISTENING, SILENCE, OBEDIENCE

The way toward the objective reality that is God and our own being requires ability to experience in the heart, to understand, to listen. This is another area where the experiences of psychology and spirituality converge. In common human experience and in psychology, nothing makes it harder to understand another than inability to listen—which is often caused by one's own inner agenda. Speaking to other psychoanalysts of their work, Elvin Semrad once said:

> The only truth you have is your patient. And the only thing that interferes with that truth is your own perception. You may not be free to observe what is there to be observed, chiefly because it evokes feelings in you that are so troublesome that you quit looking. This is one of the big things Charcot told Freud over and over again.[1]

Personal feelings, unsolved agenda, all these blur our ability truly to hear another, which is another way of saying that only the silence of the heart makes listening possible.

In the psychotherapeutic literature one can find pages on silence—as well as pages on listening—for the silences during an hour of analysis, like the silences during any human communication, can be the most fruitful moments if one lets them. They can also be the hardest. There are, of course, many silences, as in all human communication. There is a peaceful and comfortable silence that speaks of mutual understanding and can be a deeper communication than words. There is the silence in which words are being sought to express an experience or a feeling, with awareness on both sides that whatever is expressed will be received as part of a deepening relationship between the persons communicating. There is the awkward silence of resistance—when one does not wish, consciously or not, to be open with the other; and there is the responding silence which can imply issues of countertransference of the kinds mentioned in the quotation above, or others. Still, even from this silence, if it is appropriately worked with, new life can come. In all of life there are the silences of dislike or fear or inability to communicate as well as the silences of deep communication. But all of these, if allowed to live, can give birth to a creative word. It is not our silences that destroy, the great majority of times, but our inability to let silence be—that the true word or whatever is meant to come from the silence may be born in its own time.

What is true in analysis or therapy is equally true in deep relationships. How many couples—as well as others in relationship —experience the impossibility of communication, the sense of never being heard, listened to, understood, however much talking there may be. How many children find they cannot speak to parents— often because these latter seem too full of personal agenda for themselves or their child to be able to recognize a growing individual personality with personal and different aspirations and direction.

All this is to say that the ability truly to listen, truly to hear, to be still in one's own heart in order to receive the other as shared or expressed—the ability to respond only from and after that in-depth receiving and hearing—these are rare and precious gifts. Without them neither relationship nor therapy nor prayer nor love can flower.

Depth psychology suggests another form of listening as well—one already mentioned above. It is necessary to listen to oneself—to one's own heart and body and feelings and reactions to know what is really going on, in oneself or in relationships, even in relationship to God and to ultimate values.

Most of us do not find it easy to do this. For one thing, the combination of early superego development and the pressures of our society combine to encourage us to censor a considerable number of our thoughts and feelings. Secondly, as was said in discussing the shadow, it is very difficult to let oneself be—just as one is—with feelings of hatred, jealousy, laziness, lust, selfishness, as well as with the nobility, positive aspirations and desires which may seem to us quite beyond our means or "place." But, as has already been said, I can never know who I really am or see my true face except at this price. For as I find my true nobility and the desires for good I really have—as opposed to those I think I should have—I will find my own way of dealing with my own negative sides. This choice can be free and personal only on this deep level of truth and self-acceptance. It involves not only the acceptance of shadow but also the readiness to be still, silent, open to listening. All this is not a prospect for beginners.

But the beginning stage need not be as long as it often is, if truth is faced. For truth is a maturing agent par excellence—my own truth and that of others. Many of us remain beginners so long because it seems too hard to look at the truth. We palliate. We try to tell others they do not believe or feel or experience what they say they do, and we do the same to ourselves. True listening with the heart is purgatorial—but maturing.

It is precisely this point that leads one to realize the paradoxical fact that as silence is needed for communication at any real depth, so speech is needed for silence—if that silence is not to be dead. Depth psychology advocates what is called a "talking cure," which could seem the opposite pole from silence, and yet this last is not the case. Even people who find endless small-talk easy are far less vocal in a therapy situation, for here there can be little question of small-talk. It becomes far less easy to speak when one's own inner being is involved. The safety of our smoke-screens of words is then lost. Many people never want to risk such a level of communication, never want even to look at the level they would then come to express.

But if it is true that only facing my own inner truth makes it possible to hear my true self—and the Self deeper than my own —then I have to have the courage to formulate for myself, and doubtless for at least some significant other, the things inside myself that it would be easier to ignore. The "talking cure" of analysis or the self-revelation of humility in the presence of a spiritual guide becomes rather essential. This is not only so that one can ask the other for advice. Indeed, in therapy this is not at all the purpose. It is, rather, so that one can express for oneself and before another as much as one can of the "true face" that emerges to consciousness, often out of one's silence, and then deal with the response made out of another's silence and perceived truth. Thus a book on techniques of moral transformation by Pitirim Sorokin could speak of "monastic 'psychoanalysis,' counseling and therapy"[2] and could study many of the classical Eastern and Western monastic techniques in this light. Again one finds serious points of convergence in the two disciplines.

Let us look, then, at some texts of spirituality on silence. One phrase sums up beautifully and succinctly whole centuries of Christian tradition and theology. "The Father spoke one Word, which was His Son, and this Word He always speaks in eternal silence, and in silence must It be heard by the soul."[3]

The theology of this maxim needs reflection. Early and medieval Christian thought presented Christ as the Logos, the Word. Why is this Word spoken in silence?

"Eternal silence" seems to refer to the situation of the Christ-Word preexisting with the Father, as the Johannine Gospel prologue portrays Him. Early theology saw the Trinity as existing not in a void but rather in a plenitude—of each other first and then of a whole spiritual creation composed of beings preexisting the material world, beings capable of knowledge, love, and praise and perhaps far more individually unique than human persons. They were capable of sin, too, as described in the tradition concerning Lucifer, the Light-bearer. The silence in which the Word was spoken was not, then, a silence of emptiness but of receptiveness, love, adoration—a silence of plenitude and praise. One can think of Dante's "paradise" as a literary illustration, or, again, of Roublev's icon of the Trinity.

Why, then, is this Word heard only "in the silence of the soul?" Because this silence, too, is one of receptiveness, listening, love— and only such silence "hears." A spiritual daughter of John of the Cross—some centuries removed—wrote:

> There is another of Christ's songs that I would like to repeat unceasingly: "I shall keep my strength for you." My Rule tells me: "In silence will your strength be." It seems to me, therefore, that to keep one's strength for the Lord is to unify one's whole being by means of interior silence, to collect all one's powers in order to "employ" them in "the one work of love," to have this "single eye" which allows the light of God to enlighten us. A soul that debates with its self, that is taken up with its feelings,

and pursues useless thoughts and desires, scatters its forces, for it is not wholly directed toward God. Its lyre does not vibrate in unison and when the Master plays it, He cannot draw from it divine harmonies, for it is still too human and discordant. . . . Instead of persevering in praise through everything in simplicity, it must continually adjust the strings of its instrument which are all a little out of tune.[4]

While the author's youth shows in a certain idealism of tone rather different from some of what we have said above, her basic insight is profound. A musician herself, she knew the necessary conditions for an instrument to be worth playing, and they do seem applicable to the human heart.

These last two writers spoke from the Carmelite tradition, but study of earlier sources shows the same themes. In giving a list of words essential to the understanding of the thought of the desert fathers, Benedicta Ward writes:

HESYCHIA: stillness, quiet, tranquillity. This is the central consideration in the prayer of the desert fathers. On the external level it signifies an individual living as a solitary; on a deeper level it is not merely separation from noise and speaking with other people, but the possession of interior quiet and peace. Thus it is possible to use the term of many who do not actually live the hermit life. It means more specifically guarding the mind, constant remembrance of God, and the possession of inner prayer. Hesychasm is the general term and hesychast is the noun used to describe the person seeking to follow this way of prayer.[5]

The question of the remembrance of God will form a separate chapter, but what is important here is that the desert was the source of a whole current of spirituality that was to become extremely important in the Christian East and culminate in the Jesus prayer. It is not always known that this latter is the fruit of a tradition still called hesychast and still rooted in the thought of which Ward speaks. Several apophthegmata from the desert will show its beginnings:

While still living in the palace, Abba Arsenius prayed to God in these words, 'Lord, lead me in the way of salvation.' And a voice came saying to him, 'Arsenius, flee from men and you will be saved.'

Having withdrawn to the solitary life he made the same prayer again and he heard a voice saying to him, 'Arsenius, flee, be silent, pray always, for these are the sources of sinlessness.'[6]

Abba Isidore of Pelusia said, 'To live without speaking is better than to speak without living. For the former who lives rightly does good even by his silence but the latter does no good even when he speaks. When words and life correspond to one another they are together the whole of philosophy.'[7]

He [Poemen] also said, 'A man may seem to be silent, but if his heart is condemning others he is babbling ceaselessly. But there may be another who talks from morning till night and yet he is truly silent; that is, he says nothing that is not profitable.'

He also said, 'If you are silent, you will have peace wherever you live.'[8]

To understand the first quotations, one must see them in the light of Ward's explanation and in their context. Flight may be "from," but the essential is that it is "to" what is sought — God. And many of the apophthegmata bear that out well.

The desert's concern for silence as favoring union with God has been continued in the contemplative tradition of the centuries since then. Speaking of the awakening of the heart already discussed — an awakening he sees as occurring when the heart meets God's Word — Louf writes:

Now that for the first time the heart is really operative, it will try to remain always in movement. And we ourselves will have to see to it that our heart remains our dwelling place. That will not be easy; for we are always having to let go of our heart and be distracted. . . . So long as these other faculties [discursive reason, imagination] are not in complete harmony with our heart . . . assimilated and geared in to the heart's peculiar rhythm, there will be a danger that we loose our hold on Word and heart and that our heart will go back to sleep.[9]

This vigilance is essential, he adds, if one truly seeks to contemplate the Word. But

Above all, he [anyone determined to persist in prayer] must
attain to quietness, to deep, unfathomable silence. One of the
Fathers observes that the person whose life is filled with much
business and many cares and inwardly or outwardly is in a state
of uproar is like a flask with water in it that is murky because the
flask has been shaken about too much.[10]

Left still, the water in the flask clears as the scum settles. "In a
similar way, our heart, once it is restful and steeped in profound
silence, can reflect God."[11]

Contemplation of the Word of God is bound up inseparably
with silence. For the Word proceeds from the profound silence
of the Holy Trinity, the 'Trinity that is the Friend of Silence.' . . .[12]

A dead silence, however, is useless, and that is what occurs unless
silence is filled with the Word. Silence is not an end in itself but a
very important means. Louf quotes a sentence of Isaac the Syrian:
"Silence is the language of the angels and the secret of the world to
come." But he continues with a passage that will recall Jung:

We must beware of the strange and confused world inside us
with which we so readily identify. Some of the Fathers say that
to every desire arising within us we must dispatch a sentinal to
put the question: 'Who are you, where do you come from, which
side are you on?'[13]

Jung might not use the word "beware," but he insists on the
importance of not identifying with the parts of the unconscious of
which we become aware. And certainly the awareness and judgment
of what arises within is an important part of his thinking as well.
To Louf this vigilance is essential for "New space must be made
available, where we can pierce through to the source of our being."
This space is made by inner silence.

A final quotation from the pen of Thomas Merton will show the
continuance of the same tradition on silence through the centuries:

The Blessed Virgin Mary was the wisest theologian. She was the
Mother of the Word Who is at once the Theology of God and of
Men. God's Truth entered so deeply into her life as to become
incarnate in her virginal flesh. All Wisdom was centered in her
Immaculate Heart, *sedes Sapientiae*. When the angel came to her

at the Annunciation he found her in deepest silence. Few words
are recorded of her who gave us the Word. And when she had
given Him to the world, what should she do but listen to Him?
"She kept all these words, treasuring them in her heart." And so,
in every way, Our Lady is the model of contemplatives and the
mirror of mystics. Those who love the pure Truth of God in-
stinctively love the simplicity of the Immaculate Mother of God.
She draws them into the heart of her silence and of her humility.
She is the Virgin of Solitude, Whom God called His hermit. . . .
She lived as a hermit in the lofty mysteries of her Son. She lived
all the time in the sky, though she walked on the earth and swept
floors and made beds and made supper for the Carpenters. . . .

When the angel spoke, God awoke in the heart of this girl of
Nazareth and moved within her like a giant. He stirred and
opened His eyes and her soul saw that in containing Him she
contained the world besides. The Annunciation was not so much
a vision as an earthquake in which God moved the universe and
unsettled the spheres, and the beginning and end of all things
came before her in her deepest heart. And far beneath the movement of this silent cataclysm she slept in the infinite tranquillity
of God, and God was a child curled up who slept in her and her
veins were flooded with His wisdom which is night, which is
starlight, which is silence. And her whole being was embraced
in Him whom she embraced and they became tremendous
silence.[14]

This quotation sums up many of the themes we have mentioned—that of the Word spoken in silence, with its theological
import; that of the receptiveness of silence and its connection with
truth; that of simplicity, humility, and the place of silence in daily
living; and finally the relation of silence to union with God. It is
this kind of thinking through the centuries that has led to the
emphasis on silence, especially in contemplative communities and
experiences, in both East and West.

* * *

There is, however, another current intimately connected with
the concepts of silence and of listening. David Steindl-Rast, a monk,
writes as follows:

The key word of the spiritual discipline I follow is "listening."
This means a special kind of listening, a listening with one's

heart. To listen in that way is central to the monastic tradition in which I stand. The very first word of the Rule of St. Benedict is "listen!" . . .

Benedictine spirituality in turn is rooted in the broader and more ancient tradition of the Bible. But here, too, the concept of listening is central. . . . All things are brought into existence by God's creative Word; all of history is a dialogue with God, who speaks to the human heart. . . . The transcendent God communicates Self through nature and through history. . . .

Responsive listening is the form the Bible gives to our basic religious quest as human beings. This is the quest for a full human life, for happiness. It is the quest for meaning. . . . By listening deeply to the message of any given moment I shall be able to tap the very Source of Meaning and to realize the unfolding meaning of my life.

To listen in this way means to listen with one's heart, with one's whole being. . . . The daily discipline of listening and responding to meaning is called obedience. . . . The only alternative is absurdity. Ab-surdus literally means absolutely deaf. I admit implicitly that I must become ob-audiens—thoroughly listening, obedient.[15]

This quotation is long but very dense. It illustrates well the fundamental link between meaning and obedience, between silence/prayer/listening and obedience. The heart that cannot take the obedient attitude is cut off from all these other things, and that is a "hard doctrine" today.

But it is important to know what obedience means and this writer expresses it well. As he rightly says, "This concept of obedience is far more comprehensive than the narrow notion of obedience as doing-what-you-are-told-to-do."[16] Still, in some cases this latter may be part of listening attitude and a position of fundamental indocility leads to the absurd.

An Indian religious of my community writes in a study on *Gurus, Ashrams and Christians*, already mentioned above, her reflections on the Indian spiritual tradition specifically in these domains:

The guru enables a man to get direct knowledge of the Self, purifies him from sin and removes all darkness. In fact, the guru is Brahman. He promises to be with the disciple whenever he is needed. In return . . . the guru exacts a strict obedience—prompt, willing, without criticism or complaint. . . . The important thing here, however, is that this obedience be given by a mature disciple. Lack of maturity in the disciple who obeys may lead him, as indeed it often did in the past, to slavery instead of freedom. . . . [Today] the guru needs to begin by doing a task which formerly was not his, namely giving the disciple the security and education which have not been given him by way of his family life. Spiritual growth presupposes psychological soundness, emotional health and a sense of security and well-being. Only then can the guru demand and obtain a total obedience and self-surrender.[17]

The idea of the guru as Brahman may be offensive to the Judeo-Christian mind, but Vandana continues by saying that many gurus disclaim even the title of guru and certainly they stress that the power is God's, not theirs. One needs to understand such concepts in the tradition from which they come. According to this tradition, there is ultimately "but one guru . . . but one Ashram."[18] What is more important to retain from this quotation is the fact that true obedience presupposes emotional maturity. Perhaps some of the need to rebel experienced among postconciliar Christians and religious has to do with the lack of this maturity which is needed before one can require obedience. Otherwise, the one obeying can be reduced to the status of a child—and come to resent it. But the truth of this awareness does not invalidate the concept of, and need for, obedience seen above.

André Louf discusses the spiritual meaning of obedience in terms of his theology already seen. In order to understand his view it is important to remember that in German, and similarly in other Germanic languages, the word for "other" is *ander* and the word translating "to change" is *veranderen,* "to make other." This play on words is fundamental to his text.

One cannot talk about prayer without also referring to obedience. . . . We mean by obedience . . . the giving up of one's own longings and desires— My will— for the Will of another— Your will— specifically in this case the Will of the Father. This surrendering of oneself, this setting aside of one's own desires in favour of someone else, of another, puts the one who obeys in a new relationship to that Other. Obedience is a language and a sign. It also effects something in the one who obeys. It lays his life entirely open to the requirements of an Other and binds him fast to that Other. More, much more even that that. It can engender new life. By laying someone open to an Other, it alters him in the deepest sense of the word. It is a new life-style, whereby a person can detach himself more and more from his own constricted state, so as to be engrossed in the richness of an Other and to share that richness with Him. This is assuming, of course, that the obedience is spontaneous and free and never degenerates into slavery. This calls for a pure love and a great love on both sides.[19]

Louf goes on to study the false conceptions of God's Will in recent spirituality, resulting, partly, from mistranslations. Taking the Greek *thelēma* and the Hebrew *rason* to mean the same as the harsher Latin *voluntas* has brought centuries of a view of the divine will as ready to break the human, whereas in fact the Greek and Hebrew words mean: "longing, desire, love, joy . . . being 'in love' and the sexual desire that a man feels for a woman."[20] It is necessary, once again, to understand obedience in this context—and there it becomes an opening to love and to being changed by love.

If the deepest nature of obedience is to be an activity of love and of listening to the one loved, an openness of one's whole being to that love in a type of self-emptying of which only mature love is capable, then this is a far cry from some forms of obedience previously known and feared. Again, dependence, inability to make decisions or take responsibility are then seen as the caricatures they are—or rather as signs that the level of maturity needed for true obedience has not yet even been reached. But mature obedience, as a listening and opening oneself to love, does indeed *ver-anderen*, change one into the other without losing personal identity in the process.

John of the Cross, in his later tradition, speaks of transformation in God or union with Him as total willing with the Beloved. Every living being is substantially united with God, he says, or that being would not exist at all. John, however, is speaking not of that union but of the union of likeness or of transformation in love. This union "exists when God's will and the soul's are in conformity, so that nothing in the one is repugnant to the other. When the soul completely rids itself of what is repugnant and unconformed to the divine will, it rests transformed in God through love."[21] This transformation involves not only acts but habits, ways of being—and, even more, mutual surrender.

Here is an example that will provide a better understanding of this explanation. A ray of sunlight shining upon a smudgy window is unable to illumine that window completely and transform it into its own light. It could do this if the window were cleaned and polished. The less the film and stain are wiped away, the less the window will be illumined. . . . The extent of illumination is not dependent upon the ray of sunlight but upon the window. If the window is totally clean and pure, the sunlight will so transform and illumine it that to all appearances the window will be identical with the ray of sunlight. . . . Although obviously the nature of the window is distinct from that of the sun's ray (even if the two seem identical), we can assert that the window is the ray or light of the sun by participation. . . .

When God grants this supernatural favor to the soul, so great a union is caused that all the things of both God and the soul become one in participant transformation, and the soul appears to be God more than a soul. Indeed, it is God by participation.[22]

These lines remind one of the earlier story from the desert: "You can become fire."

* * *

Are there any equivalents to this issue of obedience in the field of psychology? As far as obedience goes, the attitude of the therapist is, of course, very different from that of the desert father or mother, or the guru. The aim of the therapeutic process is, in Jungian terms, individuation, so that obedience hardly seems an issue. One must, however, beware of simplistic conclusions. Part of the therapeutic process, and an essential part, is the transference. Freud remarks:

I can assure you that you are misinformed if you suppose that advice and guidance in the affairs of life play an integral part in analytic influence. On the contrary, so far as possible we avoid the role of a mentor such as this, and there is nothing we would rather bring about than that the patient should make his decisions for himself.[23]

What occurs, however, seems to run counter to this desire of the analyst. "The patient, who ought to want nothing else but to find a way out of his distressing conflicts, develops a special interest in the person of the doctor."[24] What is going on? "The patient has transferred on to the doctor intense feelings of affection which are justified neither by the doctor's behaviour nor by the situation which has developed during the treatment."[25] "The whole readiness for these feelings is derived from elsewhere"[26] — from past experiences and issues which can then be worked out in working through the transference. What has occurred, then, is that in dealing with someone recognized in some way as an authority, or, often, parental figure, the questions and feelings around these areas emerge. But the way to adulthood lies through the working through of just such issues, for which the person of the analyst has, in this case, become the focus. This is the kind of maturation process of which Vandana spoke above. So psychology here takes its place as helping to prepare for mature obedience.

These quotations were from Freud. Jung will speak also of animus/anima in connection with projection. But the process remains one of appropriating for oneself in the end what has been projected out onto others, at least if one wishes to reach personal maturity. In the desert, too, the disciple who reached maturity became, in turn, a guide.

None of these processes, though, implies a liberation from obedience but only a change in its focus. In religious terms, the prior general of the Camaldolese can write both of his Rule and of obedience that they are education toward liberty, toward the inner obedience to the Word:

> The ultimate confrontation is always with the Word of God and his love. . . . The obvious presence of this provisional understanding of the law, both in the mind of the legislator as well as in the drafting of the law itself, leads us to understand how the monk should grow in this consciousness . . . [and be] always urged toward it.[27]

> Fatherhood belongs properly to God and cannot be appropriated by anyone . . . since we are all sons of God. The abbatial charism is set forth and developed in order to protect and guarantee our sonship of God against the intrusion of any human judgment or authority which could imperil the liberty acquired for us by Christ.[28]

Obedience is always required, then, but the ultimate obedience is to God and to the deeper values in our conscience and consciousness that relate us to Him.

Jung's thoughts on the need to recognize that human consciousness and will are not the ultimate arbiters have been reviewed throughout these pages. But in her biography of Jung, Barbara Hannah demonstrates a still stronger position on this topic when she comments on one of her subject's dreams:

> It was nearly twenty years later that Jung had the dream that finally taught him that all application of self-will ("where there is a will, there is a way") not only obscures the search for truth but also impose disastrous limits to the natural development of life which can lead to the worst catastrophes.[29]

Our horizons need to be wider and deeper than our own minds and wills. We need truly to listen, in the way Steindl-Rast mentioned. We may experience the agony, the struggle, of this conflict at times. It is more comfortable in the narrow little sphere of what we see and desire and plan and can control. But both psychology and spirituality are there to tell us that the self-enclosed life ultimately stagnates. Openness to another in silence, listening, and obedience widens the heart to the horizons from which, finally, ultimate meaning flows.

·12·

SPIRITUAL GUIDE OR THERAPIST

The obverse side of silence, listening, obedience concerns the person through whom inner obedience is learned. In an earlier age, people who wanted a word of wisdom, light, peace went to the hermits in the desert or the monks or nuns in the nearest monastery, and this in the East as well as the West. As is known, the practice of confessing more than the serious sins of murder, adultery, apostasy grew up in the Western Church largely through the influence of Irish monks to whom people went for spiritual guidance. The Orthodox churches continue to value their recourse to the staretz as does the Hindu tradition its guru and the Zen its roshi.

I suggest that in a secularized world the therapist has become the secular equivalent of many of these figures. And if one goes beneath the surface, one begins to question just how "secular" this impulse —and this process—really are. Why do people come to therapy—or analysis? Those who do not use these opportunities often have a stereotype: people seeking counseling are in some way sick. (Read as a corollary that those who do not are healthy.) The facts, of course, are different. If the line from sickness to health is a continuum, people in therapy are probably not numerically lower on the scale than others. Perhaps they hurt more. Perhaps they are more conscious of hurt or need. Perhaps they are humbler and readier to admit the need for help. Perhaps they hope for something others do not hope for. Who knows what the differences are? But they come because a life option has exploded in their face; because of grief at a loss or tension in a relationship; because life seems gloomy—or full of tension—or because they seek light or meaning; because of habits they wish to change or decisions they

135

want to make; perhaps because they want to know themselves in more depth, be more in touch with their creativity or their relationship to God and others, because they want to understand their dreams and glimpse something of the riches the unconscious offers. The list is endless and contains all the material of human living.

And when they come, what happens? They may have believed, as did the visitors to the desert, that they would receive a word of wisdom or advice to change their lives. And this, as we have just seen, is even more unlikely than in the desert. There, the "abba" might prefer silence or example to speech. Here, the therapist is concerned to help a person find inner resources and guidance. Louf says that the spiritual guide passes on a spiritual tradition, a *life* that needs to be lived before it can possibly be passed on.[1] The parallel to therapy holds.

So what kind of person must the therapist be—or become? June Singer writes of the education of the Jungian analyst:

> The education of the analyst extends beyond anything that can be verbally expressed. It is, more than anything, an experience of transformation in which one comes to know one's own soul and to befriend it. In the process, it is hoped that one may become what one really is. . . . The education of an analyst is extremely personal. The psyche is divested of its protective coverings and laid bare in the personal analysis, which is also the training analysis. In this process one feels terribly alone, even though the analyst is standing by. The analyst-to-be, like anyone else, enters the dark nights with their dreams and the terrors of the day, alone and unprotected. But the difference in those who submit themselves to be trained as analysts is that they know they must go through the process no matter what, and neither turn back nor be led astray. They must confront all the difficulties and demons that beset the path, if they are to become the ones who will support others in their soul-journeys.[2]

There are personal qualities, she says, that are of prime importance, for "Analysis is nothing if it is not a way of life."[3] One essential, then, is a sense of vocation, of calling, an attraction to the mystery of the human soul. Another is the sense of the symbolic dimension of life, the ability to use "the mythic image to reflect an archetypal configuration."[4]

Also needed is commitment to continuing growth: "through reading and study, through continuing self-observation, and through ongoing analytic work with the unconscious materials that emerge."[5] But it is also necessary to go through long periods of darkness, inaction, waiting, while retaining the commitment to move toward personal integration. "This means that one is to take personal responsibility for what one says and does, not to seek excuses or scapegoats."[6] It also implies readiness for self-criticism and admission of error.

It is important not to need to be liked, for the analyst must perform tasks when confronting the darker elements in the soul of the other that will incur the anger and fear of the analysand.[7]

This requires facing one's own shadow.

Flexibility, liking for others, acceptance of others and of self, care for oneself are also listed, as well as ability "to love without possessiveness, and . . . to hate without the need for retribution." Finally, psychic energy.

Analysands want to feel that the analyst can stand the dirt and stench of another's life and not turn away. An analyst is needed who is not only wide and compassionate, but also singed, scorched, and seasoned: someone who understands how tough life really is.[8]

In other words, the issue is one of personal being and becoming. No techniques, no learning on a superficial or intellectual level prepare one for this work, but only a certain choice of how to live, and the gift to live it. In other words, the first requirement is the depth, seriousness, and perseverance of one's own journey.

All this brings us back to the issue of the secular and the sacred. If the innermost heart of the human person is the place of intersection with the divine, then truly this is holy ground. To see it as "secular," is to be unaware of its real meaning. The profound decisions of the human heart, also, involve choices of value — of good as against evil, truth as against lies, beauty or whatever else is judged as value. Are such choices "secular" because a person making them — often at the price of great struggle — does not call them a choice of God? Or because a person struggling to find a coherent and valid path through a maze of difficulties may not name this process a seeking for the will of God? Perhaps it isn't always. But drawing lines simplistically or in terms of what language people use—religious or otherwise—seems to miss the reality of what is going on.

Singer's quotations above discuss the person of the analyst. Murray Stein writes about the analytic process:

> Guggenbuhl-Craig has suggested, somewhat ironically, that changes resulting from analysis may come about in great part through the "analytic ritual": visiting an analyst once or twice a week for a number of years; attending regularly to dreams during that period; taking time for serious introspection and inner work; and, thereby, forming new habits of conscious attentiveness to the psyche and its workings.[9]

This quotation is interesting not only in itself but as it relates to spiritual discipline. Anyone familiar with classical methods of spiritual training, in religious communities for example, will recognize much from the above quotation. The "ritual" is not dissimilar. Weekly or so spiritual direction, attention to "inner movements" and impulses and to what might be considered the guidance of the Holy Spirit, efforts to grow in spiritual discernment and discretion through the experience of consulting with someone more experienced in this domain, examination of conscience/consciousness/motivations, efforts toward greater awareness of the spiritual world and its guidance—all these are to be found in various forms in many spiritual disciplines of both East and West. And these form the "work" in which the analyst is guide as well.

What is one to conclude from such resemblances? Perhaps, for one thing, that the structure of the human psyche—in whatever words one chooses to define it—has a basic universality which all these various disciplines strive to work with and train. For another, that the direction of this training seems basically much the same. The early years of human formation have socialized the human person in ways enabling him or her to operate relatively smoothly in the world, in the domain of work and of relationships. For this to happen, however, much that was individual to the person's growth, much that came strictly from within, had to be temporarily sacrificed or held back. If full "individuation," integration, fulfillment of personal calls and development are to take place, the process needs—at a given stage—to be reversed. Without totally renouncing what has been learned about the requirements of functioning in the external world, the human person needs to get in touch with the requirements of his or her own inner world and calling—and, deeper still, with the requirements of relationship with that Other found by going through the depths of one's own being. It is the experience Jung calls: "the recognition of an alien 'other' in oneself, or the objective presence of another will."[10] Increasingly, analytic psychology and spirituality seem more than akin in their ways of reaching the goal of integration.

Some lines in Jung show this resemblance still further. Speaking of psychoanalysis, he says:

> It is a catharsis of a special kind, something like the maieutics of Socrates, the "art of the midwife." It is only to be expected that for many people who have adopted a certain pose towards themselves, in which they violently believe, psychoanalysis is a veritable torture. For, in accordance with the old mystical saying, "Give up what thou hast, then shalt thou receive!" they are called upon to abandon all their cherished illusions in order that something deeper, fairer, and more embracing may arise within them. Only through the mystery of self-sacrifice can a man find himself anew. It is a genuine old wisdom that comes to light again in psychoanalytical treatment, and it is especially curious that this kind of psychic education should prove necessary in the heyday of our culture. In more than one respect it may be compared with the Socratic method, though it must be said that psychoanalysis penetrates to far greater depths.[11]

So this "work" the analyst is meant to do requires being a kind of midwife. It is "done" only by the analysand, but it requires facilitation by one who has been through the same process.

A final aspect of this work and of the analyst who guides it emerges in an article by William Goodheart. After speaking of Jung and of *imaginatio* as "the active evocation of . . . images . . . an authentic feat of thought or ideation, which does not spin aimless and groundless fantasies 'into the blue' . . . but tries to grasp the inner facts and portray them in images true to their nature,"[12] he says:

The consciousness of the therapist [in the interview of which he speaks] . . . is being challenged to perform once more for the patient this ancient act, which defines the essence of being human and guarantees that there will be a translation of the inchoate into the human, the symbolic. This is essentially the analytic attitude. It is an act that draws a line and holds that line—a line which says, "I will not respond in the kind you demand. There is another way for us to be together here, another way for us to communicate, another way for me to relate to the inchoate forces that upwell in you. I encourage, listen for, prepare the way for and respond only to *imaginatio,* the great revealer, the spellbinder who draws you into the vast complexities of your own reality. I am *not* a counselor, advisor, teacher, judge, friend, or lover! I am different from all of these: rather I am the unnatural, the anti-natural. I am the drawer of the sacred spellbinding circle in which *imaginatio* will emerge and with that alone can you discover who you are. This is my task. . . .[13]

It will be seen below that this refusal to flow with the "simply natural" is found again and again in spiritual literature as well. The analyst here is truly "Precursor" in the scriptural sense of the term. He "prepares the way of the Lord," the way for the deeper reality of the human psyche to emerge, and this is the way to consciousness of an Other than that psyche itself.

These texts have spoken of the person of the therapist. Does the literature of spirituality paint the spiritual guide very differently? Speaking once more of the Indian tradition, Vandana writes:

The Indian ideal of a spiritual man is always characterized by simplicity, humility and poverty. . . . The true guru is generally one who hides himself and comes before the public only reluctantly, usually only when forced there by the number of his disciples. The true gurus in the Himālayan foothills are often those living a hidden life in the forests or caves; silent, serene, simple, content to be unknown, undisturbed, unlauded . . . often they are slow to speak or to answer one's questions verbally. . . . 'The guru's silence is the loudest counsel (updesh).' He is one who having discovered the Source within himself, is able to let others drink of the waters of Fullness (Purnam) and Bliss (Anandam). . . . [He is] primarily one learned in the Scriptures. . . . It is the guru's function to bring the disciple to enter within . . . to touch Reality. At this point he knows himself to be unnecessary,

and often disappears. But until such time as this 'Inward' Guru
is found by the disciple, the outer guru is needed.[14]

The resemblance of this Eastern teaching with that of the Western
as begun in the desert is striking. Louf writes of the spiritual father
in the desert tradition that the term "father" carried the notion of
"transmitter of life." What was sought was the "word," closely akin
to that of Scripture. "A father's word is weighty; he does not speak
idly."[15] The atmosphere of silence, almost of roughness, is the
same as that given above.

> Witness John the Prophet's answer to a brother who insisted on
> getting advice: 'You write me again, senseless and ignorant as I
> am? . . . So I tell you the truth. I am nothing and know nothing.
> But out of obedience I tell you what is in my heart.'[16]

If the spiritual father or mother speaks out of obedience, it is also
true that the notion of obedience is important for the one guided.
"The charism of spiritual fatherhood dwells within the son's as well
as the father's heart. If, at some time, the fathers have no more to
say, this is, first of all, because there are no longer hearts disposed
as sons to receive."[17] In other words, a faith relationship is needed.

How, then, would one choose a spiritual father or mother according to Louf? It is essential to be seeking God's will and not one's
own, or one will choose according to personal desire. Then the
person chosen must be experienced in the ways of obedience — experienced, quite simply, with temptation, trial, struggle — a thought
reminiscent of Singer. If this is not the case, what will be presented
is born of theory, not of life. Again, most people chosen to be
"abba" do not wish to be such — a touchstone one could reflect on
today.

What will be the content of the relationship? "The favorite topic
for dialogue was indeed the passions and the sicknesses which affect
the soul and which the elder's word must reveal and heal."[18] This is
why experience is needed. Some present spiritualities with exclusive emphasis on optimism would not like such a view of
spiritual guidance, but, as our reflection on the shadow has shown,
it is difficult to imagine how one could begin elsewhere.

> One of the aims of the unveiling of thoughts is the bringing to
> the surface of tendencies lurking deep in the heart where they

cause havoc because they are not shared with anyone. Brought
to light they often vanish.[19]

In the light of all that has been said about analysis, this thought
makes a great deal of sense in all domains.

The purpose of all this is gradual training in personal discernment. "Discernment or acuteness of judgment, even in the humblest
details, is necessary for the monk,"[20] for every detail of life relates
with one's union with God. One remembers the desert stories about
people outstanding for their asceticism who nonetheless missed the
road—whether by excess or by pride in their own works, judgment,
will. The ability to obey with flexibility and openness was a good
test and is today, even as is in analysis the ability really to hear
sometimes hard truths.

> Whenever the elders speak of obedience, what is today called
> the 'common good' never appears on the horizon. They consider
> only the personal well-being of the brother who, facing his father,
> submits to training in obedience as he would to spiritual therapy.
> It is, above all, a way to internal freedom and spiritual matu-
> ration.[21]

Louf adds that this training may demand more than seems to be
reasonable and even set up a kind of shock-therapy "that only a
father can impose upon his own son, not only because he is supposed to know him better than anyone else, but above all because
the son trusts him totally and feels loved."[22] This is a case of being
taken beyond one's own limits—a thing one cannot do for oneself.
It is an example of the reason why one cannot be one's own spiritual
guide—or, for that matter, therapist—except in very exceptional
cases. One can do very much alone, and must, but some results of
this kind of interaction seem irreplaceable.

We return to the issue of the person of the spiritual father or
mother. Louf reemphasizes that example is more central than word.
He quotes Abba Sisoes: "Why do you insist on my speaking idly?
Do what you see."[23] And what is the most essential part of this
example? Gentleness, tenderness, mercy. Awareness of one's own
frailty makes one slow to judge another, as only dealing with one's
shadow enables one to work with another. But this theme of love is
inextricably bound up with that of firmness and strength. Otherwise

what posed as love would be weakness and would no longer image God. Finally, Louf stresses the depth of the love between spiritual father/mother and son/daughter, a love of real intimacy yet always with the judgment that prevents deviations. This love is not the end.

In his earlier work, Louf related the word of the spiritual father/mother to the word of creation spoken at the beginning of time:

> Only he who has been taught by the Spirit of God, the spiritual person, knows the things of God and understands his Word. He is also able to exercise a fatherhood-according-to-the-Spirit: to hand on the Word and watch over and see to its growth. . . . The process brings to us the Word of Creation that brought the universe into being. . . . Happy that man to whom it has been given to hear for himself, from the mouth of his spiritual father, this Word-of-the-beginning. He already carries the new world in his heart.[24]

Ultimately, then, it is a new creation, a new world, that is born of this process of obedience to the spiritual father or mother, and of the latter's obedience to the Word. I say deliberately "obedience," for this is a process of "hearing" the Word still spoken in silence. Out of this hearing is born the new creation. When, years after the above teaching of the desert, Benedict tried to codify the tradition handed down from the past, he would speak of the monastery as a "school of the Lord's service," a place where one could truly learn the ways of God. It is a good question whether this does not remain the function of religious community in the Church—for the members of those communities and for those in contact with them as well. William Johnston says the same in his thought-provoking article, "Religious Life: Contemplative Life."[25] More, it is his belief that what distinguishes religious life as a charism in the Church is its orientation to contemplation and the life of union with God. He feels that it is deviation from this call that causes the death of vocations and communities. Vandana sees an even wider conclusion:

> It was Swami Abhishiktananda's dream that the renewal of the Church in India would begin with a pilot seminary, where young volunteers would come to be trained under one or two christian gurus, live an ashram lifestyle and study 'the seed of the word,' the Indian scriptures, in the light of the Word. A tentative effort

was made to begin such a wonderful venture in Yaranasi, at Nasihi Gurukul, beginning not with seminarians but with a group of priests who felt the need of such an experience in order to be more relevant to and able to meet the needs of the contemporary Indian Church.[26]

This may, indeed, be precisely the kind of "relevance" increasingly sought by a world hungering for meaning as much as for bread, and by a West still choked by its technology. The increasing interest in psychology as well as spirituality points in some such direction. If that is so, then the work par excellence any one of us can do for others and the world has to do with attention to the Word, for when that Word is truly spoken in any one person's heart, the new Creation begins there with a dynamic power whose final ripples we cannot know but whose contact heals.

·13·

MEMORY

Great is the power of memory, exceeding great is it, O God, an inner chamber, vast and unbounded! Who has penetrated to its very bottom? Yet it is a power of my mind and it belongs to my very nature, and thus I do not comprehend all that I am. Is the mind, therefore, too limited to possess itself? Must we ask, "Where is this power belonging to it which it does not grasp?" "Is it outside it, and not within it?" "How then does it not comprehend it?" Great wonder arises within me at this. Amazement seizes me. Men go forth to marvel at the mountain heights, at huge waves in the sea, at the broad expanse of flowing rivers, at the wide reaches of the ocean, and at the circuits of the stars, but themselves they pass by.[1]

Thus Augustine of Hippo reflected on his power of memory—that power which psychoanalysis probes and which is the seat of the *memoria Dei,* the remembrance of God spiritual writers discuss. What is the importance of memory on the human journey? A whole book of the *Confessions* studies this theme, which has tempted thinkers throughout the centuries. Plato and his followers believed that all learning was remembering what was already somewhere within and previously known. Aristotle and the currents of thought following him believed instead that knowledge comes from outside, through the senses. We do not come "trailing clouds of glory" onto this earth. Not memory but sensation is primary.

But the advent of depth psychology has somewhat changed the focus on this question. Freud certainly did not believe in the "clouds of glory," but for him much of psychotherapy is concerned with bringing back to consciousness what has indeed been "forgotten" as too painful or risky to remember. In several passages he reflects on the view that these elements he suggests remembering are things in us that we consider too evil to recall.

> We have not only found that the material of the forgotten experiences of childhood is accessible to dreams, but we have also seen that the mental life of children with all its characteristics, its egoism, its incestuous choice of love-objects, and so on, still persists in dreams—that is, in the unconscious, and that dreams carry us back every night to this infantile level. The fact is thus confirmed that *what is unconscious in mental life is also what is infantile*. The strange impression of there being so much evil in people begins to diminish. This frightful evil is simply the initial, primitive, infantile part of mental life, which we can find in actual operation in children. . . . Since dreams regress to this level, they give the appearance of having brought to light the evil in us.[2]

Since Freud believes in infantile sexuality, the Oedipus complex and the other theories which have since become familiar as his, it is not difficult for him to trace all dream imagery to this source. As we have seen above,[3] Jung's dreamwork takes rather a different slant. Nonetheless, for both, the dream is a "royal road to the unconscious," and one does indeed find there both images and memories refused to the conscious mind.

As is known, for Freud the recalling of this forgotten material can also be the royal road to the healing of present psychological difficulties. What has been restored to consciousness can be dealt with in a way impossible when it is still hidden.

> We will keep to wishes for getting rid of someone, which may for the most part be attributed to the dreamer's unrestricted egoism. A wish of this kind can very often be pointed to as the constructor of a dream. Whenever anyone in the course of one's life gets in one's way—and how often this must happen in view of the complication of one's relationships in life!—a dream is promptly ready to kill that person, even if it be father or mother, brother or sister, husband or wife. This wickedness of human nature came as a great surprise to us and we were decidedly disinclined to accept this outcome of dream-interpretation without question. But as soon as we were led to look for the origin of these wishes in the past, we discovered the period of the indi-

vidual's past in which there was no longer anything strange in such egoism and such wishful impulses, directed even against his closest relatives. . . . Children love themselves first, and it is only later that they learn to love others and to sacrifice something of their own ego to others.[4]

We are well socialized, then, but in dreams our less socialized side appears—or perhaps one should say we find out how superficial our socialization may really be. Having lived through some of the events of the mid- to late-twentieth century, we should be less surprised at the news of the thinness of this civilized veneer. Where a neurosis results from the repression of the above kind of hatred, for example, remembering and facing it can help toward a cure.

Memory, then, contains the roots of our consciousness. To Jung, as we have seen, it contains more—even the memory of our race and culture.

The unconscious has a Janus-face: on one side its contents point back to a preconscious, prehistoric world of instinct, while on the other side it potentially anticipates the future. . . . In so far as no man is born totally new, but continually repeats the stage of development last reached by the species, he contains unconsciously, as an *a priori* datum, the entire psychic structure developed both upwards and downwards by his ancestors in the course of the ages.[5]

There is, then, a deeper level than the individual "memory" which would contain both remembered and forgotten personal material. There is also what could be called the "memory of the race," and this continues to live in each of us.

Is it important to be in touch with this? Jung replies:

Unconscious influences . . . are often truer and wiser than our conscious thinking. . . . Careful investigation shows how very much our conscious decisions depend on the undisturbed functioning of memory. But memory often suffers from the disturbing interference of unconscious contents. . . . Normally the unconscious collaborates with the conscious without friction or disturbance . . . but when an individual or a social group deviates too far from their instinctual foundations, they then experience the full impact of unconscious forces.[6]

Jung's answer is, then, that it is important to be in touch with this deeper level of the psyche. Losing touch bears its own intrinsic penalty in personal or collective illness. Becoming "conscious," then, involves dealing with more than the personal memory or unconscious: it involves openness to the archetypal and universal. And this, too, is "memory."

To Jung, one way of coming into touch with this "memory of the race" is through the symbolic, through myths, legends, poetry, alchemy, the thought of other ages and places. He has found extraordinary correlations in some of these fields. These "archaic and 'historical' associations and images of an archetypal nature"

> . . . evidently live and function in the deeper layers of the unconscious, especially in that phylogenetic substratum which I have called the collective unconscious. . . . They bring into our ephemeral consciousness an unknown psychic life belonging to a remote past.[7]

Therefore, memory, "rootedness," is important—and these roots are deeper than our own.

Jung continues this specific reflection by asking whether this unconscious level has a personality, a center of consciousness parallel to the ego on the conscious level. Are there, he asks, "much less fragmentary and more complete personalities," or a "dormant and hidden personality" there?[8] He responds with a conviction that evidence exists for this view and continues with a discussion of the animus or anima, the shadow, and other such personifications:

> It is our ego-consciousness that has forever a new beginning and an early end. The unconscious psyche is not only immensely old, it is also capable of growing into an equally remote future. It moulds the human species and is just as much a part of it as the human body.[9]

His conclusion, then, is that "the psyche consists of two incongruous halves which together should form a whole."[10] The dialectic involved in this process results in the forming of an "individual," in the sense in which Jung uses this term. The process involves, then, a "union of opposites"—a union which rounds out the personality into a whole:

This rounding out of the personality into a whole may well be the goal of any psychotherapy that claims to be more than a mere cure of symptoms.[11]

Individual memory, then, this "storehouse" of which Augustine speaks, opens out into a wider field than the individual. It opens not only onto the memory of the race but, deeper still, onto another Consciousness whose face we have glimpsed here and there throughout the preceding pages.

In a study written at the conclusion of training at the Jung Institute in Zurich, Russell Holmes compares the thought of Jung, as regards memory and forgetting, with that of John of the Cross. Speaking of memory as "the faculty of recollection" and concluding that "in a sense, consciousness is memory and memory is consciousness," this author reflects on the archetypal nature of memory and forgetting, notably in terms of the ladder image of ascent-descent experiences. He speaks of the Greek mythological river of Lethe, forgetting, and the spring of Mnemosyne, remembering, in the Lethian fields, "a further indication of the twin nature of forgetting and memory.[12]

> Too much water from the spring of Lesmosyne [Lethe] would leave the *ego* in an unconscious state; too much from the spring of Mnemosyne might allow the memory of unconscious contents to predominate the *ego* tasks of everyday life.[13]

Jung had already remarked, in the article just studied, that our Western culture is interested in maintaining contact with reality which forbids losing oneself in either the unconscious or simply in forgetfulness as seen above. We need both the ego and the unconscious for the union of opposites he discusses. Holmes remarks:

> If we use Jung and John of the Cross as prototypes of ascent-descent experiences, we have to conclude that a genuine descent, directed by God or the Self, carries with it a protection of the *ego*. If this were not so, we would not have their teachings, for they would never have returned and would exist now on the list of some hospital register, possibly labeled as "schizophrenic."[14]

Having delivered this warning, however, this author continues by saying that "anyone who risks analysis or a life of interior prayer must encounter these springs of forgetting and memory and discover, by experiment, the right measure to be taken from both."[15] Addiction, senility, amnesia all represent the return to the unconscious for one or other reason. But there are also myths, not the least of which is found in Genesis, of a "preexistent wholeness" from which humanity "fell." "In these myths we can see the twins, Mnemosyne and Lesmosyne, at the archetypal roots of mankind."[16] Holmes points out that these Greek myths were characteristic of the nonclassical period:

> It is in the "unmystical" and "mystical" traditions of forgetting and memory in Greek Mythology that we find the foundations of forgetting and memory in later religious traditions. They are the archetypal rungs of the "ladder of descent and ascent."[17]

This statement is extremely interesting to anyone acquainted with medieval and earlier Christian thought, for the image of the ladder and of its ascent-descent symbolism occurs time and again in that tradition. One has only to think of John Climacus's *Ladder of Ascent* or of the Benedictine ladder of humility to which we will return below. The connection of this image with the question of memory takes on new meaning in terms of that document.

> It is in religious experience that forgetting and memory find their deepest meaning. . . . In Buddhism . . . the individual must remember all his previous lives—lest he forget the lessons learned therefrom—before he reaches the state of freedom, Nirvana. . . . This dynamic is demonstrated in the psychoanalytic movement where unconscious complexes are depotentiated by exposing them to the light of consciousness. Analytical psychology goes a step further in recognizing the archetypal nucleus of the complexes and the healing power which is constellated by following the nucleus to the Self. Energetically, the healing power is reached by forgetting the personal component and becoming conscious of the eternal component.[18]

In other words, religious thought through the centuries and across the world has stressed the importance of "forgetting" things, external and internal, which are not helpful toward furthering the union with God found, as John of the Cross would say, by retiring into one's deepest center.[19] This search requires the "leaving" of such memories and attention as impede the journey inward. But, once again, common sense and daily duty provide the balance against excess in this regard. The birth of the cenobitic religious life has something to do with this discovery. Eastern thought has been stronger still on the necessity of this "forgetting": one thinks, for example, of Buddhism's four basic truths. And yet, as seen above, Buddhism, too, requires a deeper "remembering."

Once again we see the connections between spiritual and psychoanalytic thought. Remembering forgotten complexes is healing for Freud, while, for Jung, going through contact with these complexes to the archetypes to which they point is the way to individuation and healing.

> Establishing a relationship with God or Self, the *ego* enters a "mystic" state, that is a secret and unique condition at the center of the soul where the opposites are combined. To leave this state is to leave the "presence of God, Thrones and Dominations, the original energy of life." [Jung] . . . The center is arrived at by the function of forgetting and memory, and contact with it is maintained by remaining fluid in the sense of being able to recall the original energy of life and being able to forget the personal in favor of what transcends it.[20]

This is Holmes's conclusion. Both movements, then, the spiritual-mystical and the analytic, go in the same direction. They lead to a similar end. And they involve much the same dangers and risks. These points are well kept in mind as we look at the same themes in some much earlier works.

An important concept in the Rule of Benedict, which we have seen as a compendium of the earlier tradition, is that of the remembrance of God. Chapter 2 above discussed the basic stages of humility. "The first step of humility, then, is that a man keeps the *fear of God* always *before his eyes* (Ps. 35[36]:2) and never forgets it. . . . He must constantly remember everything God has commanded. . . . Let him recall that he is always seen by God."[21]

It will be recalled that this whole chapter is seen in terms of the ladder image—Jacob's ladder, which angels ascend and descend. "Without doubt, this descent and ascent can signify only that we descend by exaltation and ascend by humility."[22] In combination with our first appendix, Chapter 2 above showed while commenting on this text the depths that this descent into humility, which is an ascent, can involve. And, once again, the Benedictine text states that body and soul are the two rungs of the ladder. This remembrance of God's commands and awareness of His presence and gaze is, then, a consciousness of spiritual reality in which we believe, and has a deeper and wider perspective than that of mere sensation and intelligence. It brings, as the later degrees of humility show, an increase in gravity, seriousness, depth, purification, and inner quiet and stability, and it leads eventually to a personality unified in the love of God.

Elsewhere in the same document, the abbot is exhorted always to "remember what his title signifies. . . . He is believed to hold the place of Christ in the monastery, since he is addressed by a title of Christ"—that is, Father.[23] If he remembers this identity—if he always knows who and what he is as abbot—he will know that he "must never teach or decree or command anything that would deviate from the Lord's instructions."[24] In other words, this memory brings back a connection—one that could certainly be called archetypal—between the Christ, Father of the community, and that community, through the figure of the abbot. If he "forgets," he will deviate from that norm and do a human and personal work in the community, which is not his function.

It goes without saying that this concept can be a very delicate one. If the abbot identifies with his role exclusively, then he runs the risk of inflation, of identification with the archetype—a risk common to him and other ecclesial authority figures. He could then lose touch with his shadow, his humanity, his fallibility. When, however, he is able to remember who he is as abbot, as link with and symbol of Christ, and act accordingly and, at the same time, remember the humility of his human condition, then he can maintain the delicate balance this awareness of his title requires. When, later in the same section, he is asked also to remember the judgment of God on his own "shepherding" and the obedience of his "flock," this sobering thought can help—if he uses it, again, with the humility asked of all. The final paragraph of the chapter once again reminds him to "remember what he is and remember what he is called."[25] A memory of identity, then, is essential to such a work, but the more numinous this "identity," the more awareness of the risk of inflation must accompany it. One could reflect on the dynamism of such a principle if it were literally applied, with the above conclusions, by everyone called, in Christian terms, to the work of "father," "shepherd," or other related symbols.

The fourth chapter of the same Rule could be considered one long exercise in collective memory. Using the imagery of the monastery as a workshop in the Lord's service, it supplies "tools" the workers can choose to further their spiritual craft. One might expect something esoteric, but rather these tools include a summary of very basic teaching for all Christians. They begin with the commandments and continue with the spiritual and corporal works of mercy and other fundamental precepts of the Christian life. The monastic life is seen as simply Christian living. After some of the above comes: "Day by day remind yourself that you are going to die. Hour by hour keep careful watch over all you do . . . aware that God's gaze is upon you, wherever you may be."[26] This is about remembrance of the seriousness of life and its choices in their ultimate meaning, and, not surprisingly, is immediately followed by warnings against light and superficial conduct. The whole passage means, once more, awareness of other horizons than the immediate, external, visible. Death is not an ending but a *crisis,* in the Greek sense: a moment when our lives are tested for true values. A moment, therefore, in whose light we can live to be more spiritually real.

Then, "every day with tears and sighs confess your past sins to God in prayer . . . and change from these evil ways in the future."[27] Not a popular formula at present but one that previous reflection in these pages will suggest as very sensible, psychologically as well as spiritually. We do well not to forget our shadow and our sin.

Finally, in its concluding chapter, the Rule gives a "send-off" from its own pages into all that has been taught in Scripture and the tradition, whose phrases have been like bricks throughout the Rule, which holds them together like mortar. The whole collective memory of the People of God and, within that, of the spiritual tradition of the preceding centuries is at the root of this teaching which sends one back to this whole spiritual world. Some of our contemporary spirituality would be the richer were it not cut off from these roots in Scripture, tradition, and our early history as Church and as "God-seekers," for that tradition brings to us an experience of the ways to God common to many centuries and cultures. But the center of that entire memory is the remembrance of God, living and present, who speaks in His Word, is celebrated liturgically, is always present and acting in love.

Christian liturgical practice, too, unlike that of more ahistorical religions, is based on memory—the memory of a single paschal event made present in sacramental commemoration.

> The sacrifice of Jesus Christ will not be an isolated and transitory act, but will be perpetuated across space and time, and will always actualize the real presence of the Lord and the force of His priestly action, which will thus be able to reach all men. In this way the external acts of religion, the rites of the Christian religion, will not only arouse and foster interior devotion psychologically, but also contain and communicate grace and holiness.[28]

This text finds its own commentary in a summary of the whole plan of God:

> Here, then, is God's plan: the Word will unite with a human nature, and the human family will thereby be introduced into the divine family. As He will be Son of God and Son of man also, all men will share divine sonship in Him. At the same time, having the Son of God in their midst, they will possess Him who is the splendor and the manifestation of the Father's glory. He Himself, being appointed high Priest of mankind, will be able to present Himself to the Father as mankind's tribute of glory; and men, united in a vital way with Jesus Christ in the unity of one mystical Body, will be able to unite their worshipful acts to the sacrifice of Jesus Christ. Thus they will cooperate with Him in the formation of a single worship, the worship of the Christian religion.
> Thus the essential glory of God brings His splendors down to creatures.[29]

This text is given as an example of centuries of Christian traditional teaching on the liturgy as memory, as *anamnesis*. And also as an understanding of the liturgical moment as the point of intersection of past time with present time as seed for the future. Far more, it is seen as the place of intersection of the temporal and the eternal, the place and time where the "splendor and manifestation of the Father's glory" is made present here and now—often in a simple and not beautiful building among very simple and ordinary people in the course of a simple and ordinary day. The eternal, with its "glory," then, intersects the most humdrum. But we only see it if we remember.

> Great is the power of memory! An awesome thing, my God, deep and boundless and manifold in being! And this thing is the mind, and this am I myself: what then am I, O my God? What is my nature? . . .
>
> What . . . shall I do, O you who are my true life, my God? I will pass beyond even this power of mind which is called memory, desiring to reach you where you may be reached. . . . Even beyond memory will I pass, so that I may find you—where? . . . If I find you apart from memory, I am unmindful of you. How then shall I find you, if I do not remember you?[30]

In his search for God, Augustine struggles with this question for seven more chapters. Then he writes:

> Behold, how far within my memory have I traveled in search of you, Lord, and beyond it I have not found you! Nor have I found anything concerning you except what I have kept in memory since I first learned of you. For since I learned of you, I have not forgotten you. Wheresoever I found truth, there I found my God, truth itself . . . and since I learned about you, you abide in my memory, and I find you there when I recall you to mind and take delight in you. . . .
>
> But where within my memory do you abide? . . . I entered even into the very seat of my mind, which lies within my memory. . . . You were not there. For you are not a bodily image, nor are you an affection. . . .
>
> Where, then, did I find you, so that I might learn to know you? You were not in my memory before I learned to know you. Where then have I found you, if not in yourself and above me? There is no place, both backward do we go and forward, and there is no place. Everywhere, O Truth, you give hearing to all who consult you, and at one and the same time you make answer to them all. . . .
>
> Too late have I loved you, O Beauty so ancient and so new, too late have I loved you! Behold, you were within me, while I was outside: it was there that I sought you, and, a deformed creature, rushed headlong upon these things of beauty which you have made. You were with me, but I was not with you.[31]

His search, then, brings Augustine through his memory into the deeper places of his being where it intersects with the Presence, Truth, Beauty he is seeking. And yet, memory is an essential part of this search, or "descent" into the depths of our hearts; it is a way to be with God. It is also our way to be with ourselves, others, reality. The classical exhortation to "Flee forgetfulness" is a call to leave superficial living for the centered gravity of a life present to this Reality Augustine so earnestly sought. We have seen the same search and presence in terms of liturgy, of the thought of Benedict and of John of the Cross, and we have seen in contemporary psychology the same exhortation not to forget, not to ignore the life within stored up in the memory, the unconscious world. The next chapter will study the fruit of this search in terms of one of its culminating signs, peace.

·14·

PEACE

An earlier chapter spoke of the process of "working through," of dealing with past or present troublesome issues until, so to speak, their ghosts are laid to rest, as far as this can be. In Freudian terms, such issues may involve a past trauma, strong and unacceptable impulses, a developmental stage still incomplete. In Jungian terms the question may be a complex still too unconscious to serve a positive purpose, as its energy might when recognized. In either case, the issue involves material needing awareness, consciousness, "befriending"—which is not to say one necessarily follows its lead.

The fruit of such a process in the long run—and it may be a very long run indeed—is a certain inner integration and, in other terms, pacification. Said differently, the process of integration or individuation leads to a personality more at peace with itself and its world, though this aim remains an ideal only partially realizable by each individual according to personal gift and call. In no way, however, can such peace be born without conflict, external and internal. But it leads to greater ability to deal with conflict, greater acceptance of oneself, the other, shadow, reality.

A psychoanalytically oriented article in a recent book on marital therapy remarks:

> The ultimate aim of interpretation and working through in psychoanalytically oriented marital therapy is the neutralization and integration of aggressive and libidinal needs so that behavior is motivated more in the service of the ego and less by impulse and intrapsychic conflict.[1]

157

In other terms, the central passions around aggressivity and sexuality lead to external action and internal conflict, neither of which the deep personality desires in a unified way nor wishes to "own." Working toward integration of these tendencies leads to a more unified and free personality. The above quotation continues with remarks that such a process requires not the suppression, still less the repression, of instinctual drives and resistance—nor their encouragement either—but rather attempts to "explore the sources of these feelings" in order to understand them.

Translated into less technical language, what this implies is that our efforts to control our external behavior by will alone and by obedience to prohibitions are superficial at best and not conducive to deeper integration. The real issues are the sources of our resistances to truth and light; the sources of our anger and desires, particularly when these move in directions psychology calls ego-dystonic; when, in other words, they are not what we ourselves would wish, had we the mastery of our inner worlds. We can try to achieve this mastery by force. This is the way one is often taught— be it in childhood or in churches, schools, society. But the deeper way is exploration into causes and, one hopes, eventual healing along these lines. The result, to use the terms above, is a certain "neutralization and integration" of this instinctual level to serve what the individual really wishes and desires.

The above quotation came from a more Freudian tradition. Following a Jungian reflection on complexes can be enlightening along the same lines. In a study of Jungian thought, Edward Whitmont defines a complex as "an autonomous set of impulses grouped around certain kinds of energy-charged ideas and emotions."[2] As we have seen, in someone still not far along the road to individuation, these complexes tend to be projected outside onto people or things. Whitmont asks how one can know whether a judgment of something or someone external is accurate or projected. His answer is:

> It is the emotional coloring that will tell us whether or not we are caught in a projection. . . . In plain English, whenever projection is involved it "gets" us, it "gets under our skin." Our reaction is affect-determined and we are therefore unable to react adequately to a person or situation; we can neither accept nor modify nor leave that person or situation. This is one of the

few basic laws of the psyche which is, without exception, one-hundred-percent foolproof.[3]

The sign of projection, then, or of being caught in a complex has to do with being emotionally troubled, being caught in a kind of loss of inner freedom or equanimity. The test is clear. A projection can, however, be positive and attracting, as well as negative. In this case also, though, one is pulled out of center. We have spoken, for example, of the dynamics involved in "falling in love," as opposed to loving.

What is to be done with a complex which, in effect, prevents our being master or mistress in our own house? One can try to sublimate it, but that simply involves focussing energy elsewhere. The real aim of Jungian analysis or therapy is what is called "transformation":

> Sublimation . . . merely means that the energy which flows into the troubled area is drained away. . . . In transformation, *the drive itself* becomes changed and ceases to trouble us, because it has turned its other face, has been made into a constructive and helpful impulse. . . . Transformation indicates a change in the unconscious itself.[4]

What all this implies is that here there is a concept of a kind of peace closely related to what the Stoics—and the desert fathers after them—called *apatheia*. Unregulated emotion is a sign of a complex and a cause of greater or lesser unhappiness and mistakes in human relations. One cannot, however, "regulate" such emotion by will power, as recent decades or even centuries urged. The process of purification must go deeper and reach into the unconscious domain of the person. Once this "work" has been sufficiently done, the result is a kind of healing that shows in an ability to react more adequately and wisely, an ability not to be so troubled, in the words of the quotation above. And that is the same phraseology that one finds throughout the spiritual tradition in both East and West. What does it mean in some of these contexts?

Approaching the question partially from a theological point of view, Abbot Columba Marmion wrote in a book that served as a spiritual formation classic for decades before Vatican II:

> Now when we seek to sum up the whole of Christ's work . . . is there one word in which can be gathered up the whole substance of the mystery of the Man-God? Yes, there is such a word . . . the gift of peace condenses in itself every good which the Saviour brings to the souls He comes to redeem.
>
> Christ's life upon earth has but this one aim. When that is attained, He looks upon His work as finished. . . .
>
> It is remarkable that [Benedict] associates the seeking after peace with the seeking after God, as two ends which become but one.[5]

Defining peace primarily as inner peace, Marmion sees it in terms of a return to the inner order preceding original sin, a harmony with God and in oneself, despite personal sin and weakness. For him, such peace is born of faith, surrender to God, abandonment to Him, trust. It continues in temptation and trial and difficulty, born of an inner strength that is gift. He sees it as coming from the mediation of Christ. The tone of this thought is very Christian. Its themes, however, meet much that has been seen from other sources as well.

If we return to earlier sources of the same tradition, we find in Benedicta Ward's definitions of essential terms in desert spirituality:

> APATHEIA: the state of being unmoved by passion; this involves control of the passions rather than their destruction.[6]

This ideal will be recognized as one desired by Stoic thinkers like Marcus Aurelius. In the desert, however, the meaning was somewhat different. Hausherr writes, in his commentary on Evagrius Ponticus's *Treatise on Prayer:*

> We have already seen that peace is the place where God is. . . .
> The practical consequence is this: "Since peace is rational nature's state of impassibility, the person who wants God to dwell in him must put all his energy into purifying himself from all passions" — and thoughts, adds Evagrius in a passage where he again defines this peaceful state as *apathia* [sic]. The action of the devil has precisely the result of troubling this peaceful state which characteristically results from divine or angelic action.[7]

One has here, of course, a whole anthropology and psychology, and one that seems heavily dependent on Stoic influences. Trying to "purify oneself against all passion" seems unrealistic at best, but if one balances this view against Ward's quotation, one comes to a more reasonable interpretation of desert thinking, and of the means to attainment of this peace where God dwells and which His action produces. We may well feel that God dwells in other places than peace, and, once again, the tradition would not doubt this. But Evagrius's concern here is to further a climate conducive to prayer, and he speaks of control of passion and thought in this light. Again, our century may hesitate to attribute inner movements to angels or demons—a view that Evagrius did not hold either exclusively, for he speaks of the movements that flow from human nature as well. The discovery of the unconscious, however, suggests influences beyond our own conscious minds and wills. Perhaps we need to broaden our horizons to include these.

Two apophthegmata from the desert may suggest another slant on the question of peace:

> A brother lived in the Cells and in his solitude he was troubled. He went to tell Abba Theodore of Pherme about it. The old man said to him, 'Go, be more humble in your aspirations, place yourself under obedience and live with others.' Later, he came back to the old man and said, 'I do not find any peace with others.' The old man said to him, 'If you are not at peace either alone or with others, why have you become a monk? Is it not to suffer trials? Tell me how many years you have worn the habit?' He replied, 'For eight years.' Then the old man said to him, 'I have worn the habit seventy years and on no day have I found peace. Do you expect to find peace in eight years?' At these words the brother went away strengthened.[8]

> He [Abba Elias] also said, 'If the spirit does not sing with the body, labour is in vain. Whoever loves tribulation will obtain joy and peace later on.'[9]

Not flight from struggle, then, but perseverance in "work" and struggle is the way to peace. As the first example shows, flight into solitude from others and to others from solitude still remains flight.

Another interesting insight on the meaning of *apatheia* in the desert occurs in an article on Cassian by Adalbert de Vogue:

> The monastic life only begins when one gives oneself to *praktike*—that is, to an ascesis oriented toward the acquisition of the virtues and their queen, charity. When this latter, which is synonymous with *apatheia*, complete purity, has taken possession of the heart, then the road is free for a third renunciation in which the spirit transcends the visible to establish itself in contemplation of the invisible.[10]

Once again, these few lines are extraordinarily dense in terms both of their doctrine and of the presuppositions that lie behind them. To Cassian, the aim of life in the desert—as well as the life of those living the same ideal elsewhere—was purity of heart. This purity of heart he equates with both charity and peace. This is the aim of ascesis and also its fruit. And it is also the preparation par excellence for contemplation. The essentials of desert theology are well summarized here, and their beauty and solidity can perhaps lead us to forgive whatever semi-Pelagian nuances may be implied in dreaming of "complete purity" or too total a transcendence of the visible.

Even after saying all this, however, one can reflect on other effects of this inner peace. Discernment and clarity of judgment also become possible out of this root of peace.

> To distinguish good from evil without error is a light of true knowledge. . . . When the sea is calm, fishermen perceive the movement of its depths to such a point that hardly any of the creatures which move along its tracks escapes them; but when the sea is tossed about by winds, it hides in its sombre movement what it readily reveals in the smiling surface of its tranquillity. And then we see that the art of those who practise the wiles of fishing is of no effect.[11]

This image of a clear sea revealing its depths is a beautiful one to express what is being said here. We never see all the creatures moving in our depths! But at least we can try to keep the water a bit clear, and this is the work of honesty and humility which help peace.

The quotations here studied as a mere sampling among others suggest some interesting conclusions about peace. Once again the reflections and observations of depth psychology concerning mental and emotional health seem to point in the same direction as those of the oldest spiritual traditions of the West. The deep peace and integration that flow from examination of the roots of our psychic wounds and from struggle with and healing of what went and goes amiss at those roots is not a luxury for a few contemplatives behind cloister walls or for a few privileged analysands. Without this integration, human relationships and marriages suffer and individual happiness is made difficult. Ignatius of Loyola was to speak of peace as a criterion for the "discernment of spirits,"[12] and long before him Cassian spoke of the importance of this discernment or discretion to attain purity of heart.[13] The healing of which psychoanalysis speaks, as seen above, may not be, in its fulness, available to all, just as the union of which John of the Cross speaks may not be either on its highest levels. Not that God does not wish to give it, but that it always remains gift, not the result of human effort. Each individual on earth has specific gifts, calls, goals. But the lack of peace, rigidity, externalism, agitation that are condemned in both the psychological and the spiritual traditions do need healing and can often be at least partially helped. The importance and value of this work and struggle are suggested by the value of its goal, peace. For it seems folly to hope for a world at peace unless something of this same peace is won in the inner sphere of each person's heart.

Thomas Merton, writing on "Final Integration: Toward a 'Monastic Therapy,'" said along the same lines:

> Final integration is a state of transcultural maturity far beyond mere social adjustment, which always implies partiality and compromise. The man who is "fully born" has an entirely "inner experience of life." He apprehends his life fully and wholly from an inner ground that is at once more universal than the empirical ego and yet entirely his own. He is in a certain sense "cosmic" and "universal man." He has attained a deeper, fuller identity than that of his limited ego-self which is only a fragment of his being. He is in a certain sense identified with everybody: or in the familiar language of the New Testament . . . he is "all things to all men."

. . . With this view of life he is able to bring perspective, liberty and spontaneity into the lives of others. The finally integrated man is a peacemaker, and that is why there is such a desperate need for our leaders to become such men of insight.[14]

Jung believed the same, but in the process of waiting perhaps the most constructive thing to do is for each person to move toward this aim, as far as he or she can. To quote Jesus, who himself was a man of peace, it is the peacemakers among us who, as children of God, bring His Kingdom as far as possible on earth—and that Kingdom is first of all in people's hearts.

·15·

THE SACRED MARRIAGE

Speaking of the image of the "royal marriage," which he refers to elsewhere as *hierosgamos,* the sacred or holy marriage, Jung writes:

> We are dealing with an eternal image, an archetype, from which man can turn away his mind for a time but never permanently. Whenever this image is obscured his life loses its proper meaning and consequently its balance. . . . If he no longer sees the meaning of his life in its fulfilment, and no longer believes in man's eternal right to this fulfilment, then he has betrayed and lost his soul, substituting for it a madness which leads to destruction, as our time demonstrates all too clearly.[1]

What is this sacred marriage to which Jung refers? He speaks of it as "the mystery of the coniunctio, in which the extreme opposites unite, night is wedded with day. . . ."[2] and points out the religious use of this theme, notably in the Apocalypse. Speaking of religion, he also says of this marriage:

> It is the prefiguration and anticipation of a future condition, a glimmering of an unspoken, half-conscious union of ego and non-ego. Rightly called a *unio mystica,* it is the fundamental experience of all religions that have any life in them and have not yet degenerated into confessionalism; that have safeguarded the mystery of which the others know only the rites it produced — empty bags from which the gold has long since vanished.[3]

Earlier reflection on the unconscious seen as the animus or anima has revealed Jung's idea that to become whole each person must come into contact not only with the shadow but also with the contrasexual in him or herself. The resulting wholeness is more "androgynous" than the individual still out of contact with these deeper elements in the psyche. But there is more, for this union leads to the Self. Any brief explanation falsifies, for the concept involved is richer than any summary. One of Jung's longer and more intricate works, *Mysterium Coniunctionis,* deals with this theme—notably in terms of the alchemical tradition which so interested him. This book, too, would be impossible to summarize, but a few basic elements and lines of thought which draw heavily on symbolism much used in Christian circles can indicate some of its content and the progression toward the holy marriage in Jungian thought.

Speaking of a spirit he sees as the "exact opposite of the Christian pneuma," Jung writes: "This spirit corresponds to that part of the psyche which has not been assimilated to consciousness and whose transformation and integration are the outcome of a long and wearisome opus."[4] One comes to live the Christian spirit only by going through the "work" of which earlier pages have spoken repeatedly, but this same process is necessary for psychological wholeness. What is the movement of this process?

> The alchemists understood the return to chaos as an essential part of the opus. It was the stage of the *nigredo* and *mortificatio,* which was then followed by the "purgatorial fire" and the *albedo.*[5]

The underlying imagery here suggests the chaos "before the second day of creation, before the separation of the opposites and hence before the advent of consciousness."[6] What, then, is being said?

Jung's conviction about the importance of the opposites and their union has already been discussed, as well as the fact that humans reach a first stage of clarity by choosing one opposite rather than the other. Going into chaos involves the readiness to admit that this choice needs reinspection—that one needs, now, to make the other choice without neglecting the original one. It also involves facing the chaotic world of the shadow, of the unconscious itself.

This involves an excruciating situation to live through and one that reason alone cannot handle. For it is a matter here of going, or being brought, deeper than reason, into a domain where human clarity and will do not suffice. Hence the blackness (*nigredo*) and sense of dying (*mortificatio*) before the white (*albedo*) which is the combination of all colors can result.

This may all sound like orthodox Christian theology. In fact, the alchemical position, and Jung's, use language that hardly sounds "orthodox":

> The spirit of chaos is indispensable to the work, and it cannot be distinguished from the "gift of the Holy Ghost" any more than the Satan of the Old Testament can be distinguished from Yahweh. The unconscious is both good and evil and yet neither, the matrix of all potentialities.[7]

The concepts involved here need reflection in terms of Jung's *Answer to Job,* for example, for clarification. These will be found in Appendix 2 below, but, in the meantime, suffice it to say that Jung's point here is that the unconscious level is a- or pre-moral. Moral issues arise at a much later level in the psyche, but the morality of a person out of touch with the depths will be superficial at best. So the main point here is that the chaos of these depths must be faced and lived with, without the denial or flight that seems so much easier a solution.

Jung, referring to a work by Karl Rahner, connects the meditations on death and hell in Ignatius of Loyola's *Spiritual Exercises* with these themes. Tasting gall and wormwood and "the worm of conscience" is a contact with these depths of darkness, damnation, sin. Patristic imagery used all these themes. This is not a case of the same kind of hell-fire and damnation spirituality so well portrayed by James Joyce, among others. The purpose of the imagery is less to produce terrified compliance with the commandments out of fear of damnation than to come into touch with the kind of world-view that could inspire a Dante or many of his contemporaries. The cosmos, to them, included heaven *and* hell, virtue *and* vice, good *and* evil. This realization seems to be rare today. One wonders why.

Obviously, the whole concept of darkness, *nigredo,* is reminiscent of the imagery of John of the Cross:

This night is a painful disturbance, involving many fears, imaginings and struggles within a man. Due to the apprehension and feeling of his miseries, he suspects that he is lost and that his blessings are gone forever. The sorrow and moaning of his spirit is so deep that it turns into vehement spiritual roars and clamoring. . . . As the waters sometimes overflow in such a way that they inundate everything, this roaring and feeling so increases that in seeping through and flooding everything, it fills all one's deep affections and energies with indescribable spiritual anguish and suffering.[8]

He continues with a remark on the same theme of "work" as Jung's:

This war or combat is profound because the peace awaiting the soul must be exceedingly profound; and the spiritual suffering is intimate and penetrating because the love to be possessed by the soul will also be intimate and refined. The more intimate and highly finished the work must be, so the more intimate, careful, and pure must the labor be. . . .[9]

The imagery of water and waves is not accidental. Jung almost immediately turns to the Exodus imagery of the Red Sea—"a term for the healing and transforming baptismal water."[10]

The Red Sea drowned the Egyptians, but the Egyptians were all "non-knowers." . . . The Red Sea is a water of death for those that are "unconscious" but for those that are "conscious" it is a baptismal water of rebirth and transcendence. By "unconscious" are meant those who have no gnosis, i.e. are not enlightened as to the nature and destiny of man in the cosmos. In modern language it would be those who have no knowledge of the contents of the personal and collective unconscious.[11]

One can go through the waves and the waters without drowning, then, if one is "conscious." "Unconscious" people "who attempt to cross the sea without being purified and without the guidance of enlightenment . . . get stuck in the unconscious and suffer a spiritual death in so far as they cannot get beyond their one-sidedness."

There is no escape, then, from facing the opposites—no escape, at least, short of this kind of spiritual death. Perhaps, ultimately, it is simply a question of whether one is ready to go into the water consciously or whether one will simply be submerged. Measuring our own and our world's possibilities for evil makes this question increasingly real. But consciousness is painful. Jung remarks:

> The other side of the Red Sea is the other side of Creation. The arrival in the desert is a "genesis outside of generation." . . . There the "gods of destruction" and the "god of salvation" are all together. . . . By this is obviously meant the destructive and constructive powers of the unconscious. This *coincidentia op-positorum* forms a parallel to the Messianic state of fulfilment described in Isaiah 11:6 ff and 35:5 ff., though with one important difference: the place of "genesis outside of generation"—presumably an *opus contra naturam*—is clearly not paradise but . . . the desert and the wilderness. Everyone who becomes conscious of even a fraction of his unconscious gets outside his own time and social stratum into a kind of solitude. . . . But only there is it possible to meet the "god of salvation."[12]

It becomes increasingly apparent as one progresses with this book that all the previous themes discussed in other terms come together here—solitude, the desert, paradise, peace, as well as the shadow, the opposites, and others. Jung is not an exponent of the "return to paradise" theme dear to the Fathers of the Church. For him the departure from Eden was definitive, but, of course, it was for them, too. It is, then, all the more striking to note his Isaian imagery above. Once again, there is a paradox—the solitude of the desert and its fulfilment. The same result occurs when Jung studies another set of images—those connected with an alchemical text concerning "the chariot with four wheels."

Jung uses this image to reflect on the symbolism of the quaternity—"one of the oldest patterns of order known to man."[13] Four seems traditionally to represent perfection, totality. There are four elements, four basic functions of the personality, as well as other symbolic fours he finds in the tradition he is studying. So, he concludes, "The 'chariot of Aristotle' can be understood in this sense as a symbol of the self."[14] This chariot is placed in the "sea of the unconscious" for "incubation by means of 'self-heating'":

> By this is obviously meant a state of introversion in which the unconscious content is brooded over and digested. During this operation all relations with the outside world are broken off . . .

outside everything is quiet and still, but deep inside the psyche the wheels go on turning, performing those cyclic evolutions which bring the mandala of the total personality, the ground-plan of the self, closer to consciousness.[15]

This, then, will be the fruit of the whole process—an awareness of the deeper, truer self which is in the likeness of God in a way the surface self cannot know. This is the purpose of going through the darkness and the sea. Later Jung elaborates further:

Self-knowledge—in the total meaning of the word—is not a one-sided intellectual pastime but a journey through the four continents, where one is exposed to all the dangers of land, sea, air, and fire. Any total act of recognition worthy of the name embraces the four—or 360!—aspects of existence. Nothing may be disregarded.[16]

He goes on to say that the Ignatian recommendation of "imagination through the five senses" and the exhortation to imitate Christ "by the use of his [the retreatant's] senses" was aiming at "the fullest possible 'realization' of the object of contemplation."[17] Not separation from the material, then, nor from the ego or the body is the aim but rather their integration. One can remember in this connection the remarks of Teresa of Avila on the place of the humanity of Christ in contemplation.[18] One can also consider the following quotation from Louf:

This constant interaction between the heart and the body, which is spoken of in the monastic writings of all periods, is *the* typical feature of the technique of Christian prayer. A whole anthropology, a distinctive insight into the structure of man underlies it. The idea is certainly not that the physical is to make way for the spiritual and the material for the immaterial. . . . On the contrary, by way of grace and prayer the body returns to its original state. . . . From being a *body-of-death* it becomes the *body-of-life.*[19]

Jung writes:

In Christ's case the victory and liberation of the Primordial Man were said to be complete, so that the labours of the alchemists would seem to be superfluous. We can only assume that the alchemists were of a different opinion, and that they sought their remedy against wrath and pain in order to complete what they considered to be Christ's unfinished work of redemption.[20]

This passage suggests well what Jung himself may have seen in the writings of the alchemists. It also suggests what they may have to say to us.

The next image studied by Jung is that of ascent and descent, and it confirms, to him, the points already made. The texts speak of the importance of both movements, not just ascent.

The 'sun-moon child' who is laid in the cradle of the four elements, attains full power through them and the earth, rises to heaven and receives full power of the upper world, and then returns to earth, accomplishing, it seems, a triumph of wholeness ("gloria totius mundi").[21]

This movement of ascent to heaven and descent to earth that transfigures is repeated again and again in the texts he studies. This is about "realization," in the literal sense of that term. Some texts present the same movement in a different order: "Mylius says that the earth cannot ascend unless heaven comes down first."[22] In any case, the two opposites are always needed.

Ascent and descent, above and below, up and down, represent an emotional realization of opposites, and this realization gradually leads, or should lead, to their equilibrium. . . . This vacillating between the opposites and being tossed back and forth means being contained *in* the opposites . . . so that the painful suspension between opposites gradually changes into the bilateral activity of the point in the centre. This is the "liberation from opposites," the *nirdvandva* of Hindu philosophy, though it is not really a philosophical but rather a psychological development.[23]

Out of the duality, then, is born unity. But Jung is the first to say that, if the ascent and descent meant a "freeing of the soul from the shackles of darkness, or unconsciousness; its ascent to heaven the widening of consciousness," nonetheless finally there would be "the return to earth, to hard reality . . . endowed with the powers of the Above."[24] In this light one can once more remember Plato's cave.

Jung will summarize what has been said so far in terms of reflection on astrological or color images. The human person will pass through the darkness of "man's confusion and lostness" and, if analysis is the process of choice to continue, will reflect on the contents of the unconscious as they emerge in fantasies and dreams. Thus the narrow horizons of the conscious standpoint widen.

> The situation is now gradually illuminated as is a dark night by the rising moon. The illumination comes to a certain extent from the unconscious, since it is mainly dreams that put us on the track of enlightenment. This dawning light corresponds to the *albedo,* the moonlight which in the opinion of the alchemists heralds the rising sun. The growing redness (*rubedo*) which now follows denotes an increase of warmth and light coming from the sun, consciousness. This corresponds to the increasing participation of consciousness, which now begins to react emotionally to the contents produced by the unconscious. At first the process of integration is a "fiery" conflict, but gradually it leads over to the "melting" or synthesis of the opposites. The alchemists term this the rubedo, in which the marriage of the red man and the white woman, Sol and Luna, is consummated. Although the opposites flee from one another they nevertheless strive for balance, since a state of conflict is too inimical to life to be endured indefinitely.[25]

Before reflecting on the content of this passage, let us compare the imagery with that of John of the Cross:

> This night withdraws the spirit from its customary manner of experience to bring it to the divine experience which is foreign to every human way. . . . He is being made a stranger to his usual knowledge and experience of things so that annihilated in this respect he may be informed with the divine . . . that he may be reborn in the life of the spirit by means of this divine inflow. . . .[26]

> The very loving light and wisdom into which the soul will be transformed is that which in the beginning purges and prepares it.[27]

She (the soul) very appropriately calls this divine light "the rising dawn" which means the morning. Just as the rise of morning dispels the darkness of night and unveils the light of day, so this spirit, quieted and put to rest in God, is elevated from the darkness of natural knowledge to the morning light of the supernatural knowledge of God. This morning light is not clear, as was said, but dark as night at the time of the rising dawn.[28]

Both texts, then, speak of a progression—a beginning in darkness and chaos and a continuing process in which the very cause of the original darkness becomes a source of light. To Jung, commenting on the alchemists, this enlightenment comes from the unconscious and the eventual result to be hoped for is a new balance including both conscious and unconscious in a new unity. To John of the Cross, the night is an inflowing of God and His light and love which, at first, purify and darken—as fire blackens wood—and then enlighten and enkindle, transform. The parallelism is not difficult to see, though this is, as always, similarity combined with difference of view.

What results from this process? Jung remarks:

The ascent through the planetary spheres . . . meant something like a shedding of the characterological qualities indicated by the horoscope, a retrogressive liberation from the character imprinted by the archons. . . . The men of late antiquity . . . felt their psychic situation to be fatally dependent on the compulsion of the stars . . . a feeling which may be compared with that inspired by the modern theory of heredity, or rather by the pessimistic use of it.[29]

To have passed through all the spheres is, he adds, to be free of compulsions, to have "become like a god."[30] This may sound inflated. Jung adds at once that today's psychology makes more modest claims.

What before was a burden unwillingly borne and blamed upon the entire family, is seen by the greatest possible insight (which can be very modest!) to be no more than the possession of one's own personality, and one realizes—as though this were not self-evident!—that one cannot possibly live from anything except what one is.[31]

This sounds both realistic and very modest. It needs, however, to be seen in terms of the view it is commenting on: "The soul, which was imprinted with a horoscopic character at the time of its descent into birth, conscious now of its godlikeness, beards the archons in their lairs and carries the light undisguised down into the darkness of the world."[32] "What one is," then, needs to be seen both realistically, or humbly, and in terms of its "godlikeness" as well. Truth avoids single extremes. Jung would say both opposites are needed.

Jung reflects, then, on the notions of mystery, the secret, silence, since the text he is reflecting on now refers to prolonged conversations of importance with Mercurius, a wisdom figure, but does not reveal their content. One thinks, in this connection, of the adage that those who know do not speak, and those who speak do not know.

> In the encounter with life and the world there are experiences that are capable of moving us to long and thorough reflection, from which, in time, insights and convictions grow up. . . . The unfolding of these experiences is regulated, as it were, by two archetypes: the anima, who expresses *life*, and the "Wise Old Man" who personifies *meaning*. . . . It is therefore only logical that, towards the end of the descent he (the author) should meet Thrice-Greatest Hermes, the fount of all wisdom. This aptly describes the character of that spirit or thinking which you do not, like an intellectual operation, perform yourself, as the "little god of this world," but which happens to you as though it came from another, and greater. . . .[33]

True wisdom, then, is given. We do not produce it ourselves, and it is certainly not the fruit of the working of the intellect. "The long reflection, the 'immensa meditatio' of the alchemists is defined as an 'internal colloquy with another, who is invisible.'"[34] It is surely unnecessary to trace the parallels to this thought in spiritual tradition.

Jung concludes this chapter with a reflection on the imagery of salt and then, in the next section, discusses that of the King and Queen. The royal imagery, he notes, was originally associated with the divine, as study of early mythologies shows. The various myths concerning the death of the king also suggest archetypal themes, as do those concerning his incarnation and transformation "from an imperfect state into a perfect, whole, and incorruptible essence."[35]

This transformation often occurs through his being murdered or sacrificed. It also occurs through his relation with the queen who is his mother, sister, wife. This Queen Mother has the capacity to grant rebirth, for she is also "the water and the containing vessel . . . the feminine principle best characterized by *yin*."[36] She is, in other words, "the feminine aspect of the father-son."[37] The alchemists also used animal imagery for the king, signifying his return to his animal nature and also facilitating the use of incestuous imagery like that of brother-sister or mother-son relationships. These latter will be recognized from Egyptian as well as scriptural love poetry where the symbolic meaning of incest is different from the literal. The psychological significance of all this imagery has been discussed in the preceding chapters.

> Like the rose the figure of the mother-beloved shines in all the hues of heavenly and earthly love. She is the chaste bride and whore who symbolizes the prima materia which "nature left imperfected." It is clear from the material we have cited that this refers to the anima. She is that piece of chaos which is everywhere and yet hidden . . . a totality in the form of a *massa confusa,* yet a substance endowed with every quality in which the splendor of the hidden deity can be revealed.[38]

The king, on the other hand, stands for consciousness.

> During her pregnancy, therefore, the queen undergoes something akin to a psychotherapeutic treatment, whereby her consciousness is enriched by a knowledge of the collective unconscious, and, we may assume, by her inner participation in the conflict between her spiritual and chthonic nature. . . . Failure to know what one is doing acts like guilt and must be paid for as dearly. The conflict may even turn out to be an advantage since, without it, there could be no reconciliation and no birth of a superordinate third thing.[39]

And this is the point of the whole marriage—that from it is born this "third thing" which in some of the texts is the Christ, in others the self, and in still others various other connected symbols, notably that of the lapis, "a living being endowed with soul and spirit and an incorruptible body."[40]

The complexity of the alchemical imagery is not easy to understand. Jung uses it, however, as a study of the individuation process which he sees the alchemists as having projected out onto matter. But one must not speak too simplistically of projection: "The art is queen of the alchemist's heart . . . and in his art and its allegories the drama of his own soul, his individuation process, is played out."[41] Jung is constantly aware, however, that the process goes beyond the human level. He quotes at length a poem of Angelus Silesius of which a part reads:

> . . . God make me pregnant, and his Spirit shadow me,
> That God may rise up in my soul and shatter me.
>
> What good does Gabriel's, "Ave, Mary" do
> Unless he give me that same greeting too?[42]

Jung comments: "He was speaking of something greater than the effects of grace in the sacraments: God Himself, through the Holy Ghost, enters the work of man, in the form of inspiration as well as by direct intervention in the miraculous transformation."[43] This was something that did not occur in alchemy. So, asks Jung, why the enthusiasm of the adepts? Partly, he believes, because "There occurred during the chemical procedure psychic projections which brought unconscious contents to light"[44]—a very therapeutic experience. And partly because the seeds of what grew into Protestantism, mysticism, empirical science, and ability to appropriate the religious philosophies of the East lay here. Alchemy was a beginning. It is not possible here to trace all the details and imagery of the texts or of Jung's treatment. He stresses, however, that "the inner spiritual man bears a resemblance to Christ. . . . It [this idea] is the logical consequence of a spiritual situation in which the historical figure had long since disappeared from consciousness, while his spiritual presence was stressed all the more strongly in the form of the inner Christ or God who is born in the soul of man."[45]

Concluding the chapter on the king and queen, Jung writes:

> It would certainly be desirable if a psychological explanation and clarification could be given of what seems to be indicated by the mythologem of the marriage. But the psychologist does not

feel responsible for the existence of what cannot be known. . . .
The union of conscious and unconscious symbolized by the royal
marriage is a mythological idea which on a higher level assumes
the character of a psychological concept. . . . The psychological
union of opposites is an intuitive idea which covers the phe-
nomenology of this process. It is not an "explanatory" hypothesis
for something that, by definition, transcends our powers of conception. For when we say that conscious and unconscious unite,
we are saying in effect that this process is inconceivable.[46]

Jung's thought here meets with that of apophatic or negative
mystical theology which speaks of the impossibility of speaking
adequately of God and also, as a result, of union with him. The
union of conscious and unconscious, in Jung's understanding of
the latter, relates with this theme.

Chapter 5 of his book discusses the same question in terms of the
imagery of Adam and Eve, Primordial Man and Woman, parents
of all the living, brother and sister, spouses.

Just as the rice spoils in the defective state, so too man degenerates, whether from the malignity of the gods or from his
own stupidity or sin, and comes in conflict with his original
nature. He forgets his origination from the human ancestor,
and a ritual anamnesis is therefore required. Thus the archetype
of Man, the Anthropos, is constellated and forms the essential
core of the great religions. In the idea of the *homo maximus* the
Above and Below of creation are reunited.[47]

The reference to rice and anamnesis concerns the myths and
rituals of some religions sometimes called primitive, but Jung also
refers to the Taoist view that the prime situation of distress lies in
"the separation of heaven and earth" for unfathomable reasons, so
that they can now come together again only if the wide person
re-establishes Tao in himself by ritual meditation. He refers here
to the story of the rainmaker quoted in Chapter 7 above. The
Adam-Eve imagery, then, tends back to that of wholeness.

The subject of transformation is not the empirical man, however
much he may identify with the "old Adam," but Adam the Primordial Man, the archetype within us. The black Shulamite
herself represents the first transformation: it is the coming to

consciousness of the black anima, the Primordial Man's feminine aspect. The second, or *solificatio*, is the conscious differentiation of the masculine aspect—a far more difficult task. Every man feels identical with this, though in reality he is not. . . . It is . . . much easier to see the blackness in projected form. . . . But the masculine aspect is as unfathomable as the feminine aspect. It would certainly not be fitting for the empirical man, no matter how swollen his ego-feelings to appropriate the whole range of Adam's heights and depths. . . .[48]

This inner archetype, Adam Kadmon, is a parallel of Christ. "The coming to consciousness of Adam Kadmon" would be "an archetypal totality transcending the sexes." Nonetheless, a symbolism beyond the Christian is needed here, says Jung, for the transformation process does not end in the second Adam and the dove but in the lapis, which symbolizes the self.

This is a thought that goes beyond the Christian world of ideas and involves a mystery consummated in and through man. It is as though the drama of Christ's life were, from now on, located in man as its living carrier. As a result of this shift, the events formulated in dogma are brought within range of psychological experience and become recognizable in the process of individuation.[49]

Jung's final chapter is on the *coniunctio* itself. This was the central idea of the alchemical procedure, according to one of the first researchers in the field. The opposite chemicals used usually came from the quaternity of elements and "The alchemical description of the beginning corresponds psychologically to a primitive consciousness which is constantly liable to break up into individual affective processes—to fall apart, as it were, in four directions. . . . The result of the synthesis was consequently conceived by the adept as self-knowledge."[50]

Another very important concept emerges here—that of the *unus mundus,* personified in alchemical literature by Mercurius who also symbolizes the collective unconscious. All things came out of unity—the one world (*unus mundus*) God created. The mandala, with its central point, is seen as symbolizing "the ultimate unity of all archetypes as well as of the multiplicity of the phenomenal world, and is therefore the empirical equivalent of the metaphysical concept of a *unus mundus*."⁵¹ The alchemical *coniunctio* is seen as "a restoration of the original state of the cosmos and the divine unconsciousness of the world."⁵² It is, thus, the "union of *Yang* and *Yin* in *Tao*" and also a premonition of synchronicity, for "If mandala symbolism is the psychological equivalent of the *unus mundus*, then synchronicity is its parapsychological equivalent"⁵³ for it reveals the universal interrelationship of events.

This concept of the *unus mundus* is important because the mental union previously discussed was only a first stage to the author Jung here follows (Dorn). The second requires that this "mental union, that is the unity of spirit and soul, is conjoined with the body. But a consummation of the mysterium coniunctionis can be expected only when the unity of spirit, soul, and body is made one with the original *unus mundus*.⁵⁴ Jung links this whole imagery with that of the Assumption of Mary, seen as a wedding feast, a *hierosgamos*. And Jung repeats the above themes in his explanation of this feast. A union of reason or intellect with feeling brings increase of self-knowledge and maturity but "its reality . . . is validated only by a union with the physical world of the body."⁵⁵ This is not to deny that originally there may be need to go through a stage when the rationality of the mind is freed from disturbances arising from affectivity, but this leads to a dissociation of the personality which must later be healed. Jung points out that psychotherapy as well as spirituality requires the first stage, with its asceticism and growth in consciousness, but development must not stop here. If the second stage, of union with the body, is not attained, union with the *unus mundus* cannot be either.

Jung gives details of the alchemical process and then asks what are the psychological equivalents. The first is the therapeutic process of making conscious and dissolving projections which falsify one's view of the world and of others. "The declared aim of the treatment is to set up a rational, spiritual-psychic position over against the turbulence of the emotions." Later:

> The self as the total personality, the healing and "whole-making" medicine which is recognized even by modern psychotherapy, was combined with spiritual and conjugal love . . . sexuality . . . the whole soul. All this was united with . . . the *anima mundi* extracted from inert matter, or the God-image imprinted on the world . . . that is to say the whole of the conscious man is

surrendered to the self, to the new centre of personality which
replaces the former ego.[56]

This quotation has omitted the alchemical parallels which Jung
follows closely. He sees the alchemical process as paralleled today
by that of active imagination which he describes as bringing a kind
of solution to a problem of opposites become too strong for repression. The appropriate use of imagery can prepare a real synthesis where none seemed possible, and he strongly suggests fixing
the whole process in writing when it occurs.

Jung remarks that the alchemists called the process he sees as
coming to terms with the unconscious "meditation." Confrontation
with the shadow led to the state called *nigredo,* chaos, melancholia.
What is now called meditation in the West "where a theme is sub-
jectively chosen by the meditant or prescribed by an instructor, as
in the Ignatian *Exercitia* or in certain theosophical exercises that
developed under Indian influence" is not helpful for the end Jung
proposes. "These methods are of value only for increasing concen-
tration and consolidating consciousness, but have no significance
as regards effecting a synthesis of the personality"[57] for they are
trying to shield consciousness from the unconscious and suppress
the latter. (This observation may explain some of the alienation
found in religious circles that practice meditation in such a way.)
But where meditation opens itself to the unconscious (one can
think of the "process meditation" of Progoff, for one example), this
criticism does not hold. Jung comments further:

> The *unio mentalis* . . . means knowledge of oneself. In contradis-
> tinction to the modern prejudice that self-knowledge is nothing
> but knowledge of the ego, the alchemists regarded the self as a
> substance incommensurable with the ego, hidden in the body,
> and identical with the image of God. This view fully accords
> with the Indian idea of *purusha-atman.* . . . This "unum" is
> *nirdvandva* (free from the opposites), like the *atman* (self).[58]

Once again, then, Jung has found a conjunction of different
disciplines and cultures speaking of and moving toward a same
aim.

The same process that appears in the individual also appears in
culture. To grow, Western civilization had to move beyond "An-

cient man's sensuous delight in the body and in nature,"[59] which Christianity helped it to do. But in the process, these delights moved into the realm of sin and of shadow. Christianity led to a process of greater consciousness, but did not reach that of union with the world of the body. Jung believes it was this intuition that pushed on the alchemists in their experimentation and thirst for knowledge, and he remarks that Newman's thought on the development of dogma is important for an understanding of what has really occurred, notably in Christianity itself where the archetypes can continue to develop.

For the individual, this same process of transformation requires, first, growing knowledge of the unconscious. Active imagination (in the technical sense in which Jung uses the term) helps, as was said. So does analysis. But, as Jung points out, the transference characteristic of the early stages of analysis is something the analysand must outgrow, putting his or her hand to the plow personally in a way that no one else can do for one. The realization emerges with time that "his fantasy is a real psychic process which is happening to him personally. . . . If you recognize your own involvement you yourself must enter into the process with your personal reactions"[60] or become a mere spectator, remaining unchanged. "You will never make the One unless you become one yourself" remarks Jung, quoting his author, Dorn. One can also, of course, become a victim of one's own fantasy and lose oneself in the unconscious, but not by entering into the fantasy "as you really are." "This is where insight, the *unio mentalis*, begins to become real. What you are now creating is the beginning of individuation, whose immediate goal is the experience and production of the symbol of totality."[61]

It is this importance of imagery — and of the independence of the analyst that such a realization produces — which leads to the usefulness of artistic expression of these images. Thus integration of the unconscious is furthered and a deeper meaning to life can be found. The result is a kind of faith, of self-reliance, of inner certainty which a mandala can express, for it portrays the self in matter. This is a solution to the second stage of the *coniunctio.* The third involves "the eternal Ground of all empirical being"[62]: it is "the relation or identity of the personal with the superpersonal atman, and of the individual tao with the universal tao."[63] Jung remarks that "the visualization of the self is a window into eternity"[64] which the medievals and Oriental peoples use. The self here is "man as he is, and the indescribable and superempirical totality of that same man"[65] which no one can know completely. Empirical reality, he concludes, has a transcendental background, a fact that Plato's parable of the cave expresses well. This background is the *unus mundus.* But the body-soul split Christianity has often encouraged must be overcome to find this. But also, this stage can be reached only *"if the center experienced proves to be a spiritus rector of daily life,"*[66] and this *"experience of the self is always a defeat for the ego."*[57] (Italics Jung's.)

Jung reflects at length on the knowledge of metaphysical reality and concludes that our thinking is subjective at best. Nonetheless, this fact does not imply the nonexistence of such reality, which he regards as certain. He is aware that the human person is very much at the center of the picture in his thought, but in Christianity, "God became very man. No psychology in the world could vie with the dignity that God Himself has accorded to him."[68] These are the concluding lines of his book.

How, then, would one summarize Jung's thought on the sacred marriage? It is a union of opposites, notably the human conscious and unconscious, but by this very fact it involves more than the human. It opens out into the infinite and eternal, as well as—in Christian terms—into the very personal world that is God's transcendence. It requires the integration of the body with the psyche and the readiness to make the self, rather than the ego, central; and it passes through the stages of increasing withdrawal of projections, increasing realism—as a result—, increasing independence and readiness to deal with the reality of the psychic and spiritual until, through this process, awareness of the transcendent as a background for the whole of empirical reality occurs. This transcendent reality is, however, as near as one's self—and as real.

After this prolonged look at Jung's thought on the sacred marriage, let us reflect on the same theme in Western spirituality. In that tradition, marriage has various roots. One can remember Christ speaking of Himself as the Bridegroom[69] or John the Baptist making the same reference.[70] One can think of St. Paul speaking of marriage in terms of Christ and the Church.[71] One can, further, remember early texts on virginity speaking of consecrated virgins as brides of Christ, as was said in Chapter 3 above, and one can also remember Origen's commentary on the Song of Songs. According to Dom Cuthbert Butler, however, marriage symbolism really came into its own in the Western world with Bernard of Clairvaux's commentary on that same scriptural text.[72] Butler writes, after tracing the early history of the concept: "Though a natural step, it is a step forward in allegory to look on the union of the soul with God in contemplation as a spiritual marriage."[73]

Introducing this commentary of Bernard's in a new translation, Corneille Halflants traces the steps of progress toward such a "marriage."

> St Bernard compares the sinful soul to an unfaithful spouse who is abandoned by her lovers; the motive of her conversion is not a noble one—she is forced to return to her lawful husband. This return to God is possible because human nature, although wounded, retains a likeness to God. Moreover, if such an enterprise is manifestly beyond its strength the help granted it by the Word will supply for this.[74]

The reader familiar with Scripture will recognize in these first few lines echoes of the prophetic literature, notably Hosea. But the comparison of infidelity to God and to the Covenant with adultery is a theme recurring from the early pages of the Judeo-Christian Scriptures. Covenant love, *hesed,* is the basis of human relationship with God in this tradition. It is a choice—made first by God but ratified by the human persons involved. And there are covenants before that with Israel. These covenants, notably the later ones, involve a people, not just individuals. But it is also the individual who lives or not by this covenant. This is a major scriptural theme.

The scriptural and patristic writers who developed this thought were, then, not producing something new. They were squarely in the lines of this tradition, though later centuries developed it more. What has this thought to do with Jung's?

We have seen that Jung drew on alchemical sources which were nourished by some of the same traditions though they added other notes as well. Jung himself stresses frequently the note of the self as *imago Dei* and the nuptial imagery as well. Where does this thought converge with Bernard's and where not?

To Bernard, comments Halflants,

> The road back to God supposes love of Christ. . . . The sensible love in the heart of man for even the body of Christ and all that he has accomplished and taught in the flesh holds . . . [a] decisive place in the spiritual doctrine of the Abbot of Clairvaux.[75]

It will be remembered that Jung can be negative about what he considers externalization in devotion to Christ.[76] This may be a real point of difference between him and mystics like Bernard or Teresa of Avila. On the other hand, Bernard speaks of a progression from "sensible emotion" to a more spiritual kind of love very reminiscent of Plato's discussion of the development of love in his *Dialogues*[77] and one which lends itself to reflection on Jung's remarks on the importance of the body, though Jung places this stage later in the journey toward union than Bernard. Halflants writes again:

> St Bernard does not believe it possible to suppress with impunity the indestructible force of sense love. On the other hand, it would be illusory to believe that even with the help of grace one could quickly succeed in changing carnal into spiritual love. What is to be done? Present to carnal love an object which is proportionate to it and more delightful than any sinful creature . . . the humanity of Christ . . . dwelling place of the divinity, which will gradually reveal itself as it draws the soul into its holiness.[78]

This text bears serious reflection. Many generations of religious before the Council were frequently afraid to deal with the imagery of the Song of Songs. The early Cistercians clearly were not. They seem to have come from a time more ready to look at the reality of the senses, passions, sexuality as they found it, and to use such reality as a kind of stepping-stone toward a more spiritual love. This latter seems to have been born not of denial of the former but of a growth beyond it—once more, along the same lines mentioned by Plato. One might conclude, then, to a certain universality in the understanding of human growth in love, at least until recent times—the idea that healthy spiritual love grows out of a human base. One might also see a certain parallelism of this thought with Jung's conception of the need to develop first the ego and the tasks of the ego in this world before the human person can be ready to deal with the "marriage" of the conscious and unconscious of which he speaks. (In India, of course, marriage is an earlier stage preceding that of the total contemplative search for God.[79])

The opening lines of the Song are the Bride's request for her Lover's kiss. Commenting on Bernard in this regard, Halflants sketches the meaning of the spiritual marriage for this author. "The exceptional quality of the grace" being asked in this kiss is "a participation in the beatific life of the Trinity."[80] In Christian terms, this is both the highest grace that can be given, the goal of life, and yet also that to which anyone "born of God" is called, a grace already begun in an inchoate way.[81] Halflants remarks that Bernard constantly stresses human emotion and passion: "While knowledge and understanding are necessary, nonetheless to be converted to God and to walk upon the road that leads to salvation, it is not enough to be instructed, one must also be 'affected,' i.e. moved or seized by grace."[82] Once more, it is the issue of the heart, rather than of the head, but the heart in the sense that includes the whole of human emotional life. One does not come to God as a disembodied spirit.

Bernard speaks of the transitoriness of this grace of union:

> Always it is for so short a time! Just as one thinks he has him, he suddenly slips away. If he sometimes permits himself to be laid hold of, it is not for long. Swiftly he departs, as if fleeing from your embrace.[83]

Halflants continues his explanation of this grace of union in terms reminiscent of Evagrius and the desert:

> The purity of the soul must be so great that it is entirely freed of all sense images. In a word, there is nothing of sense or imagination in this communing of God and the soul; instead, it is privileged to receive the Word in the very depths of its being. He is there; not in figure, but in reality; he cannot be seen, but he reveals his presence by the love he rouses within the soul.[84]

Does this view contradict that of the importance of the emotions? The last line of the quotation answers. Halflants is stressing, rather, that this union is not about visions, imagination, or any such kind of perception: the place where it occurs is in the depth of the soul—in the heart as it opens out to the meeting with God.

Some of these thoughts will be recognized as not unlike Jung's in Chapter 8 above. The two authors come from different vantage points—one from the standpoint of explicit Christian faith and mysticism, the other from that of psychological experience. Nonetheless, it is important to note, despite these divergences, the place where their thoughts converge as well.

Let us come to Bernard's thought on the marriage itself. Halflants introduces it:

> When love has attained to this purity of soul, the image has regained its likeness to the Word. God is love, pure love, and when the soul by its love for him is perfectly conformed to him, the spiritual marriage is consummated.[85]

In Bernard's own words: "If it [the soul] loves God perfectly then it is wed to him."[86] His theology centers on this issue of love—a love producing conformity and union. It is time, after this long introduction, to allow him to speak for himself, in Butler's careful and deliberate translation.

> The return of the soul is its conversion, that is, its turning to the Word; to be reformed by Him and to be rendered conformable to Him. In what respect? In charity. It is that conformity which makes, as it were, a marriage between the soul and the Word. . . . And if this love is perfected, the soul is wedded to the Word.[87]

Is it that simple—that love produces spiritual marriage? If the love goes to the degree where it produces conformity, says Bernard, and we shall see the agreement in John of the Cross. Bernard explains:

> What more to be desired than this love, which makes thee, O soul, no longer content with human guidance, to draw near with confidence thyself to the Word, to attach thyself with constancy to Him, to address Him familiarly and consult Him upon all subjects, to become as receptive in thy intelligence as fearless in thy desires? This is the contract of a marriage truly spiritual and sacred. And to say this is to say little; it is more than a contract, it is embracement (complexus). Embracement surely, in which perfect correspondence of wills makes of two one spirit.[88]

This love, then, is not something to do with human will alone—far from it. While human will does enter in, desire and love in the ordinary sense of the word do as well, and this is only one side of the picture. For even more important is the receptiveness that allows one to receive the counsel, the desire, the "embrace" of the Other involved in this relationship. This is why Bernard can speak of marriage.

> Love seeks neither cause nor fruit beyond itself. Its fruit is its use. I love because I love; I love that I may love. Love, then, is a great reality. It is the only one of all the movements, feelings, and affections of the soul in which the creature is able to respond to its Creator, though not upon equal terms, and to repay like with like. . . . For when God loves He desires nought else than to be loved . . . knowing that those who love Him become blessed.[89]

Blessed, of course, is another term for happy, which suggests a certain fulfillment of the purpose for which a being was created—or, in other terms, a certain sign of having come into its own.

> This is the love of the Bride, because all that she is is only love. The very being of the Bride and her only hope is love. In this the Bride abounds; with this the Bridegroom is content.[90]

This passage is reminiscent of the lines of John of the Cross discussed in Chapter 7 above. To these two writers the aim of Christian revelation and spirituality is clearly the fulfillment of love as here described, though both agree that only some people attain that end already in this life. Bernard will explain further what such love means to him.

> . . . If she loves with her whole self, nothing is wanting where all is given. Wherefore, as I have said, to love thus is to be wedded (nupsisse); because it is not possible to love thus and yet not to be greatly loved, and in the consent of the two parties consists a full and perfect marriage (connubium). Can any one doubt that the soul is first loved, by the Word, and more dearly?[91]

One difference that will have been noted from Jung is the very personal way in which Bernard sees God relating to the "soul." This same difference has been noted between, for example, Indian and Christian mysticism, where the Trinitarian note is strong in the latter, though some Christian thought in India finds Trinitarian notes in Hindu thought as well.[92]

Bernard enables us to recognize someone who has reached this stage.

> When you shall see a soul which having left all cleaves unto the Word with every thought and desire, lives only for the Word, rules itself according to the Word, nay, becomes, as it were, fruitful by the Word; which is able to say, 'To me to live is Christ and to die is gain;' then you may have much assurance that this soul is a Bride, wedded to the Word. . . .[93]

This famous text stresses the fruitfulness of this marriage—which, once more, comes not from human effort and will but from the marriage itself, as is, in fact, the case in ordinary marriage. Once again, themes from Chapter 7 will be recognizable here. The description is a beautiful summary of the kind of person Bernard sees as truly "spouse of the Word."

Bernard preached the sermons that we have been considering to his monks in the twelfth century. What was the following history of this current of thought? One Victorine current was contemporary to him and, two hundred years later, Blessed John Ruysbroeck wrote of the same theme. But it is the two great Carmelites of the sixteenth century, Teresa of Avila and John of the Cross, who have written of the subject in terms become classical ever since.

As has been said, John of the Cross's *Spiritual Canticle* is a commentary on a poem he wrote basically paraphrasing the biblical Song of Songs. In this commentary he discusses the various stages of the spiritual life leading to the spiritual marriage through a stage he calls betrothal which we shall not take time to discuss here. Suffice it to say that the beautiful and much quoted lines that follow refer to this stage.

> My Beloved is the mountains,
> And lonely wooded valleys,
> Strange islands,
> And resounding rivers
> The whistling of love-stirring breezes,
>
> The tranquil night
> At the time of the rising dawn,
> Silent music,

Sounding solitude,
The supper that refreshes and deepens love.[94]

The commentary on these lines is hardly less beautiful than the
poetry itself, but it needs to be read in the original and not summarized. John stresses the peace of this state, but, shortly there-
after, he also refers to the "absences of the Beloved" then experienced as also "very painful."[95] The Bride invokes the Holy Spirit,
symbolized by the South Wind, to come into her garden and heal
this dryness. "The soul desires this, not for her own pleasure and
glory, but because she knows her Bridegroom delights in this."[96]

John stresses that this spiritual marriage "requires the purification of all the imperfections, rebellions, and imperfect habits of the
lower part, which, by putting off the old man, is surrendered and
made subject to the higher part."[97] One remembers Bernard on
conformity. John adds, however, the need for "a singular fortitude
and a very sublime love for so strong and intimate an embrace
from God."[98] The latter, however, produces purity, beauty, and
strength, as well as requiring them. The Holy Spirit is represented
as saying to the Father and Son in the words of the Song, followed
by John's commentary:

What shall we do for our sister on the day of her courtship, for she is
little and has no breasts? If she is a wall, let us build upon it silver
bulwarks and defenses; and if she is a door, let us reinforce it with cedar
wood. [Ct. 8:8-9] The silver bulwarks and defenses refer to the
strong and heroic virtues clothed with faith, which is signified
by the silver. These heroic virtues are those of spiritual marriage
and their foundation is the strong soul, referred to by the wall.
The peaceful Bridegroom rests in the strength of these virtues
without any weakness disturbing Him. The cedar wood applies
to the affections and properties of lofty love . . . the love proper
to spiritual marriage. The bride must first be a door in order to
receive the reinforcement of cedar wood, that is, she must hold
the door of her will open to the Bridegroom that he may enter
through the complete and true "yes" of love. This is the yes of es-
pousal which is given before the spiritual marriage. The breasts
of the bride also refer to this perfect love which she should
possess in order to appear before the Bridegroom, Christ, for
the consummation of this state.[99]

Both strength and the openness and surrender of a total "yes" are, then, required of the Bride. When she shows this strength and love, the Bridegroom

> gives the bride-soul possession of peace and tranquillity by conforming the lower part to the higher, cleansing it of all its imperfections, bringing under rational control the natural faculties and motives, and quieting all the other appetites. . . .[100]

John enumerates that "the useless wanderings of the phantasy and imaginative power" must cease; the irascible and concupiscible appetites be controlled by reason; and the four passions (joy, hope, fear, sorrow) as well as the three faculties (memory, intellect, will) be perfected in regard to their objects. The result is peace and tranquillity. The bride rests so firmly in God now that neither fear from outside nor joy can draw her out and away from what she possesses within. She can now "enjoy this gentle sleep of love [in God] at will."[101]

In the following chapter, John summarizes what he means by spiritual marriage:

> It is a total transformation in the Beloved in which each surrenders the entire possession of self to the other with a certain consummation of the union of love. The soul thereby becomes divine, becomes God through participation, insofar as is possible in this life. . . . This union resembles the union of the light of a star or candle with the light of the sun, for what then sheds light is not the star or the candle, but the sun, which has absorbed the other lights into its own.[102]

> He is for her an enchanting, desirable garden. For her entire aim in all her works is the consummation and perfection of this state. She never rests until reaching it. She finds in this state a much greater abundance and fullness of God, a more secure and stable peace, and an incomparably more perfect delight than in the spiritual espousal; here it is as though she were placed in the arms of her Bridegroom. As a result she usually experiences an intimate spiritual embrace, which is a veritable embrace, by means of which she lives the life of God. The words of St. Paul are verified in this soul: *I live, now not I, but Christ lives in me.* [Gal. 2:20][103]

John speaks of the absorption in God that results but also of the things learned in this union and of the ability to praise God for what He does in others that also follows. The bride says that now "I occupy my soul and all my energy in His service,"[104] but that service is simply love, as was said in Chapter 7 above.

One would think that this state was total bliss and John does say this. He adds, however, that it involves an intense desire to enter into the "thicket" of God's judgment and ways, which includes the thicket of suffering. For "suffering is the means of her penetrating further, deep into the thicket of the delectable wisdom of God."[105] "Deep into the thicket" means even into the agony of death to see God. John takes it as a given that there are aspects of the knowledge of God reached only through suffering. He says, also, that the bride never forgets the darkness of her sins from which God's transforming power has brought her.

> Do not despise me;
> For if, before, You found me dark,
> Now truly You can look at me
> Since You have looked
> And left in me grace and beauty.[106]

She remember, then, both the darkness and the present grace.

Finally, this union leads to knowledge of God in Himself and also in the workings of His wisdom in His creatures, the "morning" and "evening" knowledge of God.[107] It leads into transformation where what Christ has by nature the bride-soul has by participation.[108] This is, of course, true in germ of every Christian, but here the germ has come to flower. This also sounds like the fulfillment of what Jung has said about an interiorized understanding of Christ.

Looking at this doctrine as a whole, one can see how like it is, in essence, to Bernard's. To both, love is the essential. To both, the result is transformation. To both, the way involves serious and demanding asceticism carried to the point of total self-giving to God. To both, the joy involved is unspeakable and the union described is truly an embrace. For John there seems to be question of a more permanent and unclouded state than for Bernard who stresses rather its transitoriness, but John, also, is really speaking of experiences rather than of states. Reflection on the work of Teresa, John's contemporary and senior, may add further light.

Given what has been said about the shadow and given also the exalted tone of much that has been said above, some of Teresa's opening remarks in treating of this subject make enjoyable reading:

> I . . . have wondered if it will not be better for me in a few words to bring my account of this Mansion to an end. I am so much afraid it will be thought that my knowledge of it comes from experience, and this makes me very much ashamed; for, knowing myself as I do for what I am, such a thought is terrible.[109]

Past generations of readers often took such protestations as a kind of empty humility that denied the truth about her graces. Teresa did not do this—except where self-revelation in public could be both dangerous and unwise. But, when she speaks of her self-perception—or self-knowledge, to quote both Jung and her—as making her ashamed to be thought in this state, she is doubtless being honest about her feelings. After reading Jung, one has rather a good frame of reference to deal with such "opposites." (Somewhere in his writings Merton remarked that being thought to have something to say on some exalted spiritual topic made him feel he needed a shower.) In any case, Teresa consoles herself with the thought that she may be dead before it is read.

After this introduction, Teresa opens the chapter by saying that God, wanting to consummate this marriage, "brings her [the soul] into this Mansion of His, which is the seventh . . . for He must needs have an abiding-place in the soul, just as He has one in Heaven."[110] In other words, the movement here, again, is toward interiority. She remarks on the importance of not thinking "of the soul as of something dark" because God is there. This is especially so of what she calls "His own mansion," the seventh, or—in other words—the deepest, and also "its [the soul's] own centre" rather than just, as in lesser levels of union, simply one's "higher part." To understand such imagery, it is important to remember the previous chapters of her book where the experience of union with God in prayer is seen as progressively taking over, during the experience, the will, the mind, the senses. Teresa, like Bernard, speaks of the brevity of many of these experiences and the suffering this brevity causes. Here, however, it is the "centre" of the soul into which the bride is brought.

Another difference with previous stages is that there the person involved cannot understand "how or in what way that favour comes which it is enjoying,"[111] but here, this changes. Teresa writes:

> It is brought into this Mansion by means of an intellectual vision, in which, by a representation of the truth in a particular way, the Most Holy Trinity reveals itself, in all three Persons. First of all the spirit becomes enkindled and is illumined, as it were, by a cloud of the greatest brightness. It sees these three Persons, individually, and yet, by a wonderful kind of knowledge . . . the soul realizes that most certainly and truly, all these three Persons are one Substance and one Power and one Knowledge and one God alone. . . .[112]

She elaborates further and then exclaims on the uselessness of words to explain.

> Each day this soul wonders more, for she feels that They have never left her, and perceives quite clearly . . . that They are in the interior of her heart—in the most interior place of all and in its greatest depths.
>
> . . . This may lead you to think that such a person will not remain in possession of her senses but will be so completely absorbed that she will be able to fix her mind on nothing. But no: in all that belongs to the service of God she is more alert than before, and, when not otherwise occupied, she rests in that happy companionship.[113]

The contrast of temperaments of Teresa and John shows well in remarks such as these. To read the latter one would think that a person at this stage would be walking around in the kind of absorption Teresa describes. The two outlooks complement one another. It is interesting here, too, to remember Jung's remarks about the importance of staying in touch with the ego level and not getting lost in the unconscious.

Teresa adds that such a person "is walking more carefully than ever, so that she may displease Him in nothing"[114]—again, rather a contrast with John's description which sounds as if such a person is beyond needing to be careful. Teresa clarifies:

This Presence is not of course always realized so fully . . . if it
were, it would be impossible for the soul to think of anything
else, or even to live among men. . .

   We might compare the soul to a person who is with others in a
very bright room; and then suppose that the shutters are closed
so that the people are all in darkness. The light by which they
can be seen has been taken away, and, until it comes back, we
shall be unable to see them, yet we are none the less aware that
they are there. It may be asked if, when the light returns, and
this person looks for them again, she will be able to see them. To
do this is not in her power.[115]

The opening lines of this quotation are more reminiscent of
what John of the Cross says. The grace of which Teresa speaks,
however, is a preparation for yet more. "The person already referred to found herself better in every way; however numerous
were her trials and business worries, the essential part of her soul
seemed never to move from that dwelling place.[116] She adds that
she could thus feel divided, with half of herself being Martha and
the other half Mary — a struggle to which John does not refer at this
stage, as he also does not speak of concern with "business worries."
Yet he lived most of his life having to deal with serious issues in
his order.

   The spiritual marriage itself occurs, Teresa believes, through an
imaginary vision of the humanity of Christ "so that it [the soul]
may clearly understand what is taking place and not be ignorant of
the fact that it is receiving so sovereign a gift,[117] but she adds that
different people receive this grace in different ways. For Teresa the
vision took place after Holy Communion and the Lord "told her
that it was time she took upon her His affairs as if they were her
own and that He would take her affairs upon Himself."[118] This is
rather a good illustration of John's mutual surrender and self-
giving. One thing that made this vision different from others she
had had was its location "in the interior of her soul." "There is the
same difference between the Spiritual Betrothal and Spiritual
Marriage as there is between two betrothed persons and two who
are united so that they cannot be separated any more."[119]

What passes in the union of the Spiritual Marriage is very different. The Lord appears in the centre of the soul, not through
an imaginary, but through an intellectual vision. . . . The Lord

is pleased to manifest to the soul at that moment the glory that is in Heaven, in a sublimer manner than is possible through any vision or spiritual consolation. . . . The soul . . . is made one with God, Who, being likewise a Spirit, has been pleased to reveal the love that He has for us by showing to certain persons the extent of that love. . . . For He has been pleased to unite Himself with His creature in such a way that they have become like two who cannot be separated. . . .[120]

She continues on the same point. Now "The soul remains all the time in that centre with its God . . . as if the ends of two wax candles were joined so that the light they give is one." She also remarks, like John, that such a person no longer loses her peace. "It is quite certain," she adds, "that, when we empty ourselves of all that is creature and rid ourselves of it for the love of God, that same Lord will fill our souls with Himself."

She goes on in a way that rejoins the thought of John:

When Our Lord brings the soul into this Mansion of His, which is the centre of the soul itself . . . it seems, on entering, to be subject to none of the usual movements of the faculties and the imagination, which injure it and take away its peace.[121]

She does not, however, seem to agree with John that such a person is "confirmed in grace": rather, such a one is more careful than ever not to sin. She, like John, speaks of a desire for suffering. She also explains that the peace of which she speaks does not mean that there is never conflict in the "faculties," and trial and weariness as well.

Then follows a list of effects by which one can judge whether such an experience has truly taken place. They include self-forgetfulness, desire for suffering and hardship for the love of God, deep tranquillity at the center. There are no more of the "raptures" of which she spoke earlier, and humility deepens. She adds:

Do not, of course, for one moment imagine that, because these souls have such vehement desires and are so determined not to commit a single imperfection for anything in the world, they do not in fact commit many imperfections, and even sins. . . .[122]

"Let whichever of you feels surest of herself fear most," she adds. Acceptance of the shadow seems normal to her.

Why does God grant such favors, she asks. Not for our pleasure but "to strengthen our weakness." She speaks of St. Paul: he did not "shut himself up" to enjoy his visions but worked the more to serve his Lord. Once again, we see a difference of accent from John's. She closes the chapter insisting on the need for humility as a foundation for the spiritual building and on the readiness for effective conformity to Christ. Not rest but service is her final word, but her way of seeing this service is specifically hers. Writing to cloistered nuns in an age when women had less freedom than today, she makes some observations that still hold now. It is easy, she remarks, to have great desires to serve people in the other half of the world and whom one cannot reach. But love and humility are real when they touch those with whom we live. That is the test. She concludes by saying that she hopes her nuns will take delight in walking around in the Interior Castle of which she has written.

*　*　*

It is surely not necessary to belabor the differences and similarities of thought of the four authors studied in such length in this chapter. With this study of the "sacred marriage" we have come to the end of the journey of this book which has attempted to compare some of the fundamental themes of psychology and spirituality and see where, sometimes surprisingly, they point in the same directions. Both agree, finally, in this aim of union in human life—whether that union is seen in terms of the conscious and unconscious, the latter including the domain of the One who lives beyond human consciousness, or whether it is formulated explicitly in terms of union with God—though it goes without saying that not all psychology speaks of this domain.

Having worked with the themes in this last chapter, one can see how all the earlier ones are necessarily included in it. There are the notions of spiritual/psychological work and of the shadow; the question of the opposites; the importance of the heart or center of the being; the reality of the psychological and spiritual domains and of the beings one finds there, even the Supreme Being Himself. There are the inner masculine and feminine in their various forms and the questions of how we integrate these. The notions of silence, solitude, peace recur again and again as does the very important question of obedience, listening. One could enumerate in more detail, but this is not necessary, and there are surely other questions that could also be studied as part of the culminating stage seen in this chapter. Yet this, also, is not a culmination, for true completion is beyond the confines of this life.

When Augustine spoke of the restlessness of the human heart until it rests in God, he seems to have been speaking of a universal human experience. The writers, psychological as well as spiritual, studied in these pages have pointed out some of the pitfalls and false rests that do not serve this end. They have also indicated some of the ways toward it. No two journeys are alike, as none of theirs were. But faintly or more clearly one can discern patterns or maps of the road. And in the end perhaps there are no longer even any maps but only the light that burns in our hearts, the Light that shone in a darkness that would not receive it but that, by making us its image, illumines in the end even the divine darkness of God.

APPENDIX 1

An Article on Benedictine Humility in the Light of Jungian Thought

Chapter 2 mentioned a recent article on the Benedictine degrees of humility.[1] As was said, this article is a response to a talk, later an article, examining Benedictine humility in psychological terms, and taking a view of Benedict's spirituality as, among other things, a renunciation of the contemplative ideal of the desert and as lacking in the insights of contemporary creation spirituality. This appendix will summarize briefly the thought of Emmanuel Latteur, the author of the article of response, and add a few comments from a Jungian point of view.

The article comprises three sections and an introduction. In the latter appears the global view of humility, in the eyes of Benedict, as "an act of God in man."[2] In other words, the person placing him or herself totally before God and in submission to God finds that this "is exposing himself not to an objective witness but to an acting Subject." This Subject's activity tends toward the transformation of the human person exposed to it, "vivifying, beyond himself his brotherly and church relationships and even his hidden connections with the entire cosmos." Thus, for this author, what Benedict calls degrees of humility are, in fact, indices of God's invasion of the human person's heart. As a result, far from leading to individualism, this growth in humility and transformation involves "a descent into the center of the mystery of Christ . . . a penetration into the heart of the Church and the world, an opening, a passage 'through the narrow gate' opening out by the 'law of inclusion' to the human brotherhood."

But, adds the author, to bear in oneself the evil of the world, the sin and suffering of others, it is necessary — in order to avoid pharisaism—to have accepted and assumed one's own evil, to have reached reconciliation with oneself. This, he says, is what Benedict teaches (and, one might add, the tradition of the desert before him.)

> We must go to God *with* our misery, not denying it, neglecting it or hiding it. What psychoanalyses try painfully to achieve, St. Benedict proposes by a more direct way—that of the intervention of God in the heart of one who opens himself to God by faith.[3]

What is interesting about this quotation is that an author speaking totally from a spiritual standpoint finds himself saying exactly what Jung's—and other psychology teaches in this regard. And, again, there is the conception of God as supremely active, which will perhaps remind the reader of a phrase from Jung already quoted: "The individuated ego senses itself as the object of an unknown and supraordinate subject."[4]

The article continues to speak of the "invasion" of the human heart by God's action. This is language that Jung, as a psychologist, will not use. But a quotation from his reflection on the "mana-personality" may nonetheless be seen in connection with Latteur's concept:

> By affixing the attribute "divine" to the workings of autonomous contents, we are admitting their relatively superior force. And it is this superior force which has at all times constrained men to ponder the inconceivable, and even to impose the greatest sufferings upon themselves in order to give these workings their due. It is a force as real as hunger and the fear of death.[5]

Attempting to control or identify with this power emerging from the unconscious leads to the worst catastrophes, according to Jung's discussion of inflation. Rather, an attitude of suppleness and increasing awareness is important. This is not unrelated to Latteur's "divine invasion" or, at least, to receptiveness to this invasion.

Latteur sees humility not as individualism but as growth in Christlikeness that brings increasing unity with others and with the cosmos itself. Jung's notion of the collective unconscious also implies that the more in touch a person is—not only with his or her own unconscious but with the depths beyond—the more, paradoxically, that person is in touch with others, both the living who share this same inner world, perhaps unknowing, and the centuries before whose heritage we receive. In neither of these two thoughts is the human person an unconnected monad. In neither is individualism a good.

Finally, the article's stress on wholehearted acceptance of one's own evil and sin relates to Jung's view that the very first step in the process of individuation is the facing and acceptance of the shadow.

In Section 1 of his article, Latteur speaks of the first three degrees of humility. The first involves continual attention to the fact of God's presence by which one remains constantly exposed "to the unfelt but real action of God's gaze." Increasing awareness of this God who is Love leads to the desire to become freer of self-love and more "taken" by love for the Other. This becomes the second degree of humility and leads to a preference for the will of this Other over one's own.

> We know how much we need to become free of ourselves to be able to love in truth: [how much we need] to let go of our possessive or defensive attitude, our fears; to relax—adhering more and more to an Other whose plan for us invades our life and whom we consider greater than ourselves, better than ourselves, preferable to ourselves.[6]

This notion of relaxing, of giving up defensiveness, is essential to Chapter 5 in our text, and according to Latteur, it leads to a "transfiguration of desire." "In no way does he [Benedict] intend to beat down human affectivity and will or deny their fundamental value": he is simply speaking of a transformation beyond human power. This second degree, adds the article, depends on the first and "any psychoanalysis trying to abstract from this [first] can only imitate awkwardly the interior transfiguration of desire." Human desire remains present "in all its vigor but it seems now to have found its destination and its point of balance."

What does this mean? Mainly that in the monastic and spiritual tradition, desire finds its fulfillment only in God and union with Him. Preferring the will of the Other, then, is about becoming free of the possessive, defensive, cramped, tense attitudes referred to in order to relax in an awareness of and surrender to a greater love.

Why, then, the negative remarks about psychoanalysis? They may hold true of an analysis with no recognition of spiritual values but the process of individuation of Jungian analysis has to do with increasing awareness of the Self so that a "transfiguration of desire" is certainly involved.

Coming to the third degree of humility Latteur says that the firm will of union with God's will leads to

> a desiring of communion to such a point as to allow oneself, if possible, to be guided in all things by the Other and to be, as a "friend" with Him who was perfectly one with the will of the Father, Jesus Christ. . . . Thus is born a desire crazy and incomprehensible to purely human "analysis"—that of incarnating this love in submission to a very concrete superior in a monastery, in order to let oneself be more guided by Christ. Here, mysteriously, all the wild complexes of terrified defense of my independence are unleashed anew.[7]

But, he concludes, it is in the heart of this apparent menace to my "me," my liberty and tastes, that free and joyful communion takes place.

What is the root of this desire to obey? Is it only dependence, passivity, a too "feminine" nature? Many centuries after Benedict, Ignatius of Loyola wrote that, among other motives for obedience

> Even in worldly matters the greatest sages hold it to be the part of a prudent man not to trust his own wisdom, especially in his own cause, in which a man is generally too much prejudiced to be a good judge.[8]

Our subjectivity can make it difficult to discern the will of the Other from our own. The objective insight of another person, whom Benedict in no way canonizes, can help. Does this other truly represent the will of God for me more than my own mature judgment and desire? As the later sections of both this article and the Rule point out, a purified will and desire are a different story from those found at the beginnings of the journey to God. At first, the desire to control, dominate, seek one's own will are obstacles to union. Obedience to a superior is a means chosen to further union in this particular tradition, as well as in the basic spiritual tradition of both East and West.

This specifically Benedictine point finds less echo in the writings of Jung. But the need to avoid tendencies to control, to be ruled by the ego, is habitual in his works. Perhaps this monastic conception, too, he could have understood.

The article's psychological description of defensive attitudes before this type of obedience, however, seems extraordinarily accurate. Truly, Jung would say, the ego must die, not with a death that ends everything but in order to become transformed. But everyone fights death until the process of individuation has actually done its work.

Latteur considers the fourth degree so important that it alone is the subject of the middle section of his article. For him, this stage is a crisis which, if successfully lived, leads one beyond personal limits and limitations into a new and transformed way of living. It begins, however, in the most prosaic of ways.

Having chosen—for the person living in the monastic tradition —to live in a monastery and under obedience to the superior, one finds oneself plunged into the realities of that life:

> the rudeness of the monastic life, unexpected contradictions . . . difficulties of all kinds, misunderstandings, opposition, injustices, solitude, afflictions[9]

coming from those with whom one lives. The result is awareness of one's own "misery," vulnerability, powerlessness, temptation.

> Until then he could still imagine that his moments of weakness and his falls were only parenthetical episodes which did not ultimately express his deep being. . . . He was perhaps still full of illusions about himself and others, considering himself a bit as a "just man" who occasionally slips. . . . The monk is "surprised" because . . . still feeling himself to be more or less "just" he experiences as very "unjust" . . . the situations he must suffer.[10]

The crisis that results is that of self-justification, "the visceral need to defend himself . . . and demand his rights."

What is written here of the monastic life could be a description of learning to deal with the shadow in any life. One thinks of the first years of marriage after the honeymoon, the years of battling in one's work with the issues of "dream" and reality,[11] and one recognizes this coming to grips with the non-ideal concrete, with suffering and contradiction, that is part of the human condition.

The cry "Why should this happen to me?" which often occurs in moments of tragedy is connected to this issue, often on a level of very deep pain.

On the subject of defensiveness, Latteur quotes an interesting remark of Silouane, a contemporary Orthodox staretz: "Wanting to justify oneself is the act of a slave and not of a son of God."[12] The psychological parallel is doubtless the necessity, during a process of analysis or therapy, to be ready to accept the truth about oneself without excuses, defenses, shying away—a hard lesson to learn at times.

What, then, becomes of contemporary stress on assertiveness? Assertiveness, for one thing, is not self-justification; quite the contrary. It may, indeed, demand its rights but only one who knows his or her rights can relinquish them. And at times only one who is humble can assert them. There is a strong apparent contradiction between assertiveness and humility, but this contradiction is more apparent than real. Once again, grace builds on nature. A human being must first be aware of personal dignity and worth—even, in the above theology, of divine filiation—before it becomes possible to live in a healthy way the choices of this kind of humility. Unfortunately, life is not always so clearcut and progressive. People find themselves having to live this kind of petty persecution and suffering even when they have not reached the psychological and spiritual health to live it well. In this case, there is no choice but to try to work in both directions—that of a balanced human position and that of the spiritual realism of humility.

Latteur continues: "At this moment, St. Benedict asks him to guard his lips 'absolutely' in order not to revolt or complain." Why? Because, once more, inner strength comes from this refusal to dissipate energies in "murmuring" and detraction. Again and again the article repeats that this is a choice to find one's support and strength in God rather than in the human. The result?

> Discovering that his true life is situated beyond the tensions [Note: the image is one of clenching, like a fist] of turning back on the "me," henceforth "disarmed," he enters gently into peace and relaxation. He begins to know true happiness, that of the Beatitudes: "Blessed are those who mourn, who are persecuted for justice' sake, the poor, the peaceful, etc. . . ." The happiness of the "men of God" penetrates deep into his psyche showing thus

in all his being this peace and a victory which ultimately is that of God in him over evil. "If one constrains them to go a mile they go two . . . they bless those who curse them."[13]

If the psychological health that is the fruit of a process is also its validation, it would seem that what is being described above could hardly be psychologically negative. The refusal to speak mentioned here obviously does not refer to appropriate speech with the appropriate person or people—when this is done without dependence or childishness—but rather the kind of complaining victim-stance that would not be psychologically healthy either. Once again it needs to be said that the goal discussed in the article is different from the goal of analysis: even what is said about the human level proves it. Nonetheless, it is important to see that the kind of attitudes mentioned in the most traditional kind of spirituality which can so often be castigated in would-be-modern circles as negative and psychologically harmful can, in fact, be supremely healthy. A fully realistic awareness of one's shadow and limitations, one's faults and lacks of justice and holiness, and therefore the fact of being at one with a world which is equally unjust and sometimes evil is, paradoxically, an absolute requirement of a true life of faith. It is also necessary to psychological health.

The later degrees of humility deepen the awareness already found—that of being in all truth one with the Adam seen as bringing sin into the world and only from that place one with the Christ who redeems. Any other position is still superficial, has not yet plumbed the depths and can therefore not fully experience redemption, neither one's own nor another's. Living on this level makes one ready to own one's own dark sides to a spiritual father or mother (fifth degree) and it is from this level alone that the monk's hospitality (in the spiritual sense of understanding others, rather than just giving them a roof and food), compassion, speech and silence (degrees nine to eleven) can be understood.

The monastic life has no other end than to lead us back into this center of ourselves where the whole of humanity is included in Jesus Christ—in order here to have our own evil and that of all men baptized in the blood of the Lamb, that the transfiguration of Easter may shine forth.[14]

He continues to speak of "monks and all those who lend themselves to the purifications of humility," who participate in the birthpangs of a new world in the new man, Christ.

There is no room for any "privatization" in such a view. Humility, which may seem the most individual of virtues, is also the most cosmic. With the transformation of Benedict's twelfth degree of humility, the monk's behavior reflects both personal acceptance of evil in oneself and an equally deep-seated confidence in God's love and transforming power. The result is a certain gravity, tendency to silence, openness to others, peace. In this light, a story I was told in the Orient reflects exactly one traditionally told of some of the desert fathers.

It seems that there is a monastery in Japan whose abbot refuses to receive visitors. But nonetheless, people come from all over the country just to see him, so deeply does he seem established in peace and so helpful is just the sight of such a man.

Such a person has done the interior work Jung describes and has also lived Benedict's degrees of humility as well, though, as a Buddhist, he may well have heard of neither. This suggests again the common basic spiritual tradition and experience concerning the ways to union with God, or its psychological parallel, which people discover at their own time and in terms of their readiness to learn from the collective wisdom of humankind. It has been known in the East and the West. Now it begins to emerge in terms of its psychological meaning. One can only hope that, if the lesson can be learned, it will be of benefit to all humankind.

APPENDIX 2

The Problem of Evil and God: Reflections on Jung's *Answer to Job*

Few of Jung's works arouse so much controvery as his *Answer to Job*. He is speaking out of a specific psychological experience — that of God who seems to be experienced as evil as well as good — a position disconcerting for the religious person to deal with, and yet one that most people meet sooner or later, whether they wish to call it by that name or not.

In order to respond to this book, one has to understand it. In its opening pages, Jung speaks of the God of the Old Testament:

> He himself admitted that he was eaten up with rage and jealousy and that this knowledge was painful to him. Insight existed along with obtuseness, loving-kindness along with cruelty, creative power along with destructiveness. Everything was there and none of these qualities was an obstacle to the other. Such a condition is only conceivable either when no reflecting consciousness is present at all, or when the capacity for reflection is very feeble and a more or less adventitious phenomenon. A condition of this sort can only be described as *amoral*.[1]

Who is this God incapable of reflection? Is it the God of Jesus Christ — or the God of contemporary believing Judaism or Islam? Or is it, rather, the God-image of a primitive people expressed still in primitive terms which one would hope later ages would understand with more sophistication?

Jung was certainly more than aware of this question. He chooses, however, quite deliberately to use and respond to the images as they stand, seeing them as meaningful not only to primitives but also to psychological reflection. This is the religious experience of

many people, he feels—and, at times, the religious experience of
the most civilized and educated among us. Who has not heard, in
the face of tragedy, the plaint, "Why did God do this to me?" Let us
follow Jung in his exploration of this experience of a savage God,
but let us do so knowing that, in his own terms:

> The image and the statement are psychic processes which are
> different from their transcendental object: they do not posit it,
> they merely point to it.[2]

This statement must, however, be used with its accompaniment:

> Should any of my readers feel tempted to add an apologetic
> "only" to the God-images as we perceive them, he would im-
> mediately fall foul of experience, which demonstrates beyond
> any shadow of doubt the extraordinary numinosity of these
> images . . . they not only give one the feeling of pointing to the
> *Ens realissimum,* but make one convinced that they actually ex-
> press it and establish it as a fact.[3]

These images, then, express a certain universal awareness and
seem to point to a Reality. To what extent they are, as Freud
thought, projection, remains to be seen. It remains true that, as
Jung says, "The book of Job serves as a paradigm for a certain experience of God which has a special significance for us today. . . . It
is far better to admit the affect and submit to its violence than to try
to escape it by all sorts of intellectual tricks or by emotional value-
judgments."[4] Let us, then, continue this journey with him on his
own terms.

To summarize Jung's thought—insofar as this is possible for so
nuanced a presentation—Job speaks to God as just, but "cannot
deny that he is up against a God who does not care a rap for any
moral opinion and who does not recognize any form of ethics as
binding."[5] He "clearly sees that God is at odds with Himself . . . as
certain as he is of the evil in Yahweh, he is equally certain of the
good."[6] Yahweh, then, is "an *antinomy*—a totality of inner opposites."[7] By his retreat to the plane of reason, Job "shows himself
superior to his divine partner both intellectually and morally."[8]
"Yahweh fails to notice that he is being humoured, just as little as
he understands why he has continually to be praised as just."[9] In

other words, "the character thus revealed fits a personality who can only convince himself that he exists through his relation to an object."[10] "He is too unconscious to be moral."[11] Jung concludes this section by saying that this sketch is only an anthropomorphic picture.

Before continuing, let us underline this last statement. The God described in the previous paragraph is obviously offensive to faith and would even have been so to much Greek philosophy or classical metaphysics. He is more like the gods of primitive mythology that Greek philosophy left behind. But Jung is not writing metaphysics. He is writing psychology, based on empirical experience, and, as Chapter 4 above points out, one of his fundamental theories involves the interplay of opposites, the law of enantiodromia. Having felt that his psychological practice proved this principle again and again, Jung was to fall back on it constantly in the present study of religious experience. He seemed convinced that intellectual and emotional honesty required the exploration involved in this book and the terms he used for this exploration.

Section 2 of the book continues by saying that "existence is only real when it is conscious to somebody. That is why the Creator needs conscious man even though, from sheer unconsciousness, he would like to prevent him from becoming conscious."[12] Once again, this notion of God as unconscious clearly contradicts any traditional Trinitarian theology but, with this premise, one can see Jung's way to his conclusion. Despite this intention on God's part, says Jung, "the tormented though guiltless Job had secretly been lifted up to a superior knowledge of God which God himself did not possess. Had Yahweh consulted his omniscience, Job would not have had the advantage of him."[13] We have, then, a God who is omniscient but out of touch with his omniscience, a position one could surely call self-contradictory. But if one posits a God who is unconscious, one can posit also this last view. Jung seems to do it proceeding simply from his interpretation of the Scriptural text, and writing psychology, not metaphysics. Some feel that this position should forbid him to make some statements one could hardly call other than metaphysical[14] but let us, for the present, continue to follow his thought.

God's answer to Job is seen as challenging the latter as if he were himself a god, a worthy opponent, instead of a puny and suffering man. Jung sees this whole scriptural passage as showing God's desire to remain unconscious.[15] Job learns that "Yahweh is not human but, in certain respects, less than human. . . . Unconsciousness has an animal nature."[16] What has happened in the book of Job, for Jung, is that "Yahweh's dual nature has been revealed, and somebody or something has seen and registered this fact."[17] This, to him, is the significance of this scriptural work.

Jung continues the study of the God-image in Scripture with reflection on the idea of Sophia or the Wisdom of God, a "coeternal and more or less hypostatized pneuma of feminine nature that existed before the Creation."[18] Proverbs and Ecclesiasticus are quoted at length and Wisdom is seen as "Ruach, the spirit of God" who brooded over creation.

> There must be some dire necessity responsible for the anamnesis of Sophia: things simply could not go on as before, the "just" God could not go on committing injustices, and the "Omniscient" could not behave any longer like a clueless and thoughtless human being. . . . The failure of the attempt to corrupt Job has changed Yahweh's nature.[19]

Once again, theologically and even metaphysically, comment on such a view hardly seems necessary, but, once again, this view is psychological. Jung is going through Scripture, it seems, as a study in increasing consciousness of God—or rather, the changing consciousness of God. The metaphysical reality portrayed is not his issue, though conscious contents point—for him—to being. Nonetheless, he is speaking of God within the viewpoint given above, and this needs to be remembered. God is lacking in "Eros, relationship to values" in the book of Job: "the paragon of all creation is not a man but a monster!"[20] "The faithfulness of his people becomes the more important to him the more he forgets Wisdom,"[21] but "with the Job drama . . . Yahweh comes up against a man who stands firm. . . He has seen God's face and the unconscious split in his nature. God was now known."[22] Jung concludes that then, with the resulting anamnesis of wisdom,

> a momentous change is imminent: God desires to regenerate himself in the mystery of the heavenly nuptials . . . and to become man. . . . The real reason for God's becoming man is to be sought in his encounter with Job.[23]

He raises himself above his earlier primitive level of consciousness by indirectly acknowledging that the man Job is
morally superior to him and that therefore he has to catch up
and become human himself.[24]

There can be no doubt that he did not immediately become
conscious of the moral defeat he had suffered at Job's hands. In
his omniscience, of course, this fact had been known from all
eternity, and it is not unthinkable that the knowledge of it unconsciously brought him into the position of dealing so harshly
with Job in order that he himself should become conscious.[25]

What is to be thought of a God "not conscious of moral defeat," a
God morally defeated by a human person and leading the latter
to suffering for the sake of a divine growth in insight? Is such a
being God as we know him—or, again, the product of one of the
mythologies of the ancient Near East or Greece? Are the two identical for Jung? Perhaps once more following out his line of thought
may show.

The birth of Christ, sinless himself and born of a sinless mother
—a fact which Jung sees as removing both from the real human
condition—was, then, the next stage. Christ was loving toward
humankind but also "a certain irascibility is noticeable in Christ's
character, and, as is often the case with people of emotional tem-
perament, a manifest lack of self-reflection."[26] He did not confront
himself, says Jung, except in the moment when he cried out, "My
God, my God, why hast thou forsaken me?"

Here is given the answer to Job, and, clearly, this supreme
moment is as divine as it is human, as "eschatological" as it is
"psychological." And at this moment, too, where one can feel the
human being so absolutely, the divine myth is present in full
force. And both mean one and the same thing. How, then, can
one possibly "demythologize" the figure of Christ?[27]

Christ is a "myth" in the sense of his universal validity—which
does not contradict factual truth—or he is truly "beside himself."
There is no middle ground, says Jung. "The life of Christ is just
what it had to be if it is the life of a god and a man at the same time.
. . . Yahweh's intention to become man, which resulted from his
collision with Job, is fulfilled in Christ's life and suffering."[28]

One begins to see the logic of this train of thought, however offensive its early presentation may be to classical faith. The offensiveness does not, however, cease here. In the Lord's Prayer "Christ considers it appropriate to remind his father of his destructive inclinations towards mankind and to beg him to desist from them."[29] God has still not become the loving Father of the Gospels or the Summum Bonum of the philosophers.

Jung continues at some length in the following pages on a point theologians have discussed much of late—the presentation of God as an irascible Father who requires the death by torture of His Son to expiate the sins of humankind. Such a view, of course, bears out what Jung has been saying all along. "To believe that God is the Summum Bonum is impossible for a reflecting consciousness."[30] In Enoch

> the father wants to become the son, God wants to become man, the amoral wants to become exclusively good, the unconscious wants to become consciously responsible. So far everything exists only *in statu nascendi*.[31]

Job's "I know that my Vindicator lives" "can only refer to the benevolent Yahweh"[32] and so to the Christ in whom Yahweh's "benevolent aspect incarnates itself." But, if God

> had . . . only given an account of his action [incarnation] to himself, he would have seen what a fearful dissociation he had got into through his incarnation. Where, for instance, did his darkness go? . . . Does he think he is completely changed and that his amorality has fallen from him? Even his "light" son, Christ, did not quite trust him in this respect. . . . An enantiodromia in the grand style is to be expected.[33]

This last statement is surely a clue to much in Jung's thought in this whole study. To him the law of opposites is a fundamental principle of all reality—at least of all the psychological reality he studies and which he believes is real, objective. God as experienced, then, *must* be evil as well as good, unconscious as well as conscious. The very last pages of the book show his conclusions on this point and will have needed all this preceding study to be understood.

The following pages are consecrated, in this same light, to a study of the Apocalypse. John, the writer of the epistles, is seen as the author, and the Apocalypse as a resulting swing to the opposite, compensating the "goodness" of the writer in the earlier works. Archetypal contents of the kinds not emerging in the epistles did emerge with his increasing age, and the Apocalypse is the result.

> The eye of John penetrates into the distant future of the Christian aeon and into the dark abyss of those forces which his Christianity kept in equilibrium. What burst upon him is the storm of the times, the premonition of a tremendous enantiodromia. . . . It is the spirit of God itself, which blows through the weak mortal frame and again demands man's *fear* of the unfathomable Godhead.[34]

The marriage of the Lamb, the imagery of the heavenly city, suggest a final reconciliation.

> Just as the *hieros gamos* unites Yahweh with Sophia (Shekinah in the Cabala), thus restoring the original pleromatic state, so the parallel description of God and city points to their common nature: they are originally one, a single hermaphroditic being, an archetype of the greatest universality.
> No doubt this is meant as a final solution of the terrible conflict of existence. The solution, however, as here presented, does not consist in the reconciliation of the opposites, but in their final severance, by which means those whose destiny it is to be saved can save themselves by identifying with the bright pneumatic side of God. An indispensable condition for this seems to be the denial of propagation and of sexual life altogether.[35]

The reconciliation, then, is not here. What the Apocalypse was really meant to teach, according to Jung, is that Job was right: "God can be loved but must be feared."[36] And Jung moves on into the final stage of his work, where he reflects in more general terms on what has been said.

John in particular and people in general, says Jung, find it difficult to reflect on the numinous because so much affectivity is involved. "'Absolute objectivity' is more rarely achieved here than anywhere else."[37] The religious fear to doubt and to analyse. The agnostic or "enlightened" do not wish to admit the numinosity of the object lest their faith in agnosticism be shaken. "Agnosticism maintains that it does not possess any knowledge of God or of anything metaphysical, overlooking the fact that one never *possesses* a metaphysical belief but is *possessed by it.*"[38] Both are possessed by reason

> which represents the supreme arbiter who cannot be argued with. But who or what is this "reason" and why should it be supreme? Is not something that *is* and has real existence for us an authority superior to any rational judgment? . . .
> The only thing which is beyond doubt is that there are metaphysical statements which are assserted or denied with considerable affect precisely because of their numinosity. This fact gives us a sure empirical base from which to proceed.[39]

This, then, is the place from which Jung continues, as he began. He deals with statements—metaphysical or otherwise—in which people have couched their beliefs or spiritual experiences. He tries to express these statements in what he sees them to mean and to follow these expressions out to their logical conclusions, whether these latter please or displease believers or agnostics. This, surely, is what he has tried to do so far, using his own psychological principles as a means to understand but trying not to force them onto reality. Only reflection on the whole work can allow one to judge whether he succeeded.

In his final section, Jung writes:

> The paradoxical nature of God . . . tears [man] asunder into opposites and delivers him over to a seemingly insoluble conflict. What happens in such a condition? Here we must let psychology speak, for psychology represents the sum of all the observations and insights it has gained from the empirical study of severe states of conflict. . . . As experience shows, symbols of a reconciling and unitive nature do in fact turn up in dreams, the most frequent being the motif of the child-hero and the squaring of the circle, signifying the union of opposites. . . . John experienced in his vision a second birth of a son from the mother Sophia, a divine birth which was characterized by a *coniunctio oppositorum* and which anticipated the *filius sapientiae*, the essence of the individuation process.[40]

The more terrible the conflict, it seems, the more intense the fire from which the transformed gold is born. Christians had seen the opposition as lying between God and man, which made man the dark side, while in the book of Job the opposition was placed in God instead.

> Yahweh's decision to become man is a symbol of the development that had to supervene when man becomes conscious of the sort of God-image he is confronted with. God acts out of the unconscious of man and forces him to harmonize and unite the opposing influences to which his mind is exposed from the unconscious.[41]

Hiding from these awarenesses is no use at all, though it is a path people try to follow. The unconscious wants "to flow into consciousness," but it also wants to remain unconscious.

> That is to say, God wants to become man but not quite. The conflict in his nature is so great that the incarnation can only be bought by an expiatory self-sacrifice offered up to the wrath of God's dark side.[42]

Perhaps one could read this: humans conceive or experience God/the unconscious as wanting to become man/conscious but not quite. The issue, then, would be one of human experience—and of movement from the unconscious.

The incarnation of Christ is the prototype of this process and demands of us virtue and also wisdom, particularly in an era where we possess such incredible power for evil as well as good. Human wholeness, or the self

> stands for the goal of the total man, for the realization of his wholeness and individuality, with or without the consent of his will. . . . The only thing that really matters now is whether man can climb up to a higher moral level, to a higher plane of consciousness, in order to be equal to the superhuman powers which the fallen angels have played into his hand. . . . He must know something of God's nature and of metaphysical processes if he is to understand himself and thereby achieve gnosis of the divine.[43]

In other terms, humanity stands at a crossroads. It is not by denying the darkness in oneself nor, either, what Jung calls the darkness in God that it is possible to proceed. Personally, I would tend to use another terminology for the latter, since I believe that what, from a human vantage-point, is truly darkness and evil may be present in our lives for other reasons and serve other purposes than we realize with human understanding, and I believe that people experience this purposiveness for good in the end.[44] Nonetheless, that people experience God in the way that Job did and that Jung describes needs to be faced and admitted just as deeply. The pure faith viewpoint, to which I have just referred above, is not that of psychology or empirical fact, which is the view from which Jung wishes to proceed. His plea remains one for lucidity and honesty.

After speaking of the importance of the dogma of the Assumption, Jung concludes:

> The metaphysical process is known to the psychology of the unconscious as the individuation process. . . . The central symbols of this process describe the self. . . . It is only through the psyche that we can establish that God acts upon us, but we are unable to distinguish whether these actions emanate from God or from the unconscious. We cannot tell whether God and the unconscious are two different entities. Both are border-line concepts for transcendental contents. . . . There is in the unconscious an archetype of wholeness . . . and a tendency . . . to relate other archetypes to this centre . . .. which approximates it to the God-image. . . . Strictly speaking the God-image does not coincide with the unconscious as such, but with a special content of it, namely the archetype of the self. . . . Faith is certainly right when it impresses on man's mind and heart how infinitely far away and inaccessible God is; but it also teaches his nearness, his immediate presence. . . . Only that which acts upon me do I recognize as real and actual.[45]

God, then, acts on us through the unconscious. Becoming conscious brings us closer to God. Since the archetypes, as Jung adds, "are not mere objects of the mind but autonomous factors, i.e. living subjects, the differentiation of consciousness can be understood as the effect of the intervention of transcendentally conditioned dynamisms."[46] These transform us, but we only know them through our own consciousness. The concluding lines of the book read:

Even the enlightened person remains what he is, and is never more than his own limited ego before the One who dwells within him, whose form has no knowable boundaries, who encompasses him on all sides, fathomless as the abysms of the earth and vast as the sky.[47]

Is this fathomless and mysterious Being evil as well as good? I myself believe that Christian faith denies this. But it certainly does not deny psychological experience which can feel precisely this and which, Jung would say, needs to become conscious. I do not believe that being conscious requires the denial of a mystery beyond human consciousness, but Jung certainly makes no such denial. On the contrary. I think a very important part of his contribution is the awareness of how very close and how paradoxical this Mystery is.

NOTES

Abbreviations

From *The Collected Works of C.G. Jung.* Translated R.F.C. Hull. Bollingen Series XX. Princeton University Press:

C.W. VII	*Two Essays on Analytical Psychology.* 2nd ed., 1966. Paperback reprint ed., 1971.
C.W. IX	Part 1, *The Archetypes and the Collective Unconscious.* 2nd ed., 1968. Part 2, *Aion: Researches into the Phenomenology of the Self.* 2nd ed., 1968.
C.W. XI	*Psychology and Religion: West and East.* 2nd ed., 1969. This includes *Answer to Job* (separate paperback reprint edition, 1973).
C.W. XII	*Psychology and Alchemy.* 2nd ed., 1968.
C.W. XIII	*Alchemical Studies.* 1968.
C.W. XIV	*Mysterium Coniunctionis: An Inquiry into the Separation and Synthesis of Psychic Opposites in Alchemy.* 2nd ed., 1970. Paperback reprint ed., 1977.
C.W. XVI	*The Practice of Psychotherapy: Essays on the Psychology of the Transference and Other Subjects.* 2nd ed., 1966. 4th printing with corrections of 3rd, 1977.

From *The Collected Works of St. John of the Cross.* Translated K. Kavanaugh and O. Rodriquez. Washington, D.C.: Institute of Carmelite Publications, 1979:

Asc.	*The Ascent of Mount Carmel*
D.N.	*The Dark Night*
Flame	*The Living Flame of Love*
S.C.	*The Spiritual Canticle*

Other works:

Louf	André Louf. *Teach Us to Pray: Learning a Little about God.* New York: Paulist Press, 1974.
RB	*RB 1980: The Rule of St. Benedict in Latin and English with Notes.* Edited by Timothy Fry et al. Collegeville, MN: Liturgical Press, 1981.

The Sayings   *The Sayings of the Desert Fathers: The Alphabetical Collection.* Translated by Benedicta Ward. Kalamazoo, MI: Cistercian Publications. London: Mowbray, 1975.

Preface

1. See Wayne Teasdale, "The Other Half of the Soul: Dom Bede Griffiths in India," *The Canadian Catholic Review* 3, n. 6 (June 1985), 11-16.

Chapter 1. The Structure of the Human Psyche

1. *The Standard Edition of the Complete Psychological Works of Sigmund Freud,* ed. and trans. James Strachey, vol. 19, *The Ego and the Id and Other Works* (London: Hogarth Press and the Institute of Psycho-Analysis, 1961), 4.
2. Ibid., 7-10.
3. Ibid., 25.
4. Ibid., 31. For further brief explanation of the Freudian thought discussed in this chapter, see the excellent summary in Norman Cameron, *Personality Development and Psychopathology: A Dynamic Approach* (Boston: Houghton Miflin, 1963).
5. See the thought-provoking reflections of Sebastian Moore in *The Inner Loneliness* (New York: Crossroad, 1982), 51-53.
6. See Antoine Vergote, *The Religious Man: A Psychological Study of Religious Attitudes,* trans. Sr. Marie-Bernard Said (Dublin: Gill and Macmillan, 1969), 167ff.
7. E. Whitmont, *The Symbolic Quest: Basic Concepts of Analytical Psychology* (Princeton University Press, 1969), chap. 5, passim.
8. Ibid., 160.
9. *C.W.* VII, 274. In all works in this series the figure after the volume number refers to the paragraph number, not the page.
10. Ibid., 398-99.
11. I am indebted for some of the reflections that follow to Fr. Kieran Kavanaugh, O.C.D.
12. *D.N.* 1,4,4. References to this book also uses paragraphs rather than pages.
13. Ibid., 1, 9, 4.
14. Ibid., 6.
15. *C.W.* VII, 344-45.
16. Ibid., Pt. II, chap. 4, passim.
17. Ibid., 405.
18. Ibid., 400.
19. Ibid., 402-3.
20. Ibid., 405.
21. For a description of the mana-personality, see p. 30 in our text.
22. *C.W.* VII, 394.
23. Ibid., note 6.

Chapter 2. The Shadow

1. *C.W.* XVI, 452.
2. Ibid.

3. Laurens Van Der Post, *Jung and the Story of Our Time* (New York: Pantheon Books, Random House, 1975), 238.

4. June Singer, *Boundaries of the Soul: The Practice of Jung's Psychology* (New York: Anchor Press, Doubleday, 1973), 22.

5. Antoine Vergote, *The Religious Man: A Psychological Study of Religious Attitudes,* trans. Sr. Marie-Bernard Said (Dublin: Gill and Macmillan, 1969), 35ff.

6. See Albert Gelin, *The Poor of Yahweh,* trans. Mother Kathryn Sullivan (Collegeville, MN: Liturgical Press, 1964), passim.

7. Isaiah 66: 1-2.

8. See Rudolph Otto, *The Idea of the Holy: An Inquiry into the Non-Rational Factor in the Idea of the Divine and Its Relation to the Rational,* trans. John W. Harvey (New York: Oxford University Press, 1958).

9. Barnabas Ahern, C.P., in an unpublished conference given at the novitiate of the Sacred Heart, Albany, NY, ca. 1953.

10. Mt. 11:29.

11. Lk. 14: 11.

12. *RB* 7:12.

13. In *Living the Rule Today: A Series of Conferences on the Rule of Benedict* (Erie, PA: Benet Press, 1982), 76.

14. Ibid., chap. 5, passim.

15. 1 Jn. 4: 18.

16. A. Vergote, "Une approche psychologique de l'humilité dans la Règle de S. Benoît. Le chapitre vii: De l'humilité," in *Collectanea Cisterciensia* 42, no. 2 (1980), 112-35.

17. *D.N.* 1, 2, 2.

18. Ibid., 8.

19. *C.W.* VII, 391.

20. Thomas Merton, "Monastic Peace," in *The Monastic Journey,* ed. Br. Patrick Hart (New York: Image Books, Doubleday, 1978), 102.

21. Marion Woodman, "Transference and Countertransference in Analysis Dealing with Eating Disorders," *Chiron,* 1984, 64-65.

22. Ibid., 65.

23. *C.W.* VII, 221.

24. *RB* 4:62.

25. Ps. 31: 1-7, taken from *The Psalms: A New Translation from the Hebrew for Singing to the Psalmody of Joseph Gelineau* (London: Fontana Books, Collins, 1966).

Chapter 3. Work

1. The term "monk" is used throughout this book in the wide sense that includes anyone, male or female, from the time of the first hermits on (as well as before), who is trying to live the God-seeking life with a certain level of commitment and fidelity, since the monastic literature is often addressed to such a person. One finds today many who consider themselves monks without living canonical monastic profession (see Raimundo Panikkar et al., *Blessed Simplicity: The Monk as Universal Archetype* [New York: Seabury, 1982]). Many others, doubtless, are "monks" in this sense without knowing it. Panikkar writes: "By monk, *monachos,* I understand that person who aspires to reach the ultimate goal of life with all his being by renouncing all that is not necessary to it, i.e., by concentrating on this one single and unique goal. Precisely this singlemindedness . . . distinguishes the monastic way from

other spiritual endeavors toward perfection or salvation" [p. 10]. This book includes in the term "monk" those who have this single-minded attitude, even when the circumstances of life or previous choices do not enable them to incarnate it in an externally "monastic" way. This broadening of the term should not, however, be seen as minimizing the exigencies of the attitude.

2. Otto Fenichel, M.D., *The Psychoanalytic Theory of Neurosis* (New York: W.W. Norton, 1945), 573. The second part of the quotation refers to Freud's "The History of the Psychoanalytic Movement," in *Collected Papers*, vol. 1 (1924).

3. Robert Langs, M.D., *The Therapeutic Interaction*, vol. 1, *Abstracts of the Psychoanalytic Literature* (New York: Jason Aronson, 1976), 269. The abstract is of Walter A. Stewart, "An Inquiry into the Concept of Working Through," *Journal of the American Psychological Association* 11, 474-99.

The term "cathexis" means "charged with psychic energy" and this energy is usually directed toward a representation of a person or thing. See Sigmund Freud, *Introductory Lectures on Psychoanalysis*, trans. James Strachey (New York: Liveright Books, W.W. Norton, 1966), 336, note 2 and text.

4. *C.W.* VII, 113.

5. Ibid., 114.

6. Ibid., 115.

7. Ibid., 117.

8. Ibid., 122.

9. Ibid., 119.

10. Ibid.

11. Ibid.

12. See Lawrence Kohlberg, *Essays on Moral Development*, vol. 1, *The Philosophy of Moral Development: Moral Stages and the Idea of Justice* (San Francisco: Harper & Row, 1981).

13. *C.W.* VII, 252.

14. Ibid., 253.

15. *D.N.* 2, 5, 1-2.

16. *C.W.* VII, 275.

17. *The Sayings of the Desert Fathers*, trans. Benedicta Ward (Kalamazoo, MI: Cistercian Publications/London: Mowbray, 1975).

18. Ibid., xvii.

19. These sayings or apophthegmata will be referred to by the name of the person to whom they are attributed and the number of the saying in Ward's edition. This one is Theodore, 9.

20. *The Sayings*, Poemen 174.

21. *The Sayings*, Silvanus 10.

22. *Nichomachean Ethics* X, 8, 1104-7, in *The Basic Works of Aristotle*, ed. R. McKeon (New York: Random House, 1941).

23. Louf, 20-21.

24. Irenée Hausherr, "Opus Dei," *Orientalia Christiana Periodica* 13 (1947), 195-218. Translation mine throughout.

25. Jn. 6:29.

26. Hausherr, 200.

27. Origen quoted in Hausherr, 201.

28. Origen, *Iudic hom.* I, 4, quoted ibid.

29. Athanasius, *De Virginitate*, PG 28, 253 B, quoted in Hausherr, ibid.

30. Hausherr, 207.

31. John of the Cross, Letter 7: to the Discalced Carmelite Nuns of Beas, November 22, 1587, in *Collected Works* (see Abbreviations).

32. *Asc.* 2, 5, 7.
33. Ibid., 1, 5, 7.
34. Ibid., 3, 2, 8.
35. *S.C.* 39: 6.

Chapter 4. Dichotomy

1. *C.W.* VII, 243, note 1.
2. Ibid.
3. Ibid.
4. Ibid., 111.
5. Ibid.
6. Ibid., 112.
7. Ibid., 365.
8. Ibid., 360.
9. Ibid., 368.
10. See Thomas Merton, *The Ascent to Truth* (New York: Harcourt, Brace, 1951), chap. 4.
11. *C.W.* XVI, 443.
12. Ibid.
13. Ibid., 444.
14. *C.W.* XIV, 9, note.
15. John Main, *Word Into Silence* (New York: Paulist Press, 1980), vii.
16. Thomas Merton, *Contemplative Prayer* (Garden City, NY: Image Books, Doubleday, 1969), 38-39.
17. "Monastic Peace," in *The Monastic Journey,* ed. Br. Patrick Hart (Garden City, NY: Image Books, Doubleday, 1978), 88.
18. Daisetz Suzuki, Introduction to Gustie Herrigel, *Zen in the Art of Flower Arrangement,* trans. R.F.C. Hull (Boston: Routledge and Kegan Paul, 1958), xi-xii.
19. *RB* 31:10.
20. Vandana, *Gurus, Ashrams and Christians* (Madras, India: Christian Literature Society, 1980), 42.

Chapter 5. Descent to the Heart—and Defenses

1. Norman Cameron, *Personality Development and Psychopathology: A Dynamic Approach* (Boston: Houghton Miflin, 1963), 242.
2. NTL Institute, 1983 Programs, Arlington, Virginia, 7.
3. Ira Progoff, *At a Journal Workshop: The Basic Text and Guide for Using the Intensive Journal* (New York: Dialogue House Library, 1975), 47 and passim.
4. *C.W.* XII, 7.
5. Barbarah Hannah, *Jung, His Life and Work: A Biographical Memoir* (New York: G.P. Putnam's Sons, 1976), chaps. 1-5.
6. Igumen Chariton of Yalamo, compiler, *The Art of Prayer: An Orthodox Anthology* (Boston: Faber & Faber, 1966), passim.
7. John Main, *Word into Silence* (New York: Paulist Press, 1980), 14-15 (notes omitted).
8. Louf, 18.
9. Ibid., 47.

10. *The Confessions of St. Augustine*, trans. John K. Ryan (Garden City, NY: Image Books, Doubleday, 1960), X, 38.
11. Gregory the Great, *Dialogues* II, 3, quoted in Louf, 20.
12. *S.C.* 18, 4.
13. Ibid.
14. Ibid., 6-7.
15. *The Complete Works of Saint Teresa of Jesus*, trans. P. Silverio de Sta Teresa, C.D., ed. E. Alison Peers, vol. 2 (New York: Sheed and Ward, 1946), 209-10.
16. Ibid., 218.
17. Ibid., 233.
18. Ibid., 212, 229.
19. Ibid., 237. The Scripture is Ps. 118: 32.
20. Chariton, *The Art of Prayer*, 129.
21. Ibid., 128.
22. See this same book passim.
23. Thomas Keating, "Cultivating the Centering Prayer," in *Review for Religious* 37, n. 1 (January 1978), 11.
24. *The Sayings*, Poemen 63.
25. *The Sayings*, Pambo 10.
26. *RB* 66: 7.
27. *The Sayings*, Arsenius 11.
28. See Thomas Merton, "The Cell, in *Contemplations in a World of Action* (Garden City, NY: Image Books, Doubleday, 1965), 265.
29. *Opusc.* xi, c. 19, quoted in Merton, "The Cell," 268.
30. Carol Carstens, "Confessions of a Lay Contemplative," in *Spiritual Life*, Winter 1984, 222.

Chapter 6. Persona, Ego, and Self

1. *C.W.* VII, 306.
2. Ibid., 245.
3. Ibid., 246.
4. Ibid., 509.
5. Ibid., 521.
6. Ibid., 254.
7. Ibid.
8. Ibid., 260.
9. Ibid.
10. Ibid., 266.
11. Ibid., 269.
12. Ibid., 275.
13. Ibid.
14. Ibid., 373.
15. *The Sacred Books of the East*, vol. I, *The Upanishads*, trans. F. Max Mueller (Oxford University Press), 136, quoted in Barbara Hannah, *Jung, His Life and Work: A Biographical Memoir* (New York: G.P. Putnam's Sons, 1976), 47.
16. *RB* 4: 62.
17. See above p. 30.
18. Lk. 7: 35.
19. *Summa Theologiae*, Second Part.
20. *The Sayings*, Joseph of Panepbyses 7.

21. *RB* 7: 69-70.
22. *RB* Prol., 49.
23. *Flame* 1, 1.

Chapter 7. The Faces of Animus and Anima

1. Irene Claremont de Castillejo, *Knowing Woman: A Feminine Psychology* (New York: Colophon Books, Harper & Row, 1973). See "The Animus: Friend or Foe?"
2. *C.W.* VII, 296-97.
3. See Lillian B. Rubin, *Women of a Certain Age: The Midlife Search for Self* (New York: Colophon Books, Harper & Row, 1979).
4. See, for example, Castillejo, 78f., and John Sanford, *The Invisible Partners* (New York: Paulist Press, 1980), 75.
5. Castillejo, chap. 5, passim.
6. *C.W.* IX, 2, 14, quoted in Sanford, 75.
7. Castillejo, 80ff.
8. See Robert A. Johnson, *She: Understanding Feminine Psychology* (New York: Perennial Library, Harper & Row, 1977), and Erich Neumann, *Amor and Psyche: The Psychic Development of the Feminine,* trans. Ralph Manheim, Bollingen Series LIV (Princeton University Press, paperback 1971).
9. Johnson, 54.
10. Ibid., 59.
11. See Joseph Pieper, *Leisure: The Basis of Culture* (New York: Mentor Books, New American Library, 1952).
12. *Flame* 3, 34.
13. Ibid., 41-43.
14. *S.C.* 29: 2-3.
15. "Decree on the Appropriate Renewal of the Religious Life" (*Perfectae Caritatis*) in *The Documents of Vatican II,* ed. Walter Abbot, S.J. (New York: Guild Press, 1966), par. 7.
16. *St. Bernard's Sermons on the Canticle of Canticles,* trans. by a priest of Mount Melleray (Dublin: Browne & Nolan, 1920), vol. 1, pp. 176-78.
17. Evagrius Ponticus, *The Praktikos and Chapters on Prayer,* Cistercian Studies 4 (Kalamazoo, MI: Cistercian Publications, 1981), "Chapters on Prayer," n. 10.
18. I. Hausherr, *Les Leçons d'un contemplatif: Le Traité de l'Oraison d'Evagre le Pontique,* (Paris: Beauchesne et ses Fils, 1960), 23-24 (trans. mine).
19. Evagrius, chaps. 123-24. I have changed the translation of "in harmony with" to the more classical "united to."
20. *The Sayings,* Theophilus 2.

Chapter 8. Solitude, Discretion, Virtue

1. Dietrich Bonhoeffer, *Life Together: A Discussion of Christian Fellowship,* trans. John W. Doberstein (New York: Harper & Row, 1954), 77. He is quoting Luther on the second point.
2. See Thomas Merton, *Ascent to Truth* (New York: Harcourt Brace, 1951), pt. 1, chap. 1, passim.
3. See *RB* 1: 3-5.
4. Erik Erikson, *Childhood and Society,* 2nd ed. (New York: W.W. Norton, 1963), 247-51.

5. Ibid., 248-49.
6. 1 Cor. 13: 13.
7. Erikson, 251.
8. Ibid., 252.
9. Ibid., 256.
10. See C.G. Jung, "The Sacrifice," in *C.W.* V, *Symbols of Transformation: An Analysis of the Prelude to a Case of Schizophrenia,* trans. R.F.C. Hall (Princeton University Press, 2nd ed. 1967; paperback 1976); also *C.W.* XVI, 431ff.
11. Antoine Vergote, *The Religious Man: A Psychological Study of Religious Attitudes,* trans. Marie-Bernard Said (Dublin: Gill and Macmillan, 1969), chaps. 3 and 4.
12. Erikson, 262.
13. Ibid., 263.
14. Ibid., 263-64.
15. Ibid., 269.
16. Lk. 4:1.
17. *S.C.* 6.
18. Louf, 68.
19. Ibid., 72-73.
20. Ibid.
21. Ibid., 70.
22. Ibid., 71.
23. Ibid.
24. Ibid., 73-74.
25. *D.N.* 5.
26. Louf, 75.

Chapter 9. Projection and the Penance of Beasts

1. For an interesting study of Freud's religious development, see William Meissner, M.D., *Psychoanalysis and Religious Experience* (New Haven: Yale University Press, 1984).
2. Some very thorough and detailed study of this question can be found in Ana-Maria Rizzuto, M.D., *The Birth of the Living God: A Psychoanalytic Study* (University of Chicago Press, 1979).
3. *D.N.* 1, 6, 2.
4. Quoted in Rizzuto, 6 (no further information given).

Chapter 10. The Objectivity of the Psyche

1. Barbara Hannah, *Jung, His Life and Work: A Biographical Memoir* (New York: G.P. Putnam's Sons, 1976), 122.
2. Ibid., 188.
3. Ibid.
4. Ibid., 128.
5. M. Esther Harding, "The Reality of the Psyche," first article of *The Reality of the Psyche: The Proceedings of the Third International Congress for Analytical Psychology,* ed. Joseph B. Wheelwright (New York: G.P. Putnam Sons, 1968), 5.
6. Ibid.
7. Ibid., 5-6.
8. Ibid., 7.

9. Ibid.
10. Ibid., 8.
11. Ibid.
12. Ibid., 8-9.
13. Ibid., 9.
14. Ibid.
15. Ibid.
16. Ibid.
17. Ibid., 9-10.
18. Ibid., 10.

Chapter 11. Listening, Silence, Obedience

1. From *Semrad, the Heart of a Therapist,* ed. S. Rako and H. Mazer, quoted in *Psychotherapy and Social Science Review* 16, n. 6 (May 1984), 16.
2. Pitirim A. Sorokin, *The Monastic System of Techniques: Monastic "Psychoanalysis," Counseling and Therapy* (St. Meinrad, IN: Abbey Press, 1973), a reprint of two chapters of his previous book, *The Ways and Power of Love: Types, Factors and Techniques of Moral Transformation* (Boston: Beacon Press).
3. John of the Cross, *Maxims and Counsels,* n. 21, in *Collected Works* (See Abbreviations).
4. Elizabeth of the Trinity, "Last Retreat," in *I Have Found God: The Complete Works,* vol. 1, *General Introduction, Major Spiritual Writings* (Washington, D.C.: Institute of Carmelite Studies Publications, 1984), 142 (notes omitted).
5. *The Sayings,* xvi.
6. *The Sayings,* Arsenius 1 and 2.
7. *The Sayings,* Isidore 1.
8. *The Sayings,* Poemen 27 and 84.
9. Louf, 42.
10. Ibid., 43.
11. Ibid. A quotation from *The Golden Letter* (doubtless William of St. Thierry).
12. Ibid. The quotation is from Adam of Perseigne.
13. Ibid., 44.
14. Thomas Merton, *The Ascent to Truth* (New York: Harcourt, Brace, 1951), 316-17.
15. David Steindl-Rast, *A Listening Heart: The Art of Contemplative Living* (New York: Crossroad, 1983), 9-10.
16. Ibid.
17. Vandana, *Gurus, Ashrams and Christians* (Madras, India: The Christian Literature Society, 1978), 29-30.
18. Ibid., 32.
19. Louf, 27.
20. Ibid., 29.
21. *Asc.* 2, 5, 3.
22. Ibid., 2, 5, 6.
23. S. Freud, *Introductory Lectures on Psychoanalysis,* trans. James Strachey (New York: Liveright Books, W.W. Norton, 1966), 433.
24. Ibid., 439.
25. Ibid., 440-41.
26. Ibid., 442.

27. Benedetto Calati, "Spiritual Freedom and the Rule," *Monastic Studies* 9 (Autumn 1972), 104.

28. Ibid., 106.

29. Barbara Hannah, *Jung, His Life and Work: A Biographical Memoir* (New York: G.P. Putnam's Sons, 1976), 69.

Chapter 12. Spiritual Guide or Therapist

1. Louf, 40-41.

2. June Singer, "The Education of the Analyst," in *Jungian Analysis*, ed. Murray Stein, The Reality of the Psyche Series (La Salle/London: Open Court, 1982), 367.

3. Ibid., 369.

4. Ibid., 370.

5. Ibid.

6. Ibid.

7. Ibid.

8. Ibid., 371.

9. Murray Stein, "The Aims and Goals of Jungian Analysis," in *Jungian Analysis*, 42.

10. *C.W.* XIII, quoted in *Jungian Analysis*, 20.

11. C.G. Jung, 1912 paper, "Neue Bahnen der Psychologie," par. 437, quoted in Murray Stein, "Power, Shamanism, and Maieutics in the Countertransference," *Chiron*, 1984, 80.

12. *C.W.* XII, 219, quoted in Goodheart's article in the following note, 94.

13. William B. Goodheart, "Successful and Unsuccessful Interventions in Jungian Analysis: The Construction and Desctruction of the Spellbinding Circle," *Chiron*, 1984, 94-95.

14. Vandana, *Gurus, Ashrams and Christians* (Madras, India: The Christian Literature Society, 1978), 26-27.

15. A. Louf, "Spiritual Fatherhood in the Literature of the Desert," in *Abba: Guides to Wholeness and Holiness East and West*, ed. John R. Sommerfeldt, Cistercian Studies Series 38 (Kalamazoo, MI: Cistercian Publications, 1982), 38. (Henceforth referred to as *Abba*.)

16. Barsanuphius 212, in *Abba*, 41.

17. *Abba*, 40.

18. Ibid., 45.

19. Ibid., 49.

20. Ibid., 47.

21. Ibid., 49.

22. Ibid.

23. Sisoes 46, in *Abba*, 51.

24. Louf, *Teach Us to Pray*, 41.

25. William Johnston, "Religious Life: Contemplative Life," *Review for Religious* 28, no. 2 (March 1969), 291-96.

26. Vandana, 37.

Chapter 13. Memory

1. *The Confessions of St. Augustine* X, 8, 15.

2. Freud, *Introductory Lectures on Psychoanalysis*, trans. James Strachey (New York: Liveright Books, W.W. Norton, 1966), 210-11.

3. See above p. 40.
4. Freud, *Int. Lect.*, 203-4.
5. *C.W.* IX, 498-99.
6. Ibid., 504-5.
7. Ibid., 518.
8. Ibid., 509.
9. Ibid., 518.
10. Ibid.
11. Ibid., 524.
12. Russell Holmes, "A Jungian Approach to Forgetting and Memory in St. John of the Cross," in *Carmelite Studies: Contemporary Psychology and Carmel* (Washington D.C.: Institute of Carmelite Studies Publications, 1982), 189.
13. Ibid., 194.
14. Ibid., 194-95.
15. Ibid.
16. Ibid., 198.
17. Ibid., 200.
18. Ibid., 206.
19. See both *S.C.*, stanza I, 9-11, and *Flame*, stanzas 1 and 2, and commentary, passim.
20. Holmes, 214. The quotation from Jung is *The Visions Seminars* (Zurich: Spring Publications, 1976), 387.
21. *RB* 7: 10-13.
22. Ibid., 7: 7.
23. Ibid. 2: 1-2. See also note on Prol. 12 in *RB 1980*.
24. Ibid., 2:4.
25. Ibid., 2:30.
26. Ibid., 4: 47-49.
27. Ibid., 4: 57-58.
28. Gabriel M. Braso, *Liturgy and Spirituality*, trans. Leonard J. Doyle (Collegeville, MN: Liturgical Press, 1960), 65.
29. Ibid., 64.
30. Augustine, *Confessions* X, 17, 26.
31. Ibid., X, 24-27, pars. 35-38.

Chapter 14. Peace

1. Carol Cooperman Nadelson, M.D., "Marital Therapy from a Psychoanalytic Perspective," in *Marriage and Marital Therapy*, ed. T. Paolino and B. McCrady (New York: Brunner/Mazel, 1978), 146.
2. Edward C. Whitmont, *The Symbolic Quest: Basic Concepts of Analytical Psychology* (Princeton University Press, paperback 1978), 58.
3. Ibid., 60.
4. Ibid., 67.
5. Columba Marmion, *Christ, the Ideal of the Monk: Spiritual Conferences on the Monastic and Religious Life*, trans. by a nun of Tyburn Convent, 4th ed. (St. Louis: B. Herder Book Co., 1926), 428-30.
6. *The Sayings*, xvi.
7. I. Hausherr, *Les Leçons d'un contemplatif: Le Traité de l'Oraison d'Evagre le Pontique* (Paris: Beauchesne et ses Fils, 1960), 101 (translation mine). The quotations are from Evagrius, 101-4.
8. *The Sayings*, Theodore of Pherme 2.

9. The Sayings, Elias 6.

10. Adalbert de Vogüé, "Monachisme et Eglise dans la pensée de Cassien," in Théologie de la vie monastique: Etudes sur la Tradition patristique (Paris: Aubier, 1961), 230 (translation mine).

11. Diadochus of Photike, On Perfection, chaps. 6, 26, 27, 30, quoted in The Divine Office: The Liturgy of the Hours according to the Roman Rite (London: Collins, 1974), vol. 1, p. 477.

12. See "Guidelines for the Discernment of Spirits" in his Spiritual Exercises.

13. See Jean Cassien, Conférences, trans. E. Pichery, Sources Chrétiennes 46 (Paris: Editions du Cerf, 1955 [vol. 1]), Conf. 1 and 2.

14. Thomas Merton, "Final Integration: Toward a 'Monastic Therapy,'" in Contemplation in a World of Action (Garden City, NY: Image Books, Doubleday, 1973), 225-26.

Chapter 15. The Sacred Marriage

1. C.W. XIV, 201.
2. Ibid., 200.
3. Ibid., 208.
4. Ibid., 252.
5. Ibid., 253.
6. Ibid., 252.
7. Ibid., 253.
8. D.N. 2, 9,7.
9. Ibid., 2, 9, 9.
10. C.W. XIV, 256.
11. Ibid., 257.
12. Ibid., 257-58.
13. Ibid., 261.
14. Ibid.
15. Ibid., 262.
16. Ibid., 283.
17. Ibid.
18. See Interior Castle, Sixth Mansion, chap. 7, in The Complete Works of Saint Teresa of Jesus, trans. P. Silverio de Sta Teresa, C.D., ed. E. Alison Peers, vol. 2 (New York: Sheed and Ward, 1946), 302f.
19. Louf, 61.
20. C.W. XIV, 285.
21. Ibid., 290.
22. Ibid., 295.
23. Ibid., 296.
24. Ibid., 297.
25. Ibid., 307.
26. D.N. 2, 9, 5-6.
27. Ibid., 2, 10, 3.
28. S.C. 14-15, 23.
29. C.W. XIV, 308.
30. Ibid.
31. Ibid., 310.
32. Ibid., 309.
33. Ibid., 313.

34. Ibid.
35. Ibid., 356.
36. Ibid., 403.
37. Ibid., 402.
38. Ibid., 422.
39. Ibid., 428.
40. Ibid., 434.
41. Ibid., 543.
42. *Cherub. Wandersmann,* II, 103-4, quoted ibid., 444.
43. Ibid., 445.
44. Ibid., 446.
45. Ibid., 488.
46. Ibid., 541-42.
47. Ibid., 605.
48. Ibid., 647.
49. Ibid., 650.
50. Ibid., 657.
51. Ibid., 661.
52. Ibid., 662.
53. Ibid.
54. Ibid., 664.
55. Ibid.
56. Ibid., 704.
57. Ibid., 708.
58. Ibid., 711 (notes omitted).
59. Ibid., 747.
60. Ibid., 753.
61. Ibid.
62. Ibid., 760.
63. Ibid., 762.
64. Ibid., 763.
65. Ibid., 765.
66. Ibid., 777.
67. Ibid., 778.
68. Ibid., 789.
69. Mt. 9:15.
70. Jn. 3: 29.
71. Eph. 5: 31-32.
72. Dom Cuthbert Butler, *Western Mysticism: The Teaching of Sts Augustine, Gregory and Bernard on Contemplation and the Contemplative Life* (London: Constable, 2nd ed. 1927).
73. Ibid., 160-61.
74. *The Works of Bernard of Clairvaux,* vol. 2, *On the Song of Songs,* vol. 1, trans. Kilian Walsh, introduction by Corneille Halflants, Cistercian Fathers Series, no. 4 (Shannon: Irish University Press, 1971), xix.
75. Ibid.
76. See p. 64 above.
77. See Plato, *The Symposium,* trans. Walter Hamilton (Penguin Books, 1980), 92-95.
78. Halflants, xix-xx.
79. Vandana, *Gurus, Ashrams and Christians* (Madras, India: The Christian Literature Society, 1978), 40.

80. Halflants, xxi.
81. See Jn. 1:12-13.
82. Halflants, xxii.
83. Sermon 23: 2, quoted ibid., xxii-xxiii.
84. Halflants, xxiii-xxiv.
85. Ibid., xxiv.
86. Sermon 83: 3, quoted ibid.
87. Sermon 83, quoted, like the following sections, from Butler, 162f.
88. Ibid.
89. Ibid.
90. Ibid.
91. Ibid.
92. See Wayne Teasdale, "The Other Half of the Soul: Dom Bede Griffiths in India," *The Canadian Catholic Review* 3, n. 6 (June 1985), 11-16.
93. Sermon 85, quoted Butler, 165.
94. *S.C.* 14-15.
95. Ibid., 17,1.
96. Ibid., 9.
97. Ibid., st. 20-21, 1.
98. Ibid.
99. Ibid., 2.
100. Ibid., 4.
101. Ibid., 19.
102. Ibid., 22, 3.
103. Ibid., 5.
104. Ibid., 28, 3-4.
105. Ibid., 36, 12.
106. Ibid., 33.
107. Ibid., 36, 6.
108. Ibid., 39, 6.
109. *Interior Castle* VII, 1, 329-30.
110. Ibid.
111. Ibid., 331.
112. Ibid.
113. Ibid., 332.
114. Ibid.
115. Ibid.
116. Ibid., 333.
117. Ibid., VII, 2, 334.
118. Ibid.
119. Ibid.
120. Ibid., 334-35.
121. Ibid., 337.
122. Ibid., VII, 4, 344.

Appendix 1. An Article on Benedictine Humility

1. Emmanuel Latteur, "Les douze degrés d'humilité de la Règle de saint Benoît, restent-ils actuels: Echo à un article d'A. Vergote," in *Collectanea Cisterciensia* 45 (1983). (Translation mine.)
2. Latteur, 247.

3. Ibid., 248.
4. *C.W.* VII, 405.
5. Ibid., 403.
6. Latteur, 249.
7. Ibid., 250.
8. Ignatius of Loyola, *Letter... on the Virtue of Obedience,* Rome, March 26, 1553, quoted in *Constitutions and Rules of the Society of the Sacred Heart of Jesus* (privately printed, Roehampton, 1928).
9. Latteur, 250.
10. Ibid., 251.
11. See Daniel J. Levinson et al., *The Seasons of a Man's Life* (New York: Ballantine Books, 1978).
12. Mgr Sophrony, *Staretz Silouane* (Paris: Ed. Presence, 1963), 122-23, quoted in Latteur, 251.
13. Latteur, 252. The final quotation is from *RB* 7.
14. Ibid., 259.

Appendix 2. The Problem of Evil and God

1. *Answer to Job* (*CW* XI), 360.
2. *Answer to Job* (paperback ed., 1973), xv.
3. Ibid.
4. *C.W.* XI, 562.
5. Ibid., 567.
6. Ibid.
7. Ibid.
8. Ibid., 573.
9. Ibid.
10. Ibid., 574.
11. Ibid.
12. Ibid., 575.
13. Ibid., 583.
14. See Raymond Hostie, *Religion and the Psychology of Jung,* trans. G.R. Lamb (New York: Sheed and Ward, 1957), notably chap. 4.
15. *C.W.* XI, 594.
16. Ibid., 599-600.
17. Ibid., 608.
18. Ibid., 609.
19. Ibid., 617.
20. Ibid., 621.
21. Ibid., 622.
22. Ibid., 623.
23. Ibid., 624.
24. Ibid., 640.
25. Ibid., 639.
26. Ibid., 647.
27. Ibid.
28. Ibid., 648.
29. Ibid., 651.
30. Ibid., 662.
31. Ibid., 675.

32. Ibid., 684.
33. Ibid., 694.
34. Ibid., 717.
35. Ibid., 727-28.
36. Ibid., 732.
37. Ibid., 735.
38. Ibid.
39. Ibid.
40. Ibid., 738-739.
41. Ibid., 740 (notes omitted).
42. Ibid.
43. Ibid., 745-47.
44. See Justin Kelly, "God at Work," *The Way* 18, n. 3 (July, 1978), 163-73.
45. *CW* XI, 755-57.
46. Ibid., 758.
47. Ibid.